Women
in Contemporary
Muslim Societies

Women in Contemporary Muslim Societies

Edited with an Introduction by
JANE I. SMITH

Lewisburg
Bucknell University Press
London: Associated University Presses

Associated University Presses, Inc.
Cranbury, New Jersey 08512

Associated University Presses
Magdalen House
136-148 Tooley Street
London SE1 2TT, England

Library of Congress Cataloging in Publication Data

Main entry under title:

Women in contemporary Muslim societies.

   Papers presented at a workshop held at the Center for the Study of World
Religions, Harvard University, April 19, 1975.

   Bibliography: p.
   1. Women,   Muslim — Congresses.   2. Women — Near
East — Congresses.   3. Near   East — Social   conditions — Congresses.   I.
Smith, Jane I.   II. Harvard   University.   Center   for the Study of World
Religions.
   HQ1170.W57   301.41'2'0956   78-60377
   ISBN 0-8387-2263-6

PRINTED IN THE UNITED STATES OF AMERICA

Contents

Preface

The observance of 1975 as International Women's Year has engendered a great number of discussions, both formal and informal, in areas of concern to and about women on a global scale. These discussions have, it seems, helped to underline the ways in which the concerns articulated clearly by American women, particularly in the past several decades, are also being expressed by women of other cultures, yet have perhaps even more clearly spelled out the ways in which each culture and each set of contributing traditions provide a total circumstance in which questions peculiar to that configuration must be addressed.

Harvard University's Center for the Study of World Religions provides a singularly appropriate context for considering and comparing the kinds of issues that can and do arise in understanding the concerns of women in a variety of cultures. Among the several activities focusing on this theme that have taken place recently at the Center was a workshop held on April 19, 1975, on "The Role and Status of Women in Contemporary Muslim Societies." The idea for this workshop was initially conceived by Hanna Papanek (Committee for Southern Asian Studies at the University of Chicago and Department of Sociology at Boston University) and Shahida Lateef (Task Force Committee on the Status of Women in India), and developed in cooperation with Jane Smith (Center for the Study of World Religions). The papers presented in this volume are representative of issues dealt with and provide illustrative material from several areas of the Islamic world. In

7

addition to those here included, the following presentations were made at the workshop:

"Is the Subordination of Women Necessary to Islam," by Catherine Bateson (Department of Sociology and Anthropology, Northeastern University); "Changing Roles of Women in Provincial Town Life (Iran and Turkey)," by Mary-Jo Del Vecchio Good (Cambridge, Massachusetts); "Muslim Women as Part of a Minority Group," by Shahida Lateef (convener of the proceedings); "Marriage, Divorce and Marriage Law Reform in Indonesia," by Hanna Papanek (moderator).

Appended to this volume, and formulated with the help of suggestions made by the participants in the workshop as well as others, is a bibliography of books and articles in English on the general subject of women in Islam.

It was clearly the intention of those who initiated the designation of 1975 as one of concern for women that studies be expanded and that issues raised in discussion continue to be addressed. We at the Center hope that by making public some of the materials shared at our workshop we may help increase the store of resources available to those concerned with questions of women's identity in major portions of the Islamic world.

JANE I. SMITH

Notes on Contributors:

LOIS BECK holds an M.A. and a Ph.D. in anthropology from the University of Chicago. Her field work has been with pastoral nomads and tribal elite families in Iran. Currently she is Assistant Professor in the Department of Anthropology at the University of Utah, where she is also affiliated with the Middle East Study Center. She has recently coedited a book with Nikki Keddie entitled *Women in the Muslim World* (Harvard University Press, 1978).

SUSAN SCHAEFER DAVIS is a member of the Anthropology Department at Trenton State College in New Jersey. She has an M. A. and a Ph.D. from the University of Michigan in anthropology. Her field research has been in Morocco, where she has studied the various roles played by Muslim women in Moroccan society.

CAROLYN FLUEHR-LOBBAN has a Master's Degree from Temple University in Philadelphia and a Ph.D. from Northwestern University. Her field research was carried out in Khartoum in the Sudan; she is currently Assistant Professor of Anthropology at Rhode Island College.

LINA M. FRUZZETTI holds an M.A. from the University of Chicago and a Ph.D. from the University of Minnesota in anthropology. She has done four years of field work in India, North Africa, the Sudan, and with Indian Muslims in West Bengal. Presently she is teaching in the Anthropology Department at Brown University.

YVONNE YAZBECK HADDAD has a Master's Degree in history from the University of Wisconsin and is presently completing her doctorate in Islamic studies at the Hartford Seminary Foundation. She has published several articles on women in the Arab world and is currently teaching in the Department of Philosophy and Religion at Colgate University.

SHAHLA HAERI holds an M.A. in anthropology from Northeastern University, a C.A.S. in Human Development from Harvard, and is presently a doctoral candidate in anthropology at the University of California. She has done extensive research in the Middle East on modernization and family change, and recently conducted a study of Twelver Shi'ite temporary ($mut^{c}a$) marriage practices in Qum, Iran.

CARROLL McC. PASTNER is an Associate Professor of Anthropology at the University of Vermont. Her Ph.D. is from Brandeis University in anthropology, and she has done research in Trinidad in the West Indies and in Pakistani Baluchistan on the role of women in Baluch culture.

NANCY ADAMS SHILLING has an M.A. in political science from the University of Minnesota, a certificate of Arabic from Johns Hopkins and a Ph.D. from McGill University in Islamic Studies. She has done research in Lebanon and the Arabian Gulf, and serves as a consultant and conference lecturer to Western and Arab governments and private corporations. Recently she has published two guide books on the Arab world.

JANE I. SMITH is Associate Professor of History of Religions and Islamic Studies at Harvard Divinity School. She received her Ph.D. from Harvard's Center for the Study of World Religions, where she is now Associate Director, and has done research in Egypt and other areas of the Arab Middle East on modern Islamic theology.

Introduction

A good deal of attention is being given today to a consideration of the role of women in Islam, in the tradition and in contemporary terms. Despite the fact that Islam is broadly based
and represents a variety of cultural manifestations as well as a
variety of theological positions, certain basic understandings
about women and their socioreligious roles have been present
in Islam since the revelation of the Qur'ān (Koran) and the
articulation of *sharī'ah* (religious law).

While some may point to a kind of inequity in the Qur'ānic
injunctions concerning women—such as the affirmation that
the witness of a man is equivalent to that of two
women (S2:282) or that men are a step above women (S:228)—
the basic understanding of the Qur'ān is clearly that women
are equal to men in their relationship to God and that, like
men, they will be held fully accountable for their actions in the
hereafter. The suggestions that they should be chaste and
modest and reserving themselves completely for their husbands
have undoubtedly lent support to the various kinds of segregation—in the seclusion of the harem, the traditional insistence
on veiling, and the general restriction of women from many of
the activities that involve men—that have characterized the lot
of women until quite recently. And it is still true that, while in
some segments of Islamic society women are now occupying
positions of full professional responsibility on what is at least
ostensibly a par with men, in other areas things have changed
very little indeed from the way that they have operated for
many centuries.

Islamic law specifically protects the rights of women, particularly in areas of inheritance and the marriage contract. There is a wide variety of regulations concerning marriage and divorce, these having been seen as intending to improve the status of women over that of Arab customary law. In questions of dowry (*mahr*), the waiting period before remarriage (*'idda*), and the like, one can find certain protections built in for the woman. It is also true, however, that the general thrust of Islamic law (which one can find reinforced in much of the *ḥadīth* material) is such as to make women almost entirely dependent on men. Key emphasis is put on obedience of a wife to her husband; in fact, the argument can and has been made that a woman, by definition, can live a socially and religiously fulfilling life only within the structure of marriage and in relationship to her husband.

Given the fact that the *sharī'ah* has unquestionably legitimized and sanctioned the fulfillment of women through their relationships to fathers, husbands, and children, it is interesting to observe what factors have allowed for the leadership roles assumed by individual women in the history of Islam, and in what ways these and other factors are brought to bear on some of the contemporary political movements in the Islamic world. Historically Islam has allowed political and military participation of women in order to safeguard the *ummah* (community) against attacks from outside, and various contemporary instances of this can be observed (*ḥadīth* were cited in support of women fighting for God's cause in justification of the 1973 Ramadan war). Traditionally it has been the case that, once harmony has been restored, women have been expected to return to their "natural" roles in relation to family structures. Whether or not there have been any significant alterations in these kinds of expectations in the light of changes in the law is yet to be seen.

The right of divorce has always been available to a woman, but under circumstances markedly different from those in which her husband can divorce her. Rights of a mother to custody of her children, and particularly of her sons, legally always have been overshadowed by the rights of the father. It is interesting to note that, despite the changes that have occurred in regard to the legal and social situation of women in this century, and particularly recently, so eloquent a modern spokesman of Islam as Sayyid Hossein Nasr can affirm the traditional Muslim understanding of the family structure as he does in *Ideals and Realities of Islam*:

> The Muslim family is the miniature of the whole of Muslim society and its firm basis. In it the man or father functions as the imam in accordance with the patriarchal nature of Islam. The religious responsibility of the family rests upon his shoulders. He is in a sense the priest in that he can perform the rites which in other religions is reserved for the priestly class. In the family the father upholds the tenets of the religion and his authority symbolizes that of God in the world. The man is in fact respected in the family precisely because of the sacerdotal function that he fulfills. (Pp. 110-11)

Nevertheless, there can be no question that expectations are changing and with them come changes in the legal structure. Polygamy, viewed for centuries by Western antagonists as a great blot upon the face of Islam, is in some places now illegal, and monogamy tends to be considered preferable by modern Muslims. Its justification has always been in terms of the protection of unwed women and, to the extent that it is still accepted in more conservative societies, this justification is strongly reaffirmed. Education—traditionally denied to women on the grounds that greater freedom of women would inevitably contribute to a crumbling of the structure crucial to the maintenance of an ordered society—is being made increasingly available to women. Education is now providing women with a means of personal income not derived either from inheritance or from marriage, a circumstance that allows for some new kinds of flexibility in many Muslim societies.

That there have been some significant changes in the legal

structure of Islam in areas of women's rights, privileges, and responsibilities is apparent to even the most casual student of contemporary Islam. Whether or not these changes have substantially affected the role and status of Muslim women in practice, however, is quite another question and one that is raised in various ways in many of these papers. To what extent, one needs to ask, have women actually taken advantage of the changes that have been introduced into the law? (With the right to divorce their husbands, do they actually use this right? If not, why not? Does removing the veil signify to the Muslim woman what it might to the Western woman?)

The rate of change in the Islamic law, reflecting new legal opportunities for women and new interpretations of existing laws, is illustrative of the general state of flux characterizing many Islamic societies. Studies relevant today may in many cases be obsolete tomorrow; the papers that follow are an attempt to relate contemporary movements and interpretations to traditional understandings of women and their opportunities, both generally and specifically. They reflect on the one hand an increased interest in women and questions of women's identity, fostered to a great extent by recent movements in the United States, and on the other hand indicate a growing interest in singling out similar issues and concerns among women in other cultures.

There is little doubt that as a total phenomenon, if such it can be described, the "women's movement" in this culture has been concerned primarily and perhaps almost exclusively with issues directly related to the role and status of women in the United States. For some students of other cultures, however, it is becoming increasingly important to begin to consider what have been and are the major issues confronting women of different nationalities and religious traditions, and how these issues are best articulated. The immediate problem, and one for which there are no easy solutions, is to attempt to ascertain the extent to which the questions one sets about asking in relation to another culture and tradition are in any way related to the actual facts of that culture.

The recent international meeting of women in Mexico City brought out clearly the diversity of goals and variety of questions being asked by women from different areas. Hopefully, students of non-Western cultures are becoming increasingly aware of the dangers inherent in the tendency of some ethnologists, cultural anthropologists, and others to try to evaluate other cultures in terms of predefined norms formulated in an alien culture. The discussion that followed the presentation of papers at the workshop emphasized the necessity of studying cultures as they are, and attempting to frame questions in ways that are meaningful to members of those cultures. It is clear that the Islamic world itself is enormously diverse culturally, socially, and religiously. While on the one hand it may be useful, and even necessary, to generalize when dealing with descriptive material, on the other hand such generalizations may actually serve to obscure the very diversities that often lie at the heart of issues under consideration.

The tendency of many missionaries and Orientalists in the eighteenth and nineteenth centuries to urge non-Western peoples to acquire Western values as a means of measuring up to the standards of the modern world led some early modernizers in these countries to call for a blind imitation of the West. Missionaries tended to set forth the ideal of the Western home with its monogamous commitment to one wife and its relative absence of divorce as greatly preferable to the polygamous and seemingly unstable situation of the Muslim family with its easy divorce practices. Now, however, as others are viewing the increased rate of dissolution of Western families, questions are inevitably being raised about the meaning of such terms as commitment, responsibility, and liberation. Many non-Western peoples are seeing that, while their own legal systems may be constraining, the situation in the United States in fact leaves many women with little or no legal protection. Women of other cultures actually may be far less likely than before to be envious of the circumstances of American women; in many cases they are beginning to question whether or not the "liberation" achieved by women of this culture is not better understood as a kind of degradation, in much the same way that Westerners have tended to see the veil, the harem, and other Muslim customs as degrading to Islamic women. This must be understood, of course, in light of the very real fact that the struggle for equality and self-determination has been and continues to be inspired for many by the achievements of Western women.

It will be evident immediately to the reader that the papers in this collection illustrate a wide range of methodologies. The approaches can be described as literary, anthropological, sociological, and even personal insofar as some of them represent the reflections upon cultural phenomena made by members of those cultures. The following very brief set of synopses suggests the content of these articles and indicates some of the kinds of approaches possible in considering the question of women's role and status in various areas where the religion of Islam predominates:

1. "The Religious Lives of Muslim Women" (Lois Beck) provides a general introduction to the position of women in Islam and Islamic culture, both in theory and in practice. Working from the premise that women in fact are excluded from many of the religious practices traditionally reserved for men, Beck investigates some of the kinds of beliefs and practices in which women have engaged and continue to participate, such as cults of saints, tombs, and shrines, prayer gatherings, cults of curing and spirit possession and the like. The author argues that these kinds of religious activities give a woman an arena for action and power beyond the domestic one and allow her to attain status apart from that traditionally ascribed to her only in terms of her function in relation to husband and family.

2. "Traditional Affirmations concerning the Role of Women

as Found in Contemporary Arab Islamic Literature" (Yvonne Yazbeck Haddad) offers an approach quite different from the anthropological orientation that characterizes many of the papers. The author provides a survey of the major themes and arguments of contemporary Islamic writings on the subject of women and marriage. The writings cited attempt to counter the "secularists" who would remove women's role from the realm of the divinely ordained in revelation to the realm of the customary. The central theme of these writings is the affirmation that the roles of wife and mother alone provide a woman's true identity, and that all other aspects of a woman's intellectual and social life should be directed toward that dual end. The author is careful to point out that arguments repugnant to the modern feminist have actually been developed to defend Islam, not to condemn womankind. The writings reviewed stress the theme of complementarity of men and women in Islam.

3. "The Determinants of Social Position among Rural Moroccan Women" (Susan Schaefer Davis) calls into question the meaning of the term *status* in relation to Muslim women, suggesting that, before general questions of status within the society as a whole can be legitimately addressed, status within the female sex group must be considered. On the basis of fieldwork done in a medium-sized Moroccan village, the author suggests that a woman's status is determined with reference not to men but to other women. For those members of traditional society who accept sex segregation and traditional sex roles, power and prestige are available to members of both sexes. In fact, she says, the factors important in determining the status of women within their group may be more amenable to their control than those that determine the status of men. Personal acquaintance with Muslim women suggests that while a comparison between men and women in the male-dominated society might indicate that women are downtrodden, they in fact are often strong, confident, and powerful persons within the female context.

4. "The Social and Political Roles of Arab Women: A Study

in Conflict" (Nancy Adams Shilling) is divided into three sections. The first deals with the question of whether or not a minority perspective is appropriate as a framework for studying political attitudes and behavior of women; the author argues that it is. The second section deals with methodological problems of conceptualization, suggesting some of the problems that arise in studying Arab women and the kinds of technique one might profitably use. The last part of the presentation gives the author's analyses of the roles of Arab women in various strata of society, particularly in relation to Arab development programs in the 1970s. The author is particularly concerned about the relationship between women's participation in attaining government development goals and the possible escalation of social conflict that might naturally ensue.

5. "Access to Property and the Status of Women in Islam" (Carroll McC. Pastner) deals with the relationship between the status of women and female access to property. Ms. Pastner suggests that Islamic law is particularly attentive to the rights of women to acquire property through marriage and inheritance as sanctioned through religious authority. Despite these rights, she says, the general tendency has been for women to relinquish the management of their own property in favor of kinship protection, although this varies among different ethnic groups. With the introduction of women into the labor force, concomitant changes have taken place in the understanding of women owning property; patrimonial inheritance is less often forfeited in order to safeguard rights of kinship protection. Owning property is increasingly seen as a means of providing the moral and economic security that formerly came only through the family structure.

6. "Ritual Status of Muslim Women in Rural India" (Lina Fruzzetti) is based on a fieldstudy of a Muslim community in a Bengali town in which there are also a sizeable number of Hindus. The essay considers the kinds of factors that determine status in a society in which two elements come into play: the

Muslim ideal in which all persons are equal before one God, and Bengali recognition of a system of stratification that reflects the caste-oriented thinking of the larger culture. Bengali Muslims thus participate in two cultures simultaneously, and the author suggests that when men and women participate in orthodox rituals they are dealing in Muslim culture, but that when women worship saints they are dealing with peculiarly Bengali culture, with its counterpart in the Hindu worship of analogous saints or deities.

7. "Women, Law, and Social Change in Iran" (Shahla Haeri) examines the history of three laws introduced in Iran to change the social and political status of women: The Unveiling Act of 1936, the Suffrage Act of 1963, and the Family Protection Law of 1967. The author seriously questions the feasibility of trying to impose alien and foreign norms and modes of behavior on a society with deeply rooted and religiously sanctioned patterns. The social change enabled by some of these reforms has, she suggests, come about at a great cost and the reforms have not actually affected the social, educational, or economic positions of women at any meaningful level. The author does indicate, however, that there have developed among some Iranian women a new sociopolitical consciousness and an awareness of themselves as contributing members of society. A member of the society under consideration, she is able to offer some illuminating personal comment and reflection on the outcome of the introduction of these several laws.

8. "Some Suggestions Regarding the Political Mobilization of Women in the Arab World" (Carolyn Fluehr-Lobban), as the author herself observes, "is an effort to undermine the myth that Arab women are conservative or apolitical." (p. 265) It looks at the history of several women's movements in different parts of the Arab Islamic world, notably the Sudan, Egypt, Algeria, Palestine, Eritrea, Dhofar, and Iraq. The approach is that of a political historian seeking to draw from history generalizations that may also apply in the future. The

author offers a picture of women militant in the cause of national liberation and organized on their as well as their nation's behalf. She argues that women's involvement in the national struggle can give rise to a feminist movement, and illustrates the kinds of relationships between political activity and feminist issues that have actually been developed.

The *shari'ah* has always served as the great standardizing component of Islam, that which binds in a unity of practice all of the peoples from various cultures whose unity of belief is the recognition of one God and His Messenger. This very variety, however, presents problems of cultural context that often make it very difficult to isolate and identify individual phenomena. In any given instance one must determine if it is more appropriate to think in terms of Islamic culture or Middle Eastern (North African, Indian, Indonesian) culture. Several of the papers in this series suggest the problem of determining in a cultural context which elements are peculiarly Muslim and which are aspects of folk religion in which non-Mulsims of the same culture also participate. In many cases one must recognize that Islam is not to be understood as a religion per se, but rather as the dominant identifying factor in a complex cultural milieu. Since Islam functions as a kind of umbrella identity over a multitude of different manifestations and cultural identities, one must inevitably question the extent to which the conclusions of any single study or series of studies, no matter how lengthy or detailed, can be generalized to fit even one society as a whole, let alone any larger cultural or geographical unit.

Given the very nature of Islam as a religiopolitical institution and thereby a cultural phenomenon, one cannot consider questions of role and status apart from concomitant questions of social structure and cultural determinants. Changes potentially taking place under the rubrics of "modernization" and "Westernization" must be seen in the context of prevailing local customs, norms, and structures of society as well as in relation to issues of class consciousness, the holding of property, distribution of wealth, and a variety of other influencing elements. By virtue of the range of topics and approaches that they exhibit, the papers in this collection help illustrate the complexity of factors involved in considering questions of status and change.

Into this already complicated picture we must add some basic questions about feminist concerns and the possible meanings of the liberation of women in order to come to terms with the topics dealt with either implicitly or explicitly in a number of the papers in this collection. Here of course one must consider what constitutes liberation for women, first, in the context of Islam and, second, in any particular cultural context: Liberation from what and to what? Liberation for whom and determined by whom? What are the goals of liberation? And, as has been suggested in several instances, is liberation in any sense desirable by the women (or men) in any given situation? From here one can move to more particular questions: Are Muslim women seeking political power? How do women involved in national liberation movements view their role? Is there a difference between equality in status, role, and function and equality in terms of respect given and received? Is participation in political movements of liberation conducive to improving the position of women in general—or, again on a somewhat more subtle level, is that in itself a legitimate question for those about whom it is being asked, or is it in fact one that is imposed from an outside context?

We must also inquire what constitutes relative freedom and/or flexibility for women. In several of the pages to follow the argument is put forth that in fact women have more flexibility than men in raising their positions in society, or at least within the relative areas in which their roles are defined, and that in certain of their functions (for example, as purveyors of gossip) they serve as agents of social control. But here it is necessary to consider "individual" possibilities for mobility and change of status in terms of possibilities for larger groups of women or for women as a whole.

One might even raise the question of whether or not modern reform movements suggest a kind of further masculinization of Islam by moving away from emotional elements of folk religion (cults of saints and the like that have been more the province of women than of men) and emphasizing the blending of rational interpretations with traditionally acceptable understandings, the determination of which has fallen exclusively to men. If this is true, and one might make an excellent case for it, then it appears that reform itself increasingly means the denial of a feminine expression of religiosity. Do the very movements that would appear to bring with them an improvement in the situation of women in fact signal a circumstance in which those kinds of religious practices apparently most congenial to women have the least likelihood of survival? Or, is it necessary to assume that the reason why those particular practices and beliefs have lent themselves most easily to women is simply because women have been excluded from other areas of religious practice, a situation that might actually be changing?

The majority of essays in this collection are not dealing directly with religion, but are looking at the ways in which a culture in some sense identified as "religious" is responding to changes in the contemporary world. The fact remains, however, that it is because these cultures are Islamic, are what they are in large part because of the tremendous influence of a holy book considered divine and an ensuing set of legal regulations based at least in part on the dictates of that book, that the essays have the commonality to be included together in this collection. It is, therefore, not illegitimate, I think, to conclude these brief introductory considerations by raising yet another set of questions that have to do with the internal nature of Islam as a religion and with the inherent understanding of the relationship of men and women.

It is quite clear that Islam understands the role of women to be complementary to that of men. This raises, then, the following question: Is there in the institution of religion, in this case Islam, any sanction for the kinds of changes society may deem appropriate? Or is religion a kind of projected ideal that defines a cosmic order and requires that we mortals conform to it? There is a sense in which women are the maintainers of the status quo in Islam. In helping maintain the relationship of women to men, they seem thereby to have accepted it. Is there something inherent in religion itself that creates a hierarchy such that man is to God as woman is to man and child is to woman? Religion sanctions the complementarity in order to maintain a social structure with stability. And that very stability, the antithesis of chaos, is essential to an understanding of Islam that recognizes that God's creation of the world and establishing of persons in community in it is the institution of a system of order. Given this kind of starting point, one wonders what kind of sanction movements can hope to have that at least temporarily interrupt that social order, and perhaps promise to undermine it in a more permanent way. Or to pose the question from another perspective, one must ask whether or not societies that admit the kinds of changes that seem destined to occur, given the increased exposure to the West and the concerns of women in a more global context, can indeed continue to be considered Islamic.

JANE I. SMITH

Women
in Contemporary
Muslim Societies

The Religious Lives
of Muslim Women

LOIS BECK
The University of Utah

This essay has two aims: First, it provides a general introduction to the series of papers stemming from a workshop on The Role and Status of Women in Contemporary Muslim Societies[1] by attempting to outline the relationship of Islam to the socioeconomic and sociocultural bases of the position of women in Muslim societies. Second, it discusses and analyzes variations in belief and ritual found among Muslim women. Before beginning the discussion, a number of important cautionary remarks need to be made; they involve issues that are often unrecognized, ignored, or obscured in discussions of Muslim women.[2] First, the position of women in Muslim societies cannot be understood without a thorough appreciation of the contexts in which they live their lives. The various political, economic, social, and cultural factors that interact to form society and culture create, perpetuate, and change the positions of women and men in society. In any given setting, the unique way that these factors combine has particular implications for the roles, statuses, and behavioral patterns of women and men. The great variation in the cultures and societies of the Muslim Middle East, therefore, makes almost any general statement about women there false and misleading. The Muslim Middle East consists of many countries having distinct histories, cultures, customs, and laws. Each country has been differentially influenced or dominated by foreign powers, and each has been and is now undergoing different kinds and rates of change (industrialization, urbanization, modernization, secularization). Within each Muslim nation there are different ethnic, religious, tribal, and cultural groups. Each nation is class-stratified and consists of small but extremely wealthy and powerful upper and elite classes, growing and diversifying middle classes, and large and poor lower classes. The citizens of each country live in many kinds of settings and environments (cities, towns, villages, nomadic camps) and perform many different kinds of subsistence tasks. Increasing numbers of each nation's populations are now leaving rural areas to seek employment in crowded cities, sometimes without their families, and many leave their countries for work elsewhere (creating small communities of their own in many nations). Therefore, variation in the societies and communities in which women in the Muslim Middle East live defies the creation of any single "image" of women.

In order to understand the position of women in any Muslim community, specific information on various aspects of their lives is required: work and employment; ownership of property; control over income and property; education; access to health care, adequate nutrition, and birth control; decision-making abilities concerning the course of their own lives (such as whether or not to marry, have children, seek employment); and so forth. These are essentially issues of class; women of the upper and upper-middle classes have a broader and more flexible range of options in life than middle and lower-class women have; the lives of women of different classes cannot be considered to be similar.

A second reason why generalization about Middle Eastern women is difficult concerns individual variation in personality; it cannot be predicted how individual women will react to the settings in which they are found. In my interviewing of formerly pastoral nomadic women who are now living in poverty in squatter settlements on the outskirts of Shiraz in Iran, I found extreme helplessness and despair as well as great ingenuity and creativity among the settlers, and many other kinds of reactions as well. These women, too, for whom the physical conditions of life are depressingly identical, defy stereotyped images.

The third cautionary statement is that it is false to attribute to Islam the "origins" or "causes" of sexual inequality in the Middle East. Sexual inequality is not a feature exclusive to Muslim society; it is found in all parts of the world, and it has existed for millennia and long before the beginnings of Islam. That societies everywhere are based on patriarchal notions and institutions means that analysis must turn to the basic socioeconomic and sociocultural conditions of women's and men's lives. In addition, Islamic belief and practice take different forms among the various Muslim populations, and one should expect that the religion can have varying degrees of impact on women's lives. Also, many aspects of Judaism and Christianity relating to women's and men's positions are similar to those of Islam. Therefore, Islam cannot be blamed for sexual inequality, nor can any other single feature of society and culture; the phenomenon is too complex.

Fourth, women play multiple roles (in work, family life, extra-domestic life, religion, recreation), which vary as they move through the stages of the life cycle and the developmental cycle of the family. This may seem obvious, but much of the literature on women in society, especially the writings on Muslim and Middle Eastern women, treats them as if they were only "wives" and "mothers" (that is, as persons connected to others only by sexual and maternal ties). Women have many kinds of relationships and activities that extend beyond those that connect them with men and children. The multifaceted character of women's lives is usually ignored.

Fifth, focusing on the exclusion of women from political and economic power in Muslim society tends to ignore the wider perspective; most Muslim *men* (the rural and urban proletariat) are also excluded from political and economic power in society. Most Muslim men have been and continue to be subordinated to political and economic forces beyond their control. These include foreign conquerors and colonists, ruling elites, and Western and capitalistic powers and influences. While much attention has been given to the "subjugated" Muslim woman, virtually none has been given to the wider political and economic environment in which both Muslim men and women live. Also, some Middle Eastern women (generally of upper-class and elite origin) individually have greater wealth, power, and authority than do most Middle Eastern men.

The final cautionary note—one that is of increasing sensitivity for many modern Muslims—concerns the current state of the literature. The conditions that many social scientists (and most anthropologists) depict are those of "traditional," nonmodern, or modernizing Muslim populations. Many remarks about Muslim women, which take village, town, or lower-class city women as their subjects, do not apply to all Muslim women and are badly out of touch with the situations in which increasing numbers of educated and employed Muslim women exist. In addition, written accounts of the views non-Western women have of their own lives and their relationships with men are still few in number. (Notable exceptions are contained in Fernea and Bezirgan 1977. Most existing accounts tend to come from Western-educated and/or upper-class women—for example, Roy 1975; one exception is Bittari 1964.) We certainly cannot assume that the agricultural laborer in eastern Turkey or the slum dweller in Cairo feels the same way about her life as do those who read this volume. We can also say that for the non-Western world, where many populations live in abject poverty and where food, housing, and physical health are issues of *survival*, the preoccupation of the Western middle and upper classes with certain issues connected with women's emancipation and equal rights seems quite irrelevant (see Nash and Safa 1976).

The lives of some people of the Middle East are oriented toward national liberation movements and to ridding their nations or peoples of the controlling forces of Western economic and political imperialism (upper and elite classes, foreign corporations, foreign intelligence services, etc.). For most Middle Easterners, their lives are increasingly structured by world capitalism and the major industrial powers; the labor, products, and natural resources of the Middle East are largely diverted for the benefit of the world's privileged classes and nations. In some areas, such as in Algeria, Libya, Iraq, and Iran, political movements and protests have also meant pressure for the return of women to traditional roles and to veiling and seclusion. In other areas, such as in the Sudan, in the People's Democratic Republic of Yemen, and among the Palestinians, political movements and protests have allowed fuller political, economic, and social roles for women.

It is obvious, therefore, that female and male lives in the Muslim Middle East cannot be discussed in a vacuum; the central issues are the structure and organization of class inequality in the Middle East — the ways economic and political power is distributed unequally and the impact this has on the roles and status of women and men in the various socio-economic strata (Maher 1974:222).

Islam

Islam has appealed to the peoples of a wide section of the world stretching westward from Arabia to Morocco, northward to Turkey and eastern Europe, eastward to Afghanistan, Pakistan, Bangladesh, China, Indonesia, and the Philippines, and southward to the continent of Africa. There are an estimated 719 million Muslims in the world (Weekes 1978). Such a spread across geographical and cultural boundaries attests to the adaptability and flexibility of the religion. Much of the appeal of Islam for its adherents is in its message of direct monotheism. Required of Muslims are faith in and adherence to five devotional aspects: testimony that there is but one God (*shahada*), prayer five times daily (*salat*), fasting in the month of Ramadan (*saum*), giving of alms (*zakat*), and the pilgrimage to Mecca (*hajj*) (if circumstances permit). An ecclesiastical hierarchy that could rigidify and formalize the religion is lacking; Islam stresses the direct link between the individual and Allah. An institutional framework comparable to the Church in Catholicism is absent.

These facets of the religion explain not only the existence of a myriad of local forms of belief and practice within Islam but also the extreme toleration they encounter. The process of Islamization provides further explanation for variety in belief and practice:

> On the one hand, it has consisted of an effort to adapt a universal, in theory standardized and essentially unchange-able, and unusually well integrated system of ritual and belief to the realities of local, even individual, moral and metaphysical perception. On the other, it has consisted of a struggle to maintain, in the face of this adaptive flexibility, the identity of Islam not just as religion in general but as the particular directives communicated by God to mankind through the preemptory prophecies of Muhammad. (Geertz 1968:14-15)

The history of local areas is characterized by varying degrees of awareness of and adherence to Islam as exemplified in the Qur'ān, the Traditions, and the body of law, on the one hand, and by varying degrees of awareness of and adherence to local and indigenous beliefs and rituals, on the other. As a result, the religious sytems of no two Islamic communities are identical. Variation also occurs within communities according to socioeconomic class differences. For example, many individuals of the modernized upper and upper-middle classes choose to ignore most Islamic observances and perhaps consider themselves Muslims only in a general sense, while the bazaar petty bourgeois and lower classes have more traditional patterns of belief and practice (Keddie 1972:12; Fernea and Fernea 1972). In any class, women have somewhat different religious beliefs, practices, and intensities than their male relatives.

Women and Islam

In discussing women's position in Muslim society, it is not possible to disentangle those aspects originating in Islam from those stemming from broader sociocultural systems. Some authors claim that sexual inequality in Muslim society is due to Islam, and others claim that it is due instead to non-Islamic social and cultural forces (see Saleh 1972a, 1972b), but it is clear that a third approach is more informative.

The coming of Muhammad in the early seventh century A.D. clearly changed the legal positions of Islam's early female and male adherents. Pre-Islamic customs apparently included female infanticide, female abduction, and easy access for men to marriage, divorce, and concubinage, although the prevalence of such customs has undoubtedly been exaggerated by some writers. Accounts of daily life in pre-Islamic times are lacking.

Muhammad, through revelations and personal deeds, established a system of relative equality between the sexes, in which complementary, but not necessarily unequal, roles were provided for males and females. The "stronger" sex was defined as protector of the "weaker." After his death religious scholars and administrators elaborated on and exaggerated this position of protection by the male of the female, a process that reflected the patriarchal customs and attitudes of the time. Since males were the scholars and administrators, the creation and interpretation of religious law favored the male over the female. Women were rarely in a position to define through formal and legal means the parameters of their religious and social lives.

Islamic law (shari'a), in which there is no distinction between "religious" and "civil" law, stems from the Qur'ān and the Traditions (hadīth), and was compiled, through the processes of consensus ('ijma) and analogy (qiyas), by religious scholars (ulama). Variations in interpretation occurred according to the various schools within Islam and to local customs and traditions ('adat, 'urf) (see Coulson 1964; Coulson and Hinchcliffe 1978). The areas in which women's position as defined by Islamic law is most clearly illuminated are the laws that relate to questions of personal status, family life, and property rights. These laws—summarized hereafter—stipulate the rights and duties of women during each stage of the life cycle; on occasion their terms are ambiguous and subject to different interpretations. Throughout her life, a female is placed under the care and authority of males. A young girl is enjoined to be an obedient daughter and to exhibit modest and chaste behavior. A marriage guardian (wali) (in practice this is usually her father) is required in order to ensure that her marriage is properly arranged. A marriage contract (aqd) outlines the conditions of the marriage union and sets out the terms of the bridewealth and/or the sum (mahr, sadaq) provided by her husband if she is divorced by him or if he dies. The main duty of a married women is to her husband; she must obey and serve him in a respectful manner, and he in turn is obliged to provide for her welfare. Her modesty and faithfulness are prescribed. Her second duty is to produce male heir(s) for her husband. A mother is responsible for the care and nurture of her children and for their moral and religious training. Children belong by right to the legal father, and upon a certain age they are entrusted to him or his kin if the mother is divorced or widowed. A man has greater and easier rights of divorce (talaq) than does a woman. He is entitled to take as many as four wives, as long as equivalent care and attention are provided for each; this right can be restricted if his wife's marriage guardian has included a clause to this effect in the marriage contract. Inheritance rules are complex, but in general a female receives a portion half that of a male; a daughter inherits one-half the share of a son from the father's estate and a wife one-fourth or one-eighth of the husband's estate. A female is entitled to own property, and there is no community of property between husband and wife. Two women's testimony in court is equivalent to that of one man.

This summarizes a woman's legal position and the outline of her life cycle, according to the *shari'a*. The various legal schools in Islam have formulated different interpretations of these aspects, and there have been major legal reforms in this century in many of the nations in which Muslims live. In a few nations no reforms have been enacted. In others, reforms have been enacted and to varying degrees enforced (see Coulson and Hinchcliffe 1978; White 1978). Among some segments of all Muslim nations, however, Islamic law may not be observed, and legal reforms may not reach the local level. For example, Islamic laws concerning women's property rights are frequently violated. Many Muslim women are customarily denied their rights of inheritance. Since postmarital residence is often virilocal, property ownership on the part of the woman can cause alienation of agnatic wealth. The dowry that a woman carries into marriage is sometimes regarded as a substitute for her inheritance share. Possession and control of women's property, despite Islamic law to the contrary, are often assumed by their male guardians.

In all religions, an ideological basis underlies, supports, and perpetuates the codes, roles, and customs that relate to women's lives. Islam is no exception. However, "Islamic" ideology cannot be separated from the more generally ideological systems of local societies. An example of the difficulty in separating religious ideology from its sociocultural context is in the fact of the extremely low employment rates for women in Middle Eastern Muslim societies as compared with men and as compared with women in all other cultural areas of the world.

Islamic laws do not forbid women the right to seek paid employment; in fact, they allow women to own and control property. But the social realities of life for many Muslim women include: sexual segregation, emphasis on women's primary duties as wives and mothers, lack of formal education or job training, sexual discrimination in recruitment, concern over the proper behavior of women, and male dominance of the occupants, property, and some activities of the household. These customs and attitudes, which emerge from the general sociocultural systems to Muslim societies, help to keep many Muslim women from seeking paid employment (see Youssef 1974, 1978). Patterns of female employment can be better explained by economic factors (especially class) than by religious ideology. Lower-class women and women who must support their families are forced to seek employment (see Davis 1978), while the "liberated" but non-productive existence of upper-class women hinges on their ability to hire lower-class women as servants, maids, cooks, and nannies.

Another example concerns formal education. Until very recently, most females in Muslim areas have been denied opportunities for formal education; the rationale, in addition to issues relating to sexual segregation and domestic and maternal role training, is that the effects of education would be lost on them, or put to inappropriate ends. (This restriction has also applied to formal religious education, thus reducing the opportunity for women to gain an awareness of the philosophical bases of Islam and to acquire the ability to serve others in a spiritual and legal manner.) However, the current spread of formal education among females in almost all Muslim areas demonstrates that ideological and social barriers to education can be fairly quickly overcome once general societal conditions allow it.

Ideological systems have implicit components in symbolism and ritual. Some authors have written about Muslim women's ritual status, which is regarded as prohibitive to full-status social and religious roles. The biological processes associated with female maturity—menstruation and childbirth—render a woman ritually impure at regular and predictable times of her life cycle. However, other ritual restrictions affect men and women alike, and in several areas, such as prayer and fasting, females may assume full ritual status earlier in life than do males. As with previous discussions, it is clear that knowledge of particular social and cultural settings is necessary for the understanding of the particular significance that notions of ritual restrictions have on women. (Although the subject is Zoroastrian belief and ritual in Iran, an account by Boyce [1978] demonstrates what an observant and insightful social scientist can do with issues concerning the impact of ritual and religion on women's and men's lives.) Also, notions concerning ritual can be used by women to their own advantage, such as when they can avoid certain household responsibilities during their menstrual cycle. Islamic law does state that certain religious acts—such as prayer, mosque attendance, fasting, pilgrimage, contact with the Qur'ān—are forbidden or altered when women are in a state of ritual impurity. Social scientists have yet to inform us how such prohibitions actually affect women's religious and social status.

Social Patterns

The combination of legal systems, institutional mechanisms, belief systems, and social codes—many of which are *not* brought about by or directly connected with Islamic belief and ritual—serves to separate rather than to integrate females and males in Muslim society. Social patterns of sexual segregation and male guardianship over females are found in all Muslim societies, although they are most prevalent in the middle and lower classes. Muslim males are enjoined to guard and protect the female members of their families, out of notions concerning the importance of the female in terms of the honor and reputation of her family. Also, control over women helps to ensure that the children born to a woman are those of the biological and legal father. Sexual segregation separates the activities of males and females and preserves a division of labor. Females who fulfill primarily the roles of daughter, wife, mother, and kinswoman cannot easily assume roles in non-domestic spheres. Their restricted access to public places and non-relatives *can* deny them the kinds of knowledge and contacts necessary for playing active non-domestic roles in society. However, many Muslim women *do* play important non-domestic roles (see, for example, the many case studies in Beck and Keddie 1978; also, Early 1978), and patterns of segregation to allow women certain kinds of contacts and networks unavailable to men. Women's social relationships are often unrestricted by the kinds of cleavages and factions that are characteristic of men's relationships, and the networks and information available to them provide certain advantages over men.

When, in some segments of Muslim society, it is unavoidable for the spheres of females and males to overlap, the "veil" — any garb that is used to conceal parts of the head, face, or torso — provides the measure of distance and separation required for preservation of segregation. The attention given in the literature to the seclusion of women, however, has caused neglect of the fact that in sexual segregation men too are restricted in movement. While the female spends most of her time in domestic units and with other women and children, the male is denied many of the comforts of the warm intimacy of family life and is forbidden ready access to the homes of other men.

Social patterns and practices vary according to socio-economic factors (see Pastner n.d.). Those many Muslim women who must work to support themselves and their families cannot afford the "luxury" of seclusion at home (see Davis 1978). Among women in the middle socioeconomic levels, patterns of veiling and seclusion appear to be increasing. In the upper levels, veiling and seclusion are largely absent (see Keddie and Beck 1978).

Patterns of Belief and Ritual

Most writings about Islamic belief and practice concern male, not female, participants, although general recognition of this is still not made by most writers. What kinds of religious lives do women in Muslim societies lead? How do women find meaning in Islamic belief and ritual? How do religious belief and ritual relate to women's needs?

Earlier, brief mention was made of the process by which Islam adapts to various cultures and environments while retaining those features that maintain its universality. Every Muslim society is characterized by a distinctive set of traditions, customs, beliefs, and rituals having historical roots in both Islamic and indigenous systems. From both systems Muslims create their own rich and varied patterns of belief and ritual.

Belief in God and in prayer, fasting, almsgiving, and pilgrimage are common to all Muslims. But there are other aspects of religious life for Muslims, including life cycle rituals, events associated with the Great and Little Festivals, and beliefs and rituals connected with the following: the lives of early Islamic figures, contemporary religious figures, saints and saintly lineages, attendance at tombs and shrines, prayer gatherings, religious orders, spirits, curing and spirit possession cults, evil eye beliefs, spells, vows, charity, and amulets.[3] Some of these are not sanctioned within orthodox Islam, but no institution within the religion exists to condemn or remove them. Both men and women are involved in these beliefs and practices, especially among the middle and lower classes. However, reports generally indicate that, in most communities, men do not participate with the intensity nor in the numbers that do women. From the literature it appears that the strongest adherents of these forms of belief and ritual among the male populations of Muslim societies are those who are of low socioeconomic status and in economically subordinate positions. Crapanzano has written about the cult activities of rural immigrants in Moroccan shantytowns (1972, 1974); I.

M. Lewis has written of similar cults in Somalia and other Muslim societies (1971). Distance from mosques is also a factor in determining the appeal of these forms among men, and Islamic regulations and rites have local strength depending on the availability of its interpreters (*ulama, mujtaheds*) and judges (*qadis*).

Early Islamic figures. Many Muslims place a personal stake in the lives of Islam's early supporters. While Islam is a philosophically-oriented belief system for some, many others create an informal and personal faith through emotional and spiritual attachment to those individuals in Islam's past who fought, and perhaps died, for the faith. Stories of these individuals have become legends, and women were, and are today, vehicles of both the elaboration and transmission of oral tradition.

The Prophet's birthday (*maulid al-nabi*) is a day of celebration in some areas. In Turkey the story of the life of the Prophet is read at prayer gatherings (Mansur 1972:106-7). Attention is also given to the Prophet's Companions and to his immediate relatives: his daughter Fatimah, his cousin and son-in-law 'Ali, and Fatimah and 'Ali's sons Hasan and Husayn.

> There is a female element in Islam . . . in the female figure of Fatima . . . . The figure of Fatima received the greatest elaboration under Shiite auspices where it may well represent the renascence of an earlier dualist Iranian tradition. Nevertheless, Fatima is of general importance in Islam, especially in folk Islam, even in Sunni areas. The symbolism of Fatima is complex. Daughter of the Prophet, who had no male heir, she bore to Ali the only male progeny of Muhammad. Like Ali, she and her children suffered defeat and death at the hands of political rivals, thus extinguishing Muhammad's line as a continuing political force. Nevertheless, she is the fictive "mother" of the descendants of the Prophet, the *shorfa* (sing., *sherif*) who bear the *baraka* or power of the Prophet and who furnish a continuing elite from which both the heads of *tariqas* and political leaders

can be drawn. She is also, in Shiite variants of Islam, the female ancestor of the Mahdi who is to come and who will also bear the name Muhammad. In prayer she is addressed as *omm abiha*, mother of your father, a greeting used in ordinary discourse when indicating that a woman has a son who bears the name of his mother's father. (Wolf 1969:298)

The five-fingered "hand of Fatimah" is one of Islam's most widely used symbols; it is placed on the doors of homes and is worn as jewelry by many Muslim women. In Shi'a areas this symbol also represents Allah, Muhammad, 'Ali, Hasan, and Husayn, and in Muharram processions it represents 'Abbas' hand, which was severed in the battle of Karbala.

Muslim women are especially attracted to female figures, such as warriors and other early supporters of Islam, as well as the wives and sisters of Islam's male supporters, since appeal to women is believed to have greater efficacy in situations particular to women (barrenness, child mortality, sudden repudiation). Mahnaz Afkami, Iran's Minister of Women's Affairs (until the fall of 1978, when religious opposition aided in the removal of this position), explains that Islam was used by the Women's Organization of Iran to encourage sexual equality; attention was given by the Organization to early Islam's female figures such as heroes and warriors and those who were the very first supporters of the Prophet (Cobban 1977). The shrine of Bibi Hakimi (sister of Imam Reza, a Shi'a imam) in southwest Iran draws thousands of pilgrims every year, especially Qashqa'i and Luri tribal women. The shrine of Sayyida Zaynab (Umm Hashim), who is the granddaughter of the Prophet and sister of Imam Husayn, in Cairo draws many who seek cures in the oil of the tomb's lamp (for a fictionalized account, see Haqqi 1973).

Shi'a Muslims venerate their imams, including 'Ali, Husayn, and Reza, and they offer their respect to such persons as 'Abbas (Husayn's half brother who fought and died at his side at Karbala). The most important month in the religious calendar for Shi'a Muslims is Muharram; on the Tenth of Muharram in

A. D. 680, Husayn and his family were killed by Sunni Umayyids in the battle of Karbala. In villages, towns, and cities passion plays (*ta'ziyah*)—with members of traveling troupes along with local males playing the dramatic parts—reenact the battle to commemorate the deaths. The first ten days of Muharram are characterized by intense mourning. During the whole month, mourners dress in black, and celebration, music, and movies are forbidden. While women do not ordinarily participate publicly in street demonstrations, which include chest pounding and self-mutilation, they gather in private homes to express their sense of loss and horror. Male or female preachers recite the events of the tragedy, skillfully working audiences to outpourings of grief, then calming them only to raise emotions again (see Fernea 1965; Thaiss 1972, 1973; Peters 1956). It has been remarked that during these days women find emotional release from the difficulties of the year; their own troubles pale in comparison with the tragedies of Husayn and family.

Muharram observances in Iran in 1978 were combined with political and religious demonstrations against the government of the Shah. Men and women participated publicly in many forms of protest during this month.

Throughout Muslim societies women and men alike call out to Islam's early figures in times of need. For women especially, awareness of the lives of these individuals helps to personalize the religion and bring it close to daily life.

Contemporary religious figures. Another aspect of women's and men's religious lives is reliance on contemporary religious figures. These include a wide range of individuals from local religious leaders (*imam, mullah, hoca*) and respected persons in the community such as (reputed) descendants of the Prophet (*sayyid, sherif*), learned persons (*sheikh, pir*), "saints" (*marabout, sheikh igurramen*), and preachers (*qur'ān khan, rozeh khan*) to prayer writers (*du'a nevis*) and those who are itinerant mystics and ascetics (*faqir, sufi, darvish*). Although divinity or saintliness cannot be ascribed to human beings according to orthodox Islam, many local populations do so ascribe. Many of these individuals are believed to possess a divine or charismatic "grace" (*baraka*). Some of these individuals are within orthodox Muslim tradition; others are not.

Muslim women have had much less access than men to the religious education offered in mosques and religious centers, and they have had fewer opportunities to follow a religious life in the manner of these men. However, in some places there are female religious leaders (*mullah, muqaddama, sheikha*) who are trained to lead prayers and religious gatherings (see Alport 1970, Fernea 1965, Fernea and Fernea 1972, Mansur 1972, Schimmel 1974, Trimingham 1971) as well as curing sessions for spirit possession. Some of these women follow a hereditary line of women leaders. Some are women—lacking conjugal or maternal duties or occupying marginal social status—who choose to devote their lives to religious activities. Some are partly self-taught. Female religious leaders often specialize in family law and provide advice for women.

The wives of the Prophet, and in particular 'A'isha, were accessible to religious inquiries and gave advice on religious matters (Saleh 1972b), and in contemporary times the female family members of men of religious status perform similar functions. The attendants at a recently visited shrine in Tunisia were husband and wife; he ministered to the needs of men and she to the needs of women. Iran, for example, has had some important female religious leaders in the past. Some had lower class origins (Bill 1972:28), a fact that testifies both to class mobility and to the ability of some women to utilize the educational and religious training normally available only to men.

Men and women of religious status write Qur'ānic inscriptions to be used in amulets (*hijab*) and cures. Much of the ornamentation worn by women and children (and valued animals) has its origins here; most common is a small cloth packet that contains a verse of the Qur'ān or just some Arabic script on paper and is pinned onto clothes. Some men and women perform curing rituals. If the sought-for ends are consistently attained, popularity spreads and cults form around the individual. Vows are made to individuals of religious status; those who desire a particular end promise money, a piece of valued property, or sponsorship of a religious gathering, if the procured amulet or cure proves to be effective. Many individuals support themselves by the gifts of their patrons, which attests to the importance of this phenomenon.

Saints and saintly lineages. Another aspect of the religious lives of both women and men involves saints. A saint (*sayyid, wali, imam, pir*) is a venerated holy man or woman (see Schimmel 1975, Mernissi 1977, Smith 1928) who becomes elevated upon death to the rank of saint; he or she is considered to have divine grace (*baraka*) and the power to serve as an intermediary between Allah and living persons. (This is regarded by some Muslims to be heretical in terms of the Prophetic tradition.) The saint's tomb becomes a shrine and a center for pilgrimage and religious gatherings. Often that locality is the home of the saint's living descendants, who, by virtue of succession, have *baraka* also (hence, they are known as "living saints"). In some cases these saintly lineages are traced to the Prophet himself. Often a religious brotherhood or a Sufi order is connected to a saint and his or her descendants. Living saints have important political and social functions, in addition to religious ones, and they are often mediators in tribal conflicts (Gellner 1972). While many of the political functions of saintly organizations belong to men, women utilize the shrines for prayers, vows, pilgrimage, and social gatherings (see Dwyer 1978b).

Tombs and shrines. Muslim women often perform their daily prayers at home, because of patterns of sexual segregation and because of direct or indirect pressure to remain away from mosques, which in some areas are male domains only. Most mosques provide separate sections for women in balconies, in side or back rooms, or in areas shielded by lattice work. Women often find places of sanctity and worship in tombs and shrines, which usually have no corresponding restrictions (see Mernissi 1977, Trimingham 1971:232).

The Ka'ba in Meca is the most famous place of sanctity and pilgrimage in Islam; few men and fewer women, however, have the financial means to make a pilgrimage there. There are, however, throughout Muslim areas, thousands of tombs and shrines (*sayyid, zawiya, imamzadeh*) that are frequented by men and women.

> The local tradition often makes its peace with Islam by assigning its sacred tree or stone to a saint who is identified with a Koranic figure or by recognizing the saint as a *nabi* or prophet. . . .The miracles of the saints cut across denominational lines, while their various activities and the forms of their cults may well perpetuate with but slight modifications the service expected from, and offered to, them in an even remoter past. (von Grunebaum 1951:79)

A shrine may be the reputed resting place of one of Islam's well known personages, in which case it is extremely popular, or it may contain the tomb of a local person or saint who worked miracles in his or her lifetime. The shrines of female saints are often guarded by women, and men are forbidden entrance (Schimmel 1975:433). Some shrines indicate the locations of past miraculous events.

In southern Iran there is an unadorned place that nonetheless attracts dozens of villagers and nomadic people on Muslim commemorative days; a large rock has been split due to the growth of a tree and it now appears as if the tree is growing through the rock. Some people come because of the wonder of this phenomenon, others because they believe that 'Ali or Husayn once visited there. They come for the day, with a lunch, and the rock is often stained with the blood of a sheep or goat that has been sacrificed in response to a vow. Itinerant darvishes are present to give amulets and offer prayers. Charity to a poor person is believed to have greater value if it occurs on a holy day and/or at a holy place, and darvishes benefit from these good works.

Visits to shrines occur on commemorative days such as the birth and death of the Prophet and the imams, although often a local saint's day will take precedence. Muslims often combine a private ceremony such as a circumcision with a visit to a shrine (for a fictionalized account, see O' Donnell 1970). Curing rites occur at shrines, thereby adding to the efficacy of the ritual. Oaths taken at shrines are given validity. A person's reputation is enhanced if he or she has been on a pilgrimage, and in the case of the major sites an honorific title becomes attached to the name of the person (*hajji, Mashhadi, Karbalahi*). Pilgrimage is one of the few ways by which women can acquire status and respect equal to men. A person having made a pilgrimage receives divine grace from it and is often sought out for blessings.

Prayer and religious gatherings. Such gatherings (*rozehs, mersiyehs, qraya, sofrehs*) have been mentioned in the context of Shi'a mourning rites, and they are important events for women in most Muslim areas. Prayer gatherings, usually held in private homes, occur on funeral and mourning occasions and during certain Islamic months. They are sponsored by women who wish to commemorate the suffering of Husayn and family as well as the deaths in their own families. Prayer leaders — sometimes women — recite from the Qur'ān, offer sermons, and retell events in the lives of Fatimah, Zaynab, and other Muslim figures. Prayer gatherings are also offered by women who wish to ask a favor of Allah or one of the imams. Mansur writes about a religious ceremony called "The Night of the Forty-five Sultans," in which the names of holy figures are called out, in this case to ask their favor in granting the woman sponsor's wish that her daughter pass her college examinations (1972:108-9). Gatherings such as these, and the curing and spirit possession cults discussed hereafter, have important social functions, because they provide women with opportunities for social interaction and for achievement of status. Women who sponsor gatherings or who perform as leaders acquire status and respect.

Religious orders. Sufi orders and religious brotherhoods (*tariqa, zawiya*) across Muslim areas generally have fewer female than male members. Some Sufis believe that distinctions between "female" and "male" are "mere illusion," since everything is One with Allah. "Since a woman on the path of God becomes a man, she cannot be called a woman" ('Attar, as quoted in Levy 1965:132). Although few Muslim women acquire formal religious training, Sufism does allow female participation. Schimmel reports that some Sufi teaching today is carried out by women (1975:435). Women who join Sufi orders often remove themselves from or never assume conjugal and maternal roles. The person of Rabi'a al-'Adawiya (d. A. D. 801)—one of Islam's most famous Sufis and poets—is often used by contemporary Muslims as a model:

> She was reluctant to marry, but her fellow Sufis encouraged her to select a husband from one of them. She chose the most religious one and agreed to marry him if he could answer four philosophical questions. To each, he responded, "That is hidden and is known only to Allah." Her response was, "Since this is so, and I have these four questions with which to concern myself, how should I need a husband, with whom to be occupied?" And she remained unmarried (as quoted in Williams 1963:128, who cites Smith, *Rabi'a the Mystic and her Fellow-Saints in Islam,* 1928).

Zikr (remembrance) rituals of Sufi orders include prayers, ecstatic chanting and dancing, drumming, Qur'ānic recitals, incense-burning, and so forth (Fahim 1973:166). While female and male members may have separate rituals, they may also participate together (for example, see Kennedy and Fahim 1974).

Women in Somalia have their own orders, and they participate in activities in the name of the Prophet's daughter Fatimah, whom they regard as the founder of women's orders (Lewis 1955a:592). A religious institution found among Mzabite women in Algeria has important functions in social control (Alport 1970, Farrag 1971).

✓ *Spirits.* Belief in spirits (most commonly called *jinn*) is prevalent throughout Muslim areas and is an aspect of religious life that is sometimes identified with women. Many men deny the existence of spirits, even though *jinn* are mentioned and given credence in the Qur'ān. There are rituals connected with *jinn* as well as techniques of detection and exorcism. Although some *jinn* are malevolent, others are merely tricky; in each case they are believed to be the cause of many of the misfortunes and disruptions of daily life (see Donaldson 1938). A person who is acting abnormally is believed to have been "hit" or possessed by a *jinn* . Even a pot of stew knocked into the fire is the playful work of *jinn*. A desert bush that remains green is believed to be the abode of spirits, and women tie rags to its branches as offerings (Rice 1923:243). Some *jinn* take human form, with slight anatomica. abnormalities, such as in the case of a camel-footed she-demon. In Iran one way to identify a *jinn* in human form is to peek at its feet; if they are on backwards, a speedy departure is advised. Some *jinn* take animal form, and others are in drafts of air, invisible in empty bathhouses, or ready to trip an unsuspecting traveler on a dark night. It is interesting to note that the literature refers to female *jinn* more often than to male *jinn*.

Curing and spirit possession cults. Curing and spirit possession cults of various kinds (*zar, sar*) are found throughout Muslim areas (Barclay 1964, Fakhouri 1968, Lewis 1971, Morsy 1978). From a reading of the literature, it appears that the majority of participants are females; spirit possession seems to be primarily a symptom of women, and the individuals who are skilled in exorcism are often women (*kadiya*). Men sometimes criticize women for these rituals; in some places men claim to know nothing about them.

> Women stand out today as the mainstays of certain quasi-Muslim cults; the *zar* cult, the *fiqi* cult, and the cult of saints, all representing more ecstatic elements of Sudanese Islam in contrast to the restrained quality of the highly formalized orthodox rituals which are primarily the province of men. (Barclay 1963:207)

Although the expressed object of the gatherings (*zar, hadra*) is to relieve the victim of the spirit or foreign substance that is the cause of the malady, the concern shown by the gathered women cannot help but assist in the alleviation of many socio-psychologically induced symptoms. An important aspect of these and other collective rites is that they offer a means of addressing and solving problems that the other realms of women's lives may not provide. In Morocco, the activities of a cult surrounding the "worship" of 'A'isha Qandisha, the camel-footed she-demon, consist of placating her through dance and song and exorcising her from the body of sufferers (female and male) (Crapanzano 1972, 1974).

Evil eye. Another area of belief concerns the "evil eye." It is brought about unconsciously in a look or statement of praise for something attractive or desired. "Unconscious" envy is the power that can bring harm. For this reason, anything treasured or desired, like a newborn baby, a horse, a taxi, a beautiful carpet, or even a nicely arranged household, is protected with prophylactic devices such as blue beads, salt, mirrors, the Qur'ān, or some wild rue. On one level these devices serve to detract the evil that may befall the object; on another level they remind the observer to be spartan in praise or to preface praise with "bismillah . . ." ("in the name of Allah . . .") (see Spooner 1970). In most places the evil eye can only originate with an acquaintance; an outsider cannot work evil in this way. This belief system serves as a distance-creating device between individuals who, through daily contact, may be brought into such close contact that conflict is possible.

Spells. The casting of spells, for the purposes of healing, punishing thieves, or arousing passions, crosses into the realm of magic (Stirling 1965:230). Qur'ānic texts are written on pieces of paper and swallowed (or boiled in water which is then drunk) or are intoned in incomprehensible recitative (ibid.). Local individuals of ill repute may provide "evil" spells while many respected religious practitioners provide "good" spells. These practitioners may also be called upon for the exorcism of suspected spells (for an example in Turkey, see Mansur 1972:111-13).

Vows. Making a vow (*nithr, nazr*) entails a promise to perform a task if a given wish is granted. At thousands of shrines and wayside places, locks and keys, personal mementos, bits of knotted cloth, or piles of stones indicate vows. Vows are also made to holy persons. Among Shi'a Muslims, women sponsor religious gatherings (such as *sofreh hazrat-i abbas*)[4] to fulfill vows.

Discussion

Through these beliefs and practices women define Islam in terms that allow their active participation. Since women are often encouraged not to attend the mosque, they find other places of sanctity and worship, such as tombs and shrines. Since they may be excluded from men's community and public acts of worship, they have their own, more private, gatherings for prayer, curing, and mourning. Since Islam does not provide a clergy, women seek out individuals who possess knowledge about religious issues. The use of holy persons, shrines, and vows is an attempt to communicate religious feelings and beliefs. Some hope, by their acts, to find favor with the imams and saints who will intercede with God on the Day of Resurrection (Spooner 1963:87). Some rituals provide means of repentance.

The various religious responses address the particular problems of women. One set of problems is biologically imposed and relates to their important functions as mothers. Much of the effort surrounding pilgrimages, appeals to holy persons, curing sessions, amulets, and vows relates to problems of conception and child mortality (see Early 1977). This particular set of problems has a cultural component, since the burden of reproduction and nuture rests with women; a barren marriage is thought to be the fault of the wife. Women have a closer association and deeper emotional involvement with the rites of passage than men, and many of these religious activities are attempts to deal with such critical events. The second set of problems is culturally imposed and is seen in principles of social organization and in social patterns: patriarchy, patrilineality, patrilocality, child marriage, polygyny, sudden repudiation, seclusion, and male domination of economic and political systems. In societies in which women do not control the course of their own lives, religious expression allows them some degree of control. Few institutional or socially acceptable means exist for the alleviation of domestic and family difficulties, and the patterns already described provide one means of coping with various aspects of male domination. Religious participation gives women a set of activities that are not restricted to the domestic domain. They provide one, and, for some women, perhaps the only, legitimate arena outside the home, and they serve to mitigate the isolating effects of seclusion (see Papanek 1973).

Lacking full-status economic and political roles in the society at large, many women, often with unconscious intent, struggle for control and power through a "manipulation of the supernatural." Through the practice of esoteric ritual (magic potions, vows, trances) women are able to instill fear in men concerning men's powers of virility, fertility, and fatherhood (important as symbols of power in the secular world). Lewis has written of the cult activities of women in various Islamic societies that allow them to air grievances obliquely through the medium of spirits in a temporary display of defiance of male dominance, and to gain, in the end, (temporary) satisfaction from difficult domestic situations (1971:72-89).

The social functions of women's beliefs and religious activities should not be underestimated. Since some of the activities involve groups of women, essential links between and among women are created, links which can crosscut and override kin and status group barriers (barriers that continue to stand between men) (see Good 1978). Female solidarity in the form of "sub-societies" or "quasi-groups," in social systems that ordain the segregation and seclusion of women, can be a powerful social force and is one way of enhancing position vis-à-vis the male members of the community (see Sanday 1974, Tapper 1978). Female solidarity also serves to mitigate male domination by lowering the degree of dependence that women have on men (Papanek 1973:313, Pastner 1971). Effective controls within patriarchal systems work to decrease the incidence of female gatherings, for whatever purpose, but religious activities (such as mourning rites and collective prayer sessions) are thought by men to be more legitimate than others and are permitted.

In social systems in which women's status is primarily ascribed, participation or expertise in religion may allow women to achieve status (see Tapper 1978). Especially for those who are of low status, participation in a group in which social attributes are largely irrelevant provides a sense of personal validity. The principal performers in ecstatic dances in one area of Morocco were women who were widowed or otherwise stigmatized (Maher 1974:97).

Little attention has been paid in the literature to the function of variations within religious systems. Even less has been paid to the contribution of women to religion. Although social mechanisms, some of which are not connected with the Islamic tradition, serve to restrict women's roles in religious life more than they do men's roles, women do make considerable contributions to the faith. Women turn an abstract faith into a pragmatic one. They embroider on the foundations of Islam by using in unique and personal fashion its symbols, themes, and metaphors. In creating a personal and less formal system of belief and practice, women are enhancing the appeal of Islam and facilitating its continued popularity.[5] While male members of the Islamic community do not always continue the religious practices they observed as children among the female members of the household, the impact of this first contact with the religion cannot be erased; Islam was a living faith for them, and it may continue to be so, even with the professed lack of concern about religion that often comes with manhood.

An American-educated Muslim acquaintance, who does not pray or fast, still performs a few of the rituals he learned from his mother. Major journeys cannot commence without the travelers each in turn passing under a tray holding the Qur'ān, a glass of water, and some sugar; the Qur'ān is kissed and pressed to the forehead. This small but habitual ritual is a poignant expression of this individual's beliefs and of his separation from family and home.

Social scientists report that women more than men in many societies preserve traditions of all kinds from the pressures of rapid social change. Islamic scholars place great store on women as "the purity of Islam"; many women embody this spirit in action and in mind. Muslim women are often reported to be more diligent in ritual than men; their observance of prayers and the fast may be more properly and faithfully performed than men's. They are able to shame men into religious observance when inclination wavers. Women may give alms and charity in the spirit that Muhammad intended, while men may be more calculating, distributing their shares according to the economic and political ties they hope to forge (see Antoun 1968b, 1968c). Women may have more knowledge of the everyday details of Islamic belief, ritual, and history than do men, and they cause the perpetuation of these details in the next generation (see Papanek 1973:322-23).[6] As a mother, one of a woman's main duties, according to Islamic doctrine, is to provide moral and religious training for her children. She is the "consciousness" of her household, encouraging its members to engage in proper behavior. She is the guardian of the morality of her children, and she embodies in deed the purity of her father's and son's families (see Schimmel 1975:426-35).

Conclusion

Published material, in the form of personal accounts by Muslim and Middle Eastern women, ethnographic studies, and analytical essays, has only very recently become available about women's own perceptions of these issues (see, for example, Fernea and Bezirgan 1977, Beck and Keddie 1978, Dwyer 1978a). Because of sexual segregation and social restrictions, women and men are often given somewhat different views of Islam. However, an analytical separation of the many variations in patterns of belief and ritual in Islam is not possible and is not perceived in this way by its practitioners. The absence of a single religious institution, in addition to the religion's spread through many cultural zones, does not permit the emergence of any single pattern of Islamic belief and practice (Adams 1976). For the women of Islam their religious patterns should be viewed as attempts to mold a faith to their own perceptions of the world. For each Muslim woman, her particular religious beliefs and practices provide for her own special needs, and they define, in her mind, the steps that aid her in attaining status, both as a religious person and as a Muslim, in the way her particular culture defines.

Notes

1. Sponsored by the Center for the Study of World Religions, Harvard University, April 19, 1975. Appreciation is offered to Jane Smith who organized and directed the workshop. Nikki Keddie, John Petropulos, Michael Fischer, and Nancy Klepper offered helpful comments on earlier drafts of this paper. I am indebted to many individuals who have shared with me their thoughts and their writings on the position of women in Muslim society.

2. These initial remarks are included in somewhat different form in my essay in *Women in Asia* (Beck, in preparation).

3. The following examples of belief and ritual are drawn from a wide reading of ethnographic materials, fieldwork experiences in Iran, and travel throughout the Middle East.

4. "A meal for 'Abbas." 'Abbas was killed in a gruesome way at the side of his half-brother Husayn at the battle of Karbala.

5. Religious brotherhoods and other movements also play important roles in the vitalization of Islam. Interpretations similar to that given here to women can be extended to the major figures in these movements, "holy men who are interested and capable of spontaneous and creative new interpretations of Islam at all levels" (Yalman 1969:58).

6. For another religious tradition, Singer comments that men delegate to women the responsibility for household ritual (1968:439). It may be that women take on these duties on their own.

Bibliography

Adams, Charles J.
    1976   "Islamic Religious Tradition." In *The Study of the Middle East*. Edited by Leonard Binder. New York: John Wiley and Sons.

Alport, E. A.
    1970 "The Mzab." In *Peoples and Cultures of the Middle East*. Volume 2. Edited by Louise Sweet. Garden City, N.Y.: Natural History Press.

Antoun, Richard
    1968a "On the Modesty of Women in Arab Muslim Villages: A Study in the Accommodation of Traditions." *American Anthropologist* 70:671-97.
    1968b "The Social Significance of Ramadan in an Arab Village." *Muslim World* 58 (1):36-42.
    1968c "The Social Significance of Ramadan in an Arab Village." *Muslim World* 59 (2):95-104.

Barclay, Harold

1963 "Muslim Religious Practice in a Village Suburb of Khartoum." *Muslin World* 53 (3):205-11.

1964 *Buurri al-Lamaab: A Suburban Village in the Sudan.* Ithaca: Cornell University Press.

Beck, Lois

in preparation. "Female and Male Relationships in the Muslim Middle East." In *Women in Asia.* Edited by Joyce Lebra and Joy Paulson.

Beck, Lois, and Keddie, Nikki, eds.

1978 *Women in the Muslim World.* Cambridge, Mass., and London, England: Harvard University Press.

Bill, James

1972 *The Politics of Iran: Groups, Classes and Modernization.* Columbus, Ohio: Charles Merrill.

Bittari, Zoubeida

1964 *O, mes soeurs musulmanes, pleurez!* Paris: Gallimard.

Boyce, Mary

1978 *A Persian Stronghold of Zoroastrianism.* Oxford: Oxford University Press.

Cobban, Helena

1977 "Iran Women Drop Veils to Work." *Des Moines Register,* Sept. 20.

Coulson, Noel J.

1964 *A History of Islamic Law.* Edinburgh: Edinburgh University Press.

Coulson, Noel J., and Hinchcliffe, Doreen

1978 "Women and Law Reform in Contemporary Islam." In *Women in the Muslim World.* Edited by Lois Beck and Nikki Keddie. Cambridge: Harvard University Press.

Crapanzano, Vincent

1972 "The Hamadsha." In *Scholars, Saints, and Sufis.* Edited by Nikki Keddie. Berkeley: University of California Press.

1974 *The Hamadsha: A Study in Moroccan Ethnopsychiatry.* Berkeley: University of California Press.

Davis, Susan Schaefer

1978 "Working Women in a Moroccan Village." In *Women in the Muslim World.* Edited by Lois Beck and Nikki Keddie. Cambridge: Harvard University Press.

Donaldson, Bess Allen

1938 *The Wild Rue: A Study of Muhammadan Magic and Folklore in Iran.* London: Luzac and Company.

Dwyer, Daisy
1978a *Images and Self-Images: Male and Female in Morocco.*
New York: Columbia University Press.

1978b "Women, Sufism, and Decision-Making in Moroccan Islam."
In *Women in the Muslim World.* Edited by Lois Beck and Nikki Keddie. Cambridge: Harvard University Press.

Early, Evelyn
1977 "Fertility and Fate." Paper presented at the meeting of the Middle East Studies Association, New York.

1978 "Entrepreneurship among Lower Class Egyptian Women."
Paper presented at the meeting of the Middle East Studies Association, Ann Arbor, Michigan.

Fahim, Hussein
1973 "Change in Religion in a Resettled Nubian Community, Upper Egypt." *International Journal of Middle East Studies* 4:163-77.

Fakhouri, Hani
1968 "The Zar Cult in an Egyptian Village." *Anthropological Quarterly* 41 (1):49-56.

Farrag, Amina
1971 "Social Control among the Mzabite Women of Beni-Isguen."
Middle Eastern Studies (3):317-27.

Fernea, Elizabeth
1965 *Guests of the Sheik: An Ethnography of an Iraqi Village.*
Garden City, N.Y.: Doubleday.

Fernea, Elizabeth, and Bezirgan, Basima, eds.
1977 *Middle Eastern Muslim Women Speak.* Austin: University of Texas Press.

Fernea, Robert, and Fernea, Elizabeth
1972 "Variations in Religious Observance among Islamic Women." In *Scholars, Saints, and Sufis.* Edited by Nikki Keddie. Berkeley: University of California Press.

Geertz, Clifford
1968 *Islam Observed.* Chicago: University of Chicago Press.

Gellner, Ernest
1972 "Doctor and Saint." In *Scholars, Saints, and Sufis.* Edited by Nikki Keddie. Berkeley: University of California Press.

Good, Mary-Jo DelVecchio
1978 "A Comparative Perspective on Women in Provincial Iran and Turkey." In *Women in the Muslim World.* Edited by Lois Beck and Nikki Keddie. Cambridge: Harvard University Press.

Haqqi, Yahya
1973 *The Saint's Lamp and Other Stories.* Translated by M. Badawi.
Leiden: E. J. Brill.

Keddie, Nikki
1972 "Introduction." In *Scholars, Saints, and Sufis.* Edited by Nikki
Keddie. Berkeley: University of California Press.

Keddie, Nikki, and Beck, Lois
1977 "Introduction." In *Women in the Muslim World.* Edited by Lois
Beck and Nikki Keddie. Cambridge: Harvard University Press.

Kennedy, John G., and Fahim, Hussein
1974 "Nubian Dhikr Rituals and Cultural Change." *Muslim World*
64(3):205-19.

Lewis, I. M.
1955a "Sufism in Somaliland: A Study in Tribal Islam." *Bulletin of the
School of Oriental and African Studies* 17 (3):581-602.

1955b "Sufism in Somaliland: A Study in Tribal Islam." *Bulletin of the
School of Oriental and African Studies* 18 (1):145-60.

1971 *Ecstatic Religion.* Baltimore: Penguin.

Levy, Reuben
1965 *The Social Structure of Islam.* Cambridge: Cambridge University
Press.

Maher, Vanessa
1974 *Women and Property in Morocco.* Cambridge: Cambridge
University Press.

Mansur, Fatma Cosar
1972 *Bodrum: A Town in the Aegean.* Leiden: E. J. Brill.

Mernissi, Fatima
1977 "Women, Saints, and Sanctuaries." *SIGNS: Journal of Women in
Culture and Society* 3 (1):101-12.

Morsy, Soheir
1978 "Sex Differences and Folk Illness in an Egyptian Village." In
Women in the Muslim World. Edited by Lois Beck and Nikki Keddie.
Cambridge: Harvard University Press.

Nash, June, and Safa, Helen, eds.
1976 *Sex and Class in Latin America.* New York: Praeger.

O'Donnell, Terence
1970 "The Pilgrimage." *Atlantic* 226 (3):85-89.

Papanek, Hanna
1973 "Purdah: Separate Worlds and Symbolic Shelter." *Comparative
Studies in Society and History* 15 (3):289-325.

Pastner, Carroll
n.d. "Gradations of Purdah and the Creation of Social Boundaries on a
Baluchistan Oasis." Unpublished manuscript.

1971 "Sexual Dichotomization in Society and Culture: The Women of Panjgur, Baluchistan." Ph.D. thesis, Bradeis University.

Peters, Emrys
1956 "A Muslim Passion Play." *Atlantic Monthly* 198:176-80.

Rice, C. Colliver
1923 *Persian Women and Their Ways.* London: Seeley, Service and Company.

Roy, Manisha
1975 *Bengali Women.* Chicago: University of Chicago Press.

Saleh, Saneya
1972a "Women in Islam: Their Status in Religious and Traditional Culture." *International Journal of Sociology of the Family* 2 (1):35-42.

1972b "Women in Islam: Their Role in Religious and Traditional Culture." *International Journal of Sociology of the Family* 2 (2):193-201.

Sanday, Peggy
1974 "Female Status in the Public Domain." In *Woman, Culture, and Society.* Edited by Michelle Rosaldo and Louise Lamphere. Stanford: Stanford University Press.

Schimmel, Annemarie
1975 *Mystical Dimensions of Islam.* Chapel Hill: University of North Carolina Press.

Singer, Milton
1968 "The Indian Joint Family in Modern Industry." In *Structure and Change in Indian Society.* Edited by Milton Singer and Bernard Cohn. Chicago: Aldine.

Smith, Margaret
1928 *Rabi'a the Mystic and Her Fellow-Saints in Islam.* Cambridge: Cambridge University Press.

Spooner, Brian
1963 "The Function of Religion in Persian Society." *Iran* 1:83-95.

1970 "The Evil Eye in the Middle East." In *Witchcraft, Confessions and Accusations.* Edited by Mary Douglas. London: Tavistock.

Stirling, Paul
1965 *Turkish Village.* New York: John Wiley and Sons.

Tapper, Nancy
1978 "The Women's Subsociety Among the Shahsevan Nomads of Iran." In *Women in the Muslim World.* Edited by Lois Beck and Nikki Keddie. Cambridge: Harvard University Press.

Thaiss, Gustav
1972 "Religious Symbolism and Social Change: The Drama of Hussain." In *Scholars, Saints, and Sufis.* Edited by Nikki Keddie. Berkeley: University of California Press.

1973 "Unity and Discord: The Symbol of Husayn in Iran." In *Iranian Civilization and Culture.* Edited by Charles Adams. Montreal: McGill University, Institute of Islamic Studies.

Trimingham, J. Spencer
1971 *The Sufi Orders in Islam.* London: Oxford University Press.

Weekes, Richard
1978 *Muslim Peoples: A World Ethnographic Survey.* Westport,. CT: Greenwood Press.

White, Elizabeth H.
1978 "Legal Reform as an Indicator of Women's Status in Muslim Nations." In *Women in the Muslim World.* Edited by Lois Beck and Nikki Keddie. Cambridge: Harvard University Press.

Williams, John Alden
1963 *Islam.* New York: Washington Square Press.

Wolf, Eric
1969 "Society and Symbols in Latin Europe and in the Islamic Near East: Some Comparisons." *Anthropological Quarterly* 42 (3):287-301.

von Grunebaum, Gustave
1951 *Muhammedan Festivals.* New York: Schuman.

Yalman, Nur
1969 "Islamic Reform and the Mystic Tradition in Eastern Turkey." *Archives of European Sociology* 10:41-60.

Youssef, Nadia
1974 *Women and Work in Developing Societies.* Westport, CT: Greenwood Press.

1978 "The Status and Fertility Patterns of Muslim Women." In *Women in the Muslim World.* Edited by Lois Beck and Nikki Keddie. Cambridge: Harvard University Press.

Traditional Affirmations Concerning the Role of Women as Found in Contemporary Arab Islamic Literature

YVONNE YAZBECK HADDAD

*Department of Philosophy
and Religion
Colgate University*

The woman is a noble creature, she is superior in her gentle humanity. God has decreed that her nobility and happiness be concerned with her fulfillment of her role as a wife and mother.

('Abd al-Wāhid 1972:178)

These sentences published in 1972 may be regarded as summary of the conservative Muslim attitude toward women in contemporary writings. There appears to be a recent resurgence of interest in delineating and affirming the value of the Islamic foundation of the role of women and of marriage, and in defining and defending the progressive and revolutionary role that Islam has ascribed to women in society.

The material surveyed appears to be mainly apologetic in nature.[1] It is primarily aimed at women in an effort to stem the tide of imitating Western standards that is eroding the religious and legal foundations of Islamic society. In this context Islam is presented as the culmination of the historical development of the liberation of women. Surveys of the condition of women in different civilizations — Greek, Roman, Jewish, Persian, Chinese, Indian, Arab (pre-Islamic), and Christian — reveal that women were oppressed as they were treated with disdain, as nonentities, nonpersons, or as delinquent. Men were allowed an indefinite number of women. Meanwhile Islam, the religion of God, has liberated women and restored them to the role to which they were preordained. Thus Islam did not only free women from slavery, it elevated their status to that of human beings and gave them the right to live, the right to inherit, the right to learn, the right to keep their own names, and the right to have possessions.[2] One gets the feeling that most of these authors "have packed their writings with the glories of the Arab woman in all the ages. However, no matter how extensive their collection of material may be, one is incapable of discerning a correct general opinion about women in Islam. How did Islam save her? How did Islam elevate her to new heights? Rather, one finds in most of it general rhetorical words that need veracity, documentation, and evidence" (Al-Afghānī 1964:6).

For most authors, what appears to be at stake is not the role of women per se, but rather the validity of Islam as the final revelation of God for mankind. Their works appear to be the echo of conservatism reaffirming the belief that Islam is *THE WAY OF LIFE* and that all life is Islam. There is no differentiation between the secular and the sacred, between custom and law. All life in Islam is to follow the teachings of the Qur'ān and the way of the Prophet — *sunnat al-nabī*.

Thus their writings in the defense of Islam are also aimed at the secularists, men like Qāsim Amīn and Khālid Muḥammad Khālid, who ascribe the role of women to customs, making it therefore subject to change and reform. Qāsim Amīn wrote, "Yes, I come with an innovation, however, it is not of the essence of Islam, rather it is of customs and methods of interaction in which it is good to seek perfection" (Amīn 1970:31). Thus by relegating the role of women to customs rather than the tenets of religion, Amīn could call for change and progress.

This approach is conceived by the conservative leaders as contrary not only to the teachings of the Prophet, but to the revelation of God. The role of women as prescribed by the Qur'ān is part of God's blueprint for man's happiness in this world and the next. It cannot be changed or altered. Muḥammad established the perfect society in Medina. Any change that would be tolerated in Islam would be to remove vestiges of pagan customs or innovations from the West, thus purifying society from corrupt practices and returning to the Way of God as decreed in the Holy Book.

Furthermore, these works are not only aimed at secularists and the women who are led astray by them, they are also addressed to those religious leaders who tend to ignore some verses in the Qur'ān that may not sound progressive, preferring rather to emphasize some positive aspects that agree with the movement to grant women social and political equality under the law. They are probably aimed at the writings and decrees of Maḥmūd Shaltūt, rector of al-Azhar (d. 1963), who reformed that institution and allowed women to be accepted as students. He also insisted that Islam gave women political rights since the Prophet accepted the *bayᶜa* from the women of Medina, meanwhile affirming that the Qur'ān treats male and female as equal in the sight of God. Woman thus is a partner in the initial formation of humanity and has the right to education and religious responsibility before God (Amīn 1970:9-23).

Finally, the material surveyed is aimed at the government of Egypt which in its efforts to modernize and proceed with industrialization and the revolution advocated the freedom and equality of women. "Woman must be regarded as equal to man and must therefore shed the remaining shackles that impede her free movement so that she might take a constructive and profound part in shaping life."[3] In this manner the government attempted to guarantee the right of women to full participation in the planning and implementation of a new order.

At the heart of the debate is the attempt to limit the role of the woman to that ascribed to her by the traditions and to which traditional society has restricted her — that of wife and mother. This is not only her role, it is to be her sole identity. For in Islam marriage is a central institution: its importance is seen as a social duty incumbent on each individual.[4] It is prescribed by the Qur'ān (And of everything we have created pairs: that you may receive instruction) (*Sūra* 51:49), and by the Prophet who reportedly said, "If a person marries, he has fulfilled half the religion."[5] Consequently, "the individual has no right to do as he pleases . . . If one does not marry, he deprives another from getting married, thus making him susceptible to temptation and evil" (Yālgin 1972:17). In this context, marriage is seen as providing physical fulfillment for natural desires and a healthy channel for sexual and psychological needs, as well as the maintenance of society through progeny. Celibacy is reduced to a deviation, contrary to the order of the universe as created by God,[6] which renders the goals of life inoperative (Sharqāwī 1967:19; cf. Darwaza 1967:60-64). Thus a Muslim girl should be brought up and educated in preparation for these roles. Any other education is at best superfluous, if not actually harmful.[7]

Contemporary discussion concerning the education of women is centered around the content, purpose, and utility of that education. That women are to be educated (al-Abrāshī 1970:113-19) seems to be taken for granted or as a *fait accompli*. What is questioned is the policy of the department of education to provide the same academic preparation for both boys and girls,[8] thus undermining the Islamic definition of the female role.

> If a woman is to be educated, what is suitable would be to learn the principles of religion, home making, child rearing and what is necessary concerning health, worship and human relations. For she who helps her husband in his life, cleaning his house, straightening his bed, and arranging his furniture is better than she who reads newspapers, writes articles, demands voting rights and equal participation with men in Congress. By God she is not fit for that.[9]

A different education for women is necessitated, not only by the roles they have to assume, but also by the fact of basic differences between the sexes. These differences are not culturally conditioned,[10] rather they are of the essence of creation, part of God's wisdom as He provided for balance and harmony in life. Male and Female complement each other, each to fulfill the role for which they were preordained, each to uphold the other in their areas of weakness. It then becomes incumbent on Muslim society, not only to refrain from tampering with God's order by introducing innovations, but also to maintain the differences.

> We must guide boys to roles that affirm their capabilities, and likewise the girls. Thus every sex should be placed in a fitting role. The Muslim administration of the home should be centered on the principle that the man is chief and is responsible for the administration of the external matters of the home, whereas the woman is responsible for raising the children, social services and other necessities of society. (Yālgin 1972:74; cf. al-Abrāshī 1970:17)

Other authors elaborate on these differences, extolling the virtues of males and the weakness of females. The authority is given to man because he is the natural leader, and reality thus necessitates his being in control (al-Khūlī 1970:78).

> The differences between males and females are due to (a) [a woman's] menstruation, conception, giving birth, breast feeding, staying up nights and hard work during the day. [These] lead a woman to symptoms of depression and weakness of constitution. The man is free from all this. (b) Her work at home is limited in scope and experience; it is almost routine. As for the work of the man, it is wide in scope, extensive in experience and varied in relationships, full of scheming and artfulness. This leads to a marked difference in their intellectual capacity. (c) The woman in singing lullabyes to her child does not need a powerful brain, or perfect genius; rather, she needs a kind nature and a gentle disposition. Nothing gives her more joy than to descend to the level of her child and to live with him in the scope of his

world, thinking with his brain, talking in his language, playing with whatever pleases him. As for the male, he does not
need affection to deal with people outside, rather he needs
perseverance and strength of character, incisive intellect and
initiative. (Ibid.:77-78)[11]

Thus Islam gives precedence to man because of the way he is
created, for he has been endowed with characteristics and
capabilities—both physical and intellectual (which have not
been given to women)—that enable him to earn a living. Furthermore, scientific research has found that there are
biological, physiological, and psychological differences that
account for the "higher percentage of geniuses among men and
the higher incidence of imbeciles among women."[12]

These elaborations on the shortcomings of women must not
be seen as an indictment of the female sex, nor are they an attempt to subjugate women because of an innate chauvinistic
outlook. They must be viewed within the context of the faith
and the defense of Islam. They are a response to condemna-
tions from the outside—of missionaries and Orientalists, and of
revolt from the inside—of secularists and women's libera-
tionists, who accused Islam of relegating women to an inferior
status. The imitation of the West is seen as social imperialism.
It is not imposed by the outside, but rather is generated from a
feeling of inferiority and psychic servitude on the part of the
women in the Arab world who appear to have no confidence in
the validity and adequacy of the Arab civilization. Thus where
the missionary and the Orientalist have failed in undermining
the culture, the women and their supporters are carrying the
banner of insubordination. They are responding to acquired
values, and flirting with alien and un-Islamic standards.
Hence, the appeal is to women to preserve the Islamic society
and protect it from Western influences and fluctuating institutions. It is a plea to stand united in defending Islam against innovation and change, a desperate appeal against participation
in self-destruction.

Thus, to contemporary writers, Islam does not say that

women are inferior, rather, that they are different. They have been created for a specific function in which they can excel.[13] Liberation should not mean acquiring male characteristics or performing masculine functions, which is reprehensible;[14] rather, liberation for the woman is to be herself and to fulfill the destiny for which God has created her.

Liberation is not freedom from obedience to men, or freedom from the restrictions of the faith; rather, liberation must be from corruption and alienation that have been brought about by Western impingement on the East. It must be a liberation from measuring up to Western standards that erode the basic foundations of the community of God, a liberation from colonial status and imperialistic politics, a liberation to be onself as God has willed for the welfare of humanity within the *ummah* of Islam.

At the heart of the argument is the traditional interpretation of *Sūra* 4:34 of the Qur'ān (Men are in charge of women, because God has preferred the one over the other and because they spend (on them) of their wealth. Therefore, the righteous women are obedient, guarding the secret God would have them guard. As for those women from whom you fear disobedience, admonish them and boycott their beds and beat them. If they obey you, do not seek a way against them. God is High and Exalted.)

This verse has led contemporary authors not only to emphasize the traditions that medieval Islam ascribed to the Prophet, but also to quote selective material that may substantiate an interpretation to the effect that man is in charge of the woman, that the wife must obey her husband, and that the husband has the right to discipline his wife.

Thus the emphasis on differences between the sexes upholds the necessity of men being responsible for women and defends the relevance and validity of the teachings of the Qur'ān for today. Islam is the natural religion, and as such it affirms the goodness of human instincts and needs.

There seems to be a consensus that man is in charge of

woman (Yālgin 1972:64); however, there are differences about what that involves. For some, a literal interpretation of the verse in the Qur'ān would imply superiority for the male as he is the provider of financial support.[15] Others (al-'Aqqād 1959:7-9; Sharqāwī 1967:2; cf. Wāfī 1972:116) see a potential threat in that interpretation. For if superiority is contingent on capability to provide, the whole structure would be undermined if a woman acquired independent means and was able to support herself or her husband. Consequently, they ascribe superiority to physical and other differences.

Meanwhile those who refuse to interpret the verse as an indicator of superiority of the husband over the wife interpret "in charge" to mean having responsibility for.[16] Every social institution, no matter how small, needs a leader; and in the case of the family, the role of leadership belongs to the husband, not because of extra merit, but as a responsibility assigned to him by God to safeguard society. This does not deny that the financial support of the family is the husband's responsibility, it just affirms that it is expected of him. (For where there is no leadership, chaos and disintegration take over.)

The insistence of most authors on the necessity of confining the woman to the house and not allowing her outside employment may stem from the contemporary situation in some Arab countries. One can see, for example, in socialist Syria how the power of the husband over his wife and his absolute authority over the administration of the house and its finances is seen as being undermined. As more women seek employment and supplementary means of support, they are not only breaking the restrictions of seclusion by coming in contact with other people, both male and female, but they are also flirting with independence. The fact that the government guarantees the jobs of all who are employed provides more security than the marital status, which is threatened by divorce. Furthermore, social security benefits liberate the employed female from being dependent on her children for support. It is reported that some women refuse to resign their jobs despite the insistence of their husbands. Thus independence breeds disobedience.

As mentioned, that the wife should obey her husband is seen as the second teaching of *Sūra* 4:34 of the Qur'ān. This is usually bolstered by traditions ascribed to the Prophet that stipulate obedience as the means by which a wife attains heaven (Smith and Haddad 1975). Asked who the best woman is, the Prophet is reported to have said, "She is the one whose sight gives you pleasure and the one who obeys your order without contradiction" (Yālgin 1972:42). At another occasion it is reported that he said, "If it were permissible to have a human being worship another, I would order the woman to prostrate herself before her husband" (Ibid.:77; also Sharqāwī 1967:65 and Bayhānī 1973:23).

Thus constant obedience is seen as sanctioned by the Qur'ān and the *hadīth*. It is part of the innate nature of things and the way a wife finds fulfillment and meaning in her life.

> The happiest hour for a woman is the hour of her surrender and obedience to the man. Her greatest desire is to have a husband whose power she can feel . . . Being subservient is painful to a living being generally; however, for the woman, subservience fulfills the purpose of her femininity. She is grateful in her pain and victorious in her obedience.[17]

Furthermore, obedience to the husband does not demean the woman or detract from her self-respect, for that is the order of things.[18] She should not be in a position of authority because she is not qualified for that role. She lacks experience as well as ability, for she has not been capable of maintaining a position of responsibility despite opportunities to do so over the years. Thus:

> The best wife is she who is lively but obedient, affectionate and bears children, has a short tongue, obedient to the reins, faithful when he is absent, modest when in company, reverent in her appearance, self-effacing when standing,

sincere in her service of her husband, increasing his little into abundance and removing his sorrow with her good conduct and gentle conversation. (Sharqāwī 1967:69)

The authority of the husband is not limited to the administration of the house and the finances. The wife is required to be totally obedient concerning who visits her and where she can go. Her obedience is especially imperative in matters of sex, for the Prophet is reported to have said, "If a man calls his wife to his bed and she does not come and he sleeps in anger, the angels shall curse her until the morning" (Yālgin 1972:77).

Al-Bayhānī notes that Islam does not require of women more than was required of the Prophet's wives. Thus:

The greatest thing in which obedience is imperative is intercourse, which is the goal of marriage. It is the most important thing the man asks of his wife. It is not permissible for her to refuse it except for a legal purpose such as menstruation, sickness and childbirth. For if she does, she commits sin, and her right of clothing, housing and upkeep from her husband becomes invalidated and God's curse will be upon her. (Al-Bayhānī 1973:23)

Meanwhile, not all wives live up to the ideal. In fact, some authors note that women are incapable of doing so because of their innate nature, for the female tends to be obsessed with what is forbidden. "The story of the fall is the eternal symbol of the nature of woman which never changes: i.e., she does whatever she is told not to do" ('Aqqād, n.d.:7). Consequently, one notes that women are prone to depravity if left to their natural instincts. For

Men are the sole source of every accepted definition of good conduct whether for men or for women. Woman has never been a true source of anything to do with ethics or good character even though she brings up the children. The guidelines are provided by the male. ('Aqqād 1959:30)

Consequently, the woman should be disciplined by her husband. His right to discipline is derived from his superior knowledge of what is good and beneficial. This right has been recognized and sanctioned by the Qur'ān and the Prophet and upheld by centuries of Islamic law.[19] Thus if she disobeys and is hard to manage, he should talk to her. If she "fails to respond to her husband's kind reproach, he should admonish her, for that is a sign that she has lost her human sensitivity and probably considers kindness as weakness in the man's character" (Yālgin, 1972:163). If she does not respond to admonition, he is to boycott her bed, for

> that is a treatment that restrains women from persisting in being contrary. [It is] humiliating to her pride, for the thing she values most is her femininity, and the strongest thing for attack she uses against man is this weapon. Thus by with-holding sex from her and showing her that he is above her, that he does not care for her, he disarms her and cheapens her wares. That is the worst defeat she could suffer. (Al-Khūlī 1970:130)

If these methods do not work, physical punishment must be used, for it is now clear that she has become like an animal. Most of the sources do insist that the husband must beat her gently (Yālgin 1972:163; Abrāshī 1970:35-36; Baltājī 1974:279; 'Aqqād 1959:131). If these methods do not work, he should seek arbitration. His final weapon, of course, is divorce.

A review of the contemporary literature on the role of women in Islam presupposes the husband-wife relationship as one threatened by antagonism, or at best a struggle for self-assertion and dominance. This is generally based on the idea of the polarity of the sexes who represent different instincts and needs. Islam has provided the legislation that eradicates contention and leads to harmony and peace.

Parallel to the discussion of the role of the wife, the sources attempt to answer questions raised about polygamy. Generally there is a consensus in defense of the custom. Several authors justify it as a means of safeguarding the family, since it does not necessitate divorce of the first wife as a prerequisite of marrying another as is the custom in the West. For, whereas Western man practices polygamy through multiple marriages contracted successively, in Islam the possibility of having four wives concurrently protects these innocent women from the pain of separation and the shame of divorce.

The Modernists' interpretation of *Sūra* 4:3 (And if you fear that you will treat the orphans unjustly, marry what pleases you of women, two, three or four. If you fear that you will not be just, then one, of what your right hand possesses. This will prevent you from acting unjustly) puts the emphasis on one woman, since the marriage of multiple wives is contingent on justice, and the verse says that ". . . you will not be just . . . " Thus modernists like Muḥammad ᶜAbduh and his students have emphasized the necessity of limiting the number of wives to one. This interpretation is surprisingly contested by Shaltūt, who attacks the Egyptian Ministry of Social Affairs for its attempt in 1945 to introduce legislation that would restrict the number of wives to one. This legislation gives the judge the right to grant permission for marrying more wives after examination and verification that the man's character and financial means would support a second wife. (Shaltūt 1964:207).

> Anyone who interprets the verse about plurality of wives and restricting their number to one is falsifying the revelation . . . Polygamy is Islamic and the Sharī ᶜa has sanctioned it. As for the question of justice, that is left for the individual. (Ibid.: 201, 203)

Shaltūt's objection to restrictive polygamy or conditional monogamy is based on his sense of social justice. If the law stipulates that the man has to have the means to support more than one wife before he is allowed to marry another, only the rich can benefit. Consequently he suggests that "the leaders of the nation should seek legislation not to limit or restrict polygamy, but rather to put a limit on celibacy and to produce legislation to aid (financially) those who marry more than one to encourage others to follow suit and to help them pay for their wives and progeny."(Ibid.:204).

Restrictive polygamy is also contested by Bint Al-Shāṭi' (ᶜĀ'isha ᶜAbd al-Raḥmān) in her *al-Qur'ān wa-al-Tafsīr al-ᶜAṣrī* (1970:57-58). Here she attacks Muṣṭafā Maḥmūd's interpretation of *Sūra* 4:3 as restricting marriage to one person contingent on the question of justice. To her this raises an old theological question of the possibility of God's enjoining two contradictory principles, on the one hand ordering the marrying of up to four wives, while on the other maintaining that only one is all He meant. Thus her support of polygamy is in defense of the Qur'ān and the inviolability of God, who does not contradict Himself.

Others see *Sūra* 4:3 as restricting polygamy to four wives. Thus the Qur'ān did not initiate polygamy, they say, nor give license to multiple marriages; rather Islam limited, restricted, and regularized polygamy, which is the law of nature. Furthermore, the virtues of polygamy allow justice for the husband in cases where the wife is barren, when she is sick, or is sexually frigid. It also has social benefits as it helps restore population in underpopulated areas, especially when there is an abundance of women after a war (Al-Khūlī, 1970:90-93; Yālgin 1972:169-70; Al-Abrāshī, 1970:58-59).

Polygamy also helps solve social problems, such as when the wife is sick or suffering from a contagious or debilitating disease:

> What should a man do in this condition? Should he abstain for the rest of his life, and abstinance after marriage — as they say — is harder on the soul than before marriage? Should he divorce his sick wife and abandon her or expel her from the house in order to marry another? How could he send her out when she is in this condition? Where would she go, and where would she find shelter? What religion, what human conscience accepts that he would do this

contemptible act, what could be more unjust than this?
Should he bother the sick woman on her bed when she is in
her weakest and least capable condition? What should the
husband do . . . etc. (Yālgin 1972: 169-70)[20]

Another interpretation of the verse that is offered is that God
made marrying more than one wife contingent on solving the
problem of orphans (Al-Madanī, *Ra'ī*, pp. 21-25), especially
after a war. The verse was revealed because these Muslims had
obeyed God and refrained from burying their daughters when
young; this legislation was intended to solve the problem of the
abundance of women. Multiple wives ensure that orphan girls
are not left unmarried. This is consistent with the Islamic
injunction against celibacy. Hence we note that current
writings on the role of women tend to insist on polygamy as
Islamic, as right and as necessary.

One of the reasons given in defense of polygamy is the
problem of the barren wife. A wife should be capable of
bearing children. The Prophet is reported to have said, "A
black woman who can bear children is better than a beautiful
woman who is barren."[21] Children fulfill man's instinct for
procreation and for the preservation of the species. They also
provide support for the parents in their old age.[22]

The role of the mother in Islam is highly respected. It is
attained by those who have persevered and fulfilled their duties
as wives. The Qur'ān prescribes that parents should be
respected and honored. Some *hadīths* suggest that the role of
the mother is superior to that of the father.

A man came to the Prophet and asked him "Who should I
respect and obey?" The Prophet answered, "Your mother."
Then he asked, "Who then?" The Prophet answered, "Your
mother." Then he asked, "Who then?" The Prophet
answered, "Your mother." Then he asked "Who then?" He
answered, "Your father." Thus obedience comes three times
to the mother before the father. (Al-Abrāshī 1970: 39-40)[23]

The relation between a mother and her son is considered a

very deep and special one, a spiritual endowment that makes her the sole "source of life". (al-Khūlī 1970:139-42). It is a relationship that does not involve the father. Whereas the husband-wife relationship is seen as a polarity of two elements often in tension, that of mother and son is one of serene harmony. The son not only obeys his mother but provides for her needs and protects her from whatever disturbs her:

> For the mother has suffered a great deal for her son. Long has she stayed up so he can sleep, and labored and become tired that he may rest, and suffered so he can be happy, gone hungry so he can eat, she put him above herself. Her happiest moment is when she sees him happy, smiling, healthy, intelligent. She is always ready to ransom him with whatever she possesses — no matter what the price is. Can the son forget her good deeds? (al-Abrāshī 1970: 44-45)

Thus the patience of the wife pays off in great dividends. She is recompensed by the devotion and obedience of her children. As a mother, her life is fulfilled and her identity is established. For a careful observation of Arab society reveals that the dual and complementary role of wife and mother present a generally accurate picture of the way a woman is perceived and of the way she perceives herself.

The special role of the mother may be attributed to the fact that in most cases the son is the only man in her life with whom she has a love relationship. This may be caused by the general attitudes and sanctions of society concerning male-female relationships. These include the tendency to segregate the sexes, the emphasis that any association between male and female can only be or lead to a sexual relationship,[24] the restrictions against women openly expressing emotions toward men, the predominance of arranged marriages, the frequent discrepancy in the age of the couples, and the woman's fear of divorce and its contingent stigma.

Thus the only free love relationship is that between a mother and her son. It is free because it is the only one sanctioned by society. By the time the son is in his late teens or early twenties, he assumes the role of the provider. Thus the older the son becomes the greater the increase in the status of the mother as she tends to centralize power and assume the running of the household. Where there is a great discrepancy in age between husband and wife, the old and tired husband retires while the wife comes into her own.

When the son marries, the daughter-in-law is initiated into the role of the wife who labors patiently and obeys silently, waiting for the day of her liberation through her son. Meanwhile, the mother having survived the test of being a wife can now become a member of the elite — those who supervise and regulate the mores, customs, and sanctions of society.

The traditional role of the mother includes the supervision of her son's wife and making sure that her daughter-in-law adheres to her role as defined by society and sanctioned by Islam. It will be interesting to observe how this role of the mother changes as the incidence of nuclear families increases and that of extended families declines.

One wonders whether the shift in emphasis in contemporary literature from the superiority of the male per se to an analysis of differences and an affirmation of religious models for the roles of women is an attempt to maintain a status quo in a society that is changing rapidly, or whether it is a traditional Islamic attempt at recapturing an "idealized reality" in a situation of flux.

The latter alternative would explain the current discussion and debate concerning social and political rights of women. That women have been given these rights in Egypt is a matter of fact. Furthermore, there are professional women working as secretaries, engineers, lawyers, hostesses, congresswomen, doctors (even taking care of male patients), and so forth. What is surprising is the amount of literature published during the last ten years that condemns these achievements, affirming that such "innovations" undermine society and lead to its disintegration.

These authors tend to view the demands for social and political rights as at best misguided:

> Women have misunderstood the Islamic principle. The decrease in the woman's responsibility does not mean a decrease in her worth. Justice means that each should do what is best for him and this is what Islam has decreed. (Yālgin 1972:76)

That the witness of a woman in Islamic law is equated to half that of a man is cited by several authors as the proof of the inability of a woman to be rational, detached, and fair. As a female she is overcome by emotion, which is the single governing factor in her life. Consequently al-Ghazzālī asks, "How can half a witness be a judge?" (Ghazzālī n.d.:200). And al-ʿAqqād repeats that being a judge is not within the realm of her role, nor are social and political rights:

> Women have rights other than those of voting — these are the rights of a mother, the rights of a wife, of a fiancee, of a friend, who inspires the mind, the emotion and the imagination. If these rights are paralyzed in her hands, that would be the bankruptcy of femininity which cannot be replaced by law or by voting rights. (al-ʿAqqād, n.d.:145)

The fairness of the discrepancy between the rights of husbands and wives is justified, for

> Justice is well served in this system, for a woman always knows that the child she is bearing is definitely hers, whereas the man never has that certainty concerning those that are called his children. (Ibid.:22)

In this manner, we note that the contemporary conservative arguments are necessarily repetitious inasmuch as they are an affirmation of an inalienable truth. Male and female they were created by God; they may be equal in His sight, but He did create them as male and female, distinct — each for a specific purpose and function to fulfill His will in creation. The roles have been defined and delineated by Islamic law to uphold the community of God, the community of the faithful.

Hence Westerners attempting to understand the contemporary liberation of women in the Arab world must seek to comprehend the objections and restrictions that these movements face. The "liberated" Arab woman must seek to find her identity within the community, for Islam exists as the intersection of the individual and the communal. What this means in practical terms is that one cannot be a Muslim outside of the context of the community; consequently the emphasis is on cooperation versus competition. God's word, the Qur'ān, was not made manifest to redeem the individual as an individual and set him free; its primary goal was the establishment of a community living under the law and guidance of God, a community committed in prayer and obedience to His will.

In this context, liberation is not seen as freedom from "oppression" of men; rather it is seen in cosmic dimensions as rebellion against God and His order for the world and mankind.

This is not to disregard the fact that several reformers have called for equality and the emancipation of women. Nazīrah Zayn al-Dīn in *Al-Sufūr wa-al-Hijāb* in 1928 talks about the necessity of the freedom of each individual in order to build a progressive society. Her appeal is directed towards men in Egypt because they were in control.

In a similar manner, Qāsim Amīn, one of the pioneers of women's liberation through education in Egypt, wrote:

Ask the married people if they are loved by their wives. Their answer is "Yes." However, the truth is other than what they think. I have searched extensively in families where it is said that there is total harmony, but I have not found till now a man who loves his wife, nor a woman who has loved her husband. As for the apparent harmony between the pair, it is due either to the fact that the man is tired and has left, or that the wife has permitted her husband to treat her as though she were his private property, or that both of them are ignorant and not aware of the value of life. This latter is the condition of most Egyptians . . .

As for the first two kinds, harmony has been bought at a high price — the disintegration of one of the partners for the sake of the other. All that I will admit is that it is possible at times to see what appears like affection between married couples. This is the exception that proves the rule, which is lack of love. It is lack of love on the part of the husband because his wife is below him in mentality and education — so that there is almost no communication that would lead to an instant of mutual happiness. There is almost nothing on which they agree. That is because she is so distant from his emotions, understandings and matters that appeal to him, while she indulges in things in which he has no interest. (Amīn 1970:56)

In this commentary, Qāsim Amīn isolated one of the factors that plagued Egyptian society at his time. The education of women, he argued, would lead to mutual respect, understanding, and compatibility. He had to appeal to men and convince them of the utility of the education of women as leading to a happier homelife — for the man.

The importance of male acceptance appears to continue to be central in the aims of the woman's movement in Egypt. During International Women's Year, a special Preparation Committee was organized from the female members of the People's Congress, the labor and vocational unions, the communication industry, and the social and benevolent societies. The aims set forth were as follows: (1) Equality between males and females, (2) Total integration of women in the effort for national development, (3) Acknowledgment of the place of women in the preservation of world peace. That these aims are acceptable even to the conservative Muslim must be clear at the outset. It is when they are articulated in specifics, which are often controversial, that questions arise. Such specifics include the eradication of illiteracy, the raising of the standards of women both socially and economically, and family planning. The last two in particular are seen by conservatives as potentially subversive to the order of society; Mrs. Sadat thus advocates the attempt to proceed with care and caution, moving toward the achievement of these goals one at a time (*Majallat al-Musawwar*, December 1969).

A general perusal of recent periodical literature in Egypt reveals that there is a great emphasis on the International Women's Year. This excerpt from an interview with Mrs. Sadat may highlight the difference between the goals of liberation of women in the United States and those in Egypt. Mrs. Sadat said, "The role of the woman is to be with the man, to be at his side in his struggle for a better life" (Ibid.). Thus while women's liberation in the United States strives for the liberation of the woman as a person in her own right, in Egypt the woman continues to seek her liberation within the confines of the role assigned to her by Islam, that of a wife and a mother.

Notes

1. Among the several treatises on the subject, this paper will make use of the writings of Saᶜīd al-Afghānī, Maḥmūd Shaltūt, Muḥammad Nāṣir al-Dīn al-Albānī, Aḥmad al-Sharabāṣī, Abū Radwān Zaghlūl Bin al-Sanūsī, Muḥammad ᶜIzzat Darwaza, ᶜUthmān Saᶜīd al-Sharqāwī, ᶜAbd al-Nāṣir Tawfīq al-ᶜAṭṭār, al-Bahi al-Khūlī, Muḥammad ᶜAṭiyya al-Abrāshī, Muḥammad Ismāᶜīl Ibrāhīm, ᶜAlī ᶜAbd al-Wāhid Wāfī, Miqdād Yālgin, Muḥammad Abdul-Rauf, ᶜAbd al-Nāṣir Tawfīq al-ᶜAṭṭār, Muḥammad al-Aḥmadī Abū al-Nūr, Muṣṭafā ᶜAbd al-Wāhid, Muḥammad bin Sālim al-Bayhānī, Muḥammad Balṭājī, Zakarīya Aḥmad al-Barrī, Muḥammad ᶜAmārah, ᶜAbd Allāh ᶜAfīfī.

2. Al-Abrāshī, *Makānat*, 1970:7-35; Abdul-Rauf, *Marriage*, 1972; Al-Khūlī, *Al-Islām*:1970:10-2. The latter goes on to say that in Sparta women were allowed an indefinite number of husbands, "a most repulsive custom!" cf. Ben al-Sanūsī, *al-Mar'ah*:13-16; cf. Darwaza, *al-Mar'ah*, 1967:15ff.

The material surveyed included every book dealing with women and the family in Islam published since 1964 that is in the collection of the Hartford Seminary Foundation and Widener Library of Harvard University. Popular material written by secularists and socialists was not consulted since that was outside the scope of the research.

3. *The National Charter*, May 1962, p. 74.

4. "Marriage is the foundation of the family, the family is the foundation of society . . . It is the highest form of safeguarding society. It is a door to happiness. It is loved and held dearly by those with a healthy nature" Abū al-Nūr, *Minhāj*, 1972:30, 34.

5. Al-Khūlī, *Al-Islām, 1970:44.* On page 47, he reports that the Prophet said, "You who say so and so, by God, I fear for you from God . . . I fast and break my fast . . . I pray and I sleep . . . I marry women . . . That is my *WAY,* he who chooses another way than mine is not one of us."

6. Abū al-Nūr, *Minhāj,* 1972:35 and 38, where he quotes S. 5:87 (O you who believe! Do not forbid the good things that God has made lawful for you, and do not transgress. For God does not love transgressors.)

7. Ibrahīm, *al-Zawāj,* 1971:208; Abd al-Wāhid, *al-Islām,* 1972:188, "Nature necessitates that the path of each girl, whether educated or not, is the house and marriage . . ."

8. At the turn of the century Qāsim Amīn called for equality of the sexes and for the liberation of women through education. That he had to appeal to men to allow women to learn, led him to present education as a means of preparing a better wife and a more congenial companion for the husband. In *Tahrīr al-Mar'ah,* p. 58, he wrote:

> Even in things that are her domain, things for which she is created, there is nothing in her that appeals to her husband. For most women have not made a habit of combing their hair every day, or taking more than one bath a week. They do not know how to use a toothbrush, nor do they take care of their clothing whose quality and cleanliness have a great impact on appealing to the man. They do not know how desire is generated in the man and how to maintain it and how to fulfill it. That is because the ignorant woman is unaware of the inner movements of the soul. She cannot comprehend the causes of attraction and repulsion. If she seeks to stimulate the man, she usually arouses the opposite reaction.

Contemporary writers are concerned that education is not preparing women for their role in the home.

> What is the need of a girl for all the study of science and the arts, etc. . . . when she does not know how to take care of the house and family? ('Abd al-Wāhid, *al-Islām* 1972:188)

The official opinion of the Muslim Brotherhood was spelled out by Muḥammad al-Ghazzālī, *Min Huna Na'lam,* Cairo, n.d.:204.

> A woman's mission is to be a good wife and a compassionate mother . . . an ignorant rural woman is better for the nation than one thousand female lawyers or attorney generals.

And again:

> Girls are to be educated in areas that belong to them and not to men. We do not want *at all* to educate women to be secretaries or managers of offices or a minister of government (Ibid.:207).

Another author warns about the evils of educating women to be equal with men:

You who persist in educating women: strengthen yourselves before you begin your task, make religion her banner waving over her head, and her crown shining over her forehead . . . or you would lose her character . . . and would find her education, a path to evil and a way to corruption (^{C}Afīfī, al-Mar'ah:13).

9. Al-Bayhānī, Ustādh, 1973:75. The author affirms that between the two covers of the book is *all* that a women needs to know. This includes details on such things as what to do when a woman gets in contact with a dog and the necessity of refraining from using a toothbrush (efficacy of using siwāk), etc. . . . The only roles a woman could take outside the house would be those of gynecologist or midwife.

10. Margaret Mead's studies showing that male and female roles may be culturally conditioned are cited and condemned as false because they are based on the study of three tribes rather than the total experience of mankind. See Yālgin, al-Bayt, 1972:71; cf. Wāfī, al-Usra, 1972:117.

11. Cf. Yālgin, al-Bayt 1972:84:

It should be known that a woman cannot be ideal in all her behavior and conduct, because her biological constitution makes her weak in initiative, will and personality in a general way.

This is what makes her deficient in her work, which she does not complete, and she does not fulfill her duties as she should. In this case, [the man] must bear with her as much as possible. Meanwhile she should not be left freedom of action for that would lead to further deviation and she would ignore her duties and not fulfill them to the utmost of her capacity.

See also 'Aqqād, 'Abbas Mahmūd, Hādhihi al-Shajarah, Cairo, n.d.:23.

Women enjoy the pain of childbirth and childbearing, a feeling men do not share as they rebel against pain, whereas it is in the nature of women not to be able to distinguish between pleasure and pain (as they are the same thing to them).

12. Yālgin, al-Bayt, 1972:63-66; on page 68 he says:

A look at the present and the past and at human history shows that the most famous were men. Science has developed on the shoulders of men. The most famous philosophers, physicians, mathematicians are men and not women, even until this day and even though women have had opportunities for learning for over a hundred years . . .

Cf. al-'Aqqād, 'Abbas Mahmūd, Al-Mar'ah fī al-Qur'ān, Cairo, 1959, where he elaborates on the same theme.

The superiority of men over women is evident in professions in which women have had exclusive domain . . . For the woman has busied herself with the preparation of food since humanity began, she has cooked food since prehistory. She learns it at home from her childhood. She loves food and craves for it and demands appetizers during her pregnancy, while seeking larger quantities of it during breast feeding. However, even after inheriting this profession for thousands of years, she does not reach the proficiency of a man who dedicates a few years for it, nor is she able to compete with him in the excellence of common meals, or in the creation of new tastes or the improvement of the old. She also is incapable of administering a kitchen where there are several workers, whether male or female.

13. Al-Abrāshī, *Makānat* 1970:17, says: "Man is responsible for the demands of life outside the home. The woman is responsible for things she can do with skill, e.g. raising children, sewing their clothes, feeding them and bathing them."

Cf. 'Aqqād, n.d. *Hādhihi*:141: "A woman has every right that does not distract her from her primary duty, which is a duty in which she solely excels and which no one else can perform — i.e., her house and the new generation." See also pp. 146-47, where he says, "Her role is that of mother, housewife and family. These are things that she can do that do not distort her mission, e.g., raising birds and chickens, making cheese and yogurt, growing fruits and flowers."

14. "It is despicable for the woman to wear men's clothes — such as pants which they wear now — for in it is an effort to draw attention to herself or to arouse . . . Islam goes also beyond that for male and female are the creation of God according to the laws of the universe. We do not know why God created people as male and female; however, we know that it was in His wisdom . . . For the man to imitate the woman and the woman to imitate the man is not only a transgression of a custom, rather, it is the trampling of law, and the invalidation of what God willed in His wisdom" (al-Khūlī, *al-Islām*, 1970:166.

Cf. al-Albānī, *Hijāb*:66-67.

15. Yālgin, *al-Bayt* 1972:64; *cf.* Wāfī, *al-Mar'ah:* 43-75 isolates six distinctions between males and females — in religious duties, economic responsibilities, inheritance, witness, obedience, and family responsibility.

16. Shaltūt, *al-Qur'ān* 1959:60; cf. al-Khūlī, *al-Islām* 1970:73.

> The authority in the house belongs to the man. The children belong to him and he spends on them. He is the owner of the house, he furnishes it and spends on it. Thus the authority comes from responsibility, not because of a desire to detract from justice, equality and consensus of the woman. It is his responsibility to pay for the home and to protect.

17. 'Aqqād, *Hādhihi,* n.d.:90; cf. Abū al-Nūr, *Minhāj,* 1972:35.

> God has established the relation between man and woman; if observed, one notes that the woman is weaker than the man. She comes to him and surrenders to him, knowing full well that he is capable of abusing her rights.

18. Yālgin, *Al-Bayt,* 1972:64, cf. Ibid.:85.

> The woman should obey the husband "because of what God created in him of superior capabilities and powers for administration and guidance of the affairs of life with wisdom, patience and vigor. She must also obey him for religious reasons, for such an obedience is a part of the application of Islam. If she disobeys, she will be punished on the day of judgment. However, this obedience is contingent that he

does not ask her to commit the forbidden, such as drink wine, refrain from prayer, dance with men, etc. . . . ."

19. The Prophet said, "the woman is created from a crooked bone. She will not be straightened on a way for you. If you enjoy her, you enjoy her with her curvature (crookedness). If you attempt to straighten her, you will break her and what breaks her is divorce" (Yālgin, al-Bayt: 84).

20. Cf. Al-'Attār, Ta'addud:15: "The nature of women is repelled by a multiplicity of husbands. The woman who marries several husbands legally is exposed — more than other women — to contacting cancer of the uterus, while the dishonorable woman is susceptible to venereal disease. . . .etc. Meanwhile, the man is not susceptible to these diseases if he has several legal wives."

21. Yālgin, al-Bayt, p. 42. He also reports that the Prophet said, "The best of your women is the child bearer, the compassionate who keeps the secret, the chaste, the dignified in her work, the submissive to her husband, the one who adorns herself in the presence of her husband, the inaccessible to anyone but her husband who listens to his words, obeys his commands and when they are alone offers to him whatever he desires of her and does not display the vulgarity of men."

22. The Prophet is reported to have said, "You and your property are your fathers'. Your children are your best earnings. Eat of your children's earnings." He also said, "The best that you eat is of your earning. Your children are of your earning" (Abū al-Nūr, Manhāj, 1972:96).

23. Cf. 'Abd al-Wāhid, al-Usrah, p. 84, where the Prophet is reported to have said, "Heaven is under the feet of mothers," and a sign of the imminence of the eschaton is when "the woman will give birth to her master," i.e., a son who would treat her as a slave.

24. Bin al-Sanūsī, al-Mar'ah, 1967:32: The Prophet is reported to have said, "Whenever a man meets with a woman alone, Satan is inevitably their third."

Bibliography

ᶜAbd al-Rahmān, ᶜĀisha
      1970 Al-Qur'ān wa-al-Tafsīr al-ᶜAsrī. Cairo.
ᶜAbd al-Wāhid, Mustafā
      1972 Al-Islām wa-al-Mushkilah al-Jinsiyyah. Cairo.
ᶜAbd al-Wāhid, Mustafā
      1972 Al-Usrah fī al-Islām. Cairo.
Abdul-Rauf, Muhammad
      1972 Marriage in Islam. Jerico, N.Y.: Exposition Press.
Al-Abrāshī, Muhammad ᶜAtiyyah
      1970 Makānat al-Mar'ah fī al-Islām. Cairo.

ᶜAbū al-Nūr, Muhammad al-Ahmadī
1972 *Minhāj al-Sunnah fī al-Zawāj*. Cairo.

Al-Afghānī, Saᶜīd
1964 *Al-Islām wa-al-Mar'ah*. Damascus.

ᶜAfīfī, ᶜAbd Allāh
n.d. *Al-Mar'ah al-ᶜArabiyyah fī zilāl al-Islām*. Beirut.

Al-Albānī, Muhammad Nāsir al-Dīn
1965 *Hijāb al-Mar'ah al-Muslimah fī al-Kitāb wa-al-Sunnah*. Cairo.

ᶜAmārah, Muhammad
1975 *Al-Islām wa-al-Mar'ah fī Ra'ī al-Imām Muhammad ᶜAbduh*. Cairo.

Al-ᶜAttār, ᶜAbd al-Nāsir Tawfīq
1968 *Dirāsat fī Qadiyyat Taᶜaddud al-Zawjāt min al-Nawāhī al-Ijtimāᶜiyyah wa-al-Dīniyyah wa-al Qānūniyyah*. Cairo.

Al-ᶜAttār, ᶜAbd al-Nāsir Tawfīq
1972 *Taᶜaddud al-Zawjāt*. Cairo.

Baltājī, Muhammad
1974 *Dirāsāt fī Ahkām al-Usrah*. Cairo.

Al-Barrī, Zakariyyah Ahmad
1974 *Al-Ahkām al-Asāsīyah li-l-Usrah al-Islāmīyyah*. Cairo.

Al-Bayhānī, Muhammad bin Sālim
1973 *Ustādh al-Mar'ah*. Cairo.

Bin al-Sanūsī, Abū Radwān Zaghlūl
1967 *Al-Mar'ah bayn al-Hijāb wa-al-Sufūr*. Beirut.

Darwaza, Muhammad ᶜIzzat
1967 *Al-Mar'ah fī al-Qur'ān wa-al-Sunnah*. Beirut.

Ibrāhīm, Muhammad Ismāᶜīl
1971 *Al-Zawāj*. Cairo.

Al-Khūlī, al-Bahī
1970 *Al-Islām wa-Qadāyā al-Mar'ah al-Muᶜāsirah*. Kuwait.

1969 *Majallat al-Musawwar*. Cairo, December 1969.

1962 *The National Charter*. Cairo, May, 1962.

Shaltūt, Mahmūd
1964 *Al-Islām ᶜAqīdah wa-Sharīᶜah*. Cairo.

1964 *Min Tawjīhāt al-Islām*. Cairo.

Al-Sharabāsī, Ahmad
1965 *Al-Dīn wa-Tanzīm al-Usra*. Cairo.

Al-Sharqāwī, ᶜUthmān Saᶜīd
1967 *Al-Islām wa-al-Hayāt al-Zawjiyyah*. Cairo.

Smith, J.I. and Y.Y. Haddad
    1975 "Women in the Afterlife: The Islamic View as Seen from Qur'ān and Tradition." *Journal of the American Academy of Religion,* vol. 43, no.1.

Wāfī, ᶜAlī ᶜAbd al-Wāḥid
    1971   *Al-Mar'ah fī al-Islām.* Cairo.

Yālgin, Miqdād
    1972   *Al-Bayt al-Islāmī.* Cairo.

Zayn al-Dīn, Nazīrah
    1928   *Al-Sufūr wa-al-Ḥijāb.* Cairo.

The Determinants of Social Position among Rural Moroccan Women

SUSAN SCHAEFER DAVIS

Trenton State College

In both the popular image of traditional Muslim women and in much of the literature concerning them, it is assumed that the status of these women is based solely on that of their husbands or male kin; the women as individuals are said to have no control over their own status. In an article on change and the Arab village family, for example, Henry Rosenfeld states that men have "rights to property, the definitive factor for village status. Women, tied to the village, without property and relegated to the lowest status, tied to dependence on the brother-protector and the honor of their patrilineage, remain in the realm of kin relations only" (1968:745). It is suggested here that such views are androcentric and lead to the neglect of a great deal of information concerning women that emerges upon closer examination of the female realm in which they exist. I feel that there is much more than kinship involved in the determination of the status of traditional Muslim women, as evidenced in a particular Moroccan village where the data for this paper were collected. A closer look at the women's world will also help solve the paradox of why these apparently weak and statusless females often seem, to the observer who knows them well, to be the strongest members of the society.

In attempting to discuss the status of Muslim women, one is immediately faced by the problem of a suitable definition of *status*. Until a clear meaning for this term is articulated, it will be difficult to discuss the comparative status of men and women within a culture or to compare each sex across cultures. The use of the term *status* regarding women presents certain problems not encountered when men are discussed, and it is further suggested here that determining the status of Muslim women presents special problems.

The most commonly used meanings of *status* and *role* are those set forth by Ralph Linton. In this schema, a status is a position (specifically, a collection of rights and duties) in a particular pattern of reciprocal behavior between individuals or groups of individuals. Since each individual has many statuses, his or her general status connotes the sum total of all the status positions he or she occupies. A role is the dynamic aspect of a status, that is, the actions involved in fulfilling a status, and the two are quite inseparable (Linton 1936). It is probable that Rosenfeld uses status in this sense.

However, authors who have focused their research on the females in a society have found that it was necessary to further refine their definition of status. Thus Sanday states that

> female status is generally defined in terms of (1) the degree to which females have authority and/or power in the domestic and/or public domains; and (2) the degree to which females are accorded deferential treatment and are respected and revered in the domestic and/or public domains. An analysis of variation in female status and the causes of variation in any one of these conceptual domains is a legitimate and interesting task. (1974:191)

To this I would add that the same definition could also be applied to males, whose status until now has been considered mainly in the public domain.

Unfortunately, it seems that even this more refined definition of status will not completely solve the problems encountered in studying Muslim women, because Sanday's definition of the domestic domain does not exactly coincide with the female realm in which most Muslim women primarily function. Sanday's domestic domain "includes activities performed within the realm of the localized family unit. The public domain includes political and economic activities that take place or have impact beyond the localized family unit and that relate to the control of persons or the control of things" (1974:190). While a cursory glance may suggest that Muslim males function in the public domain and females in the domestic, this is not entirely true. Males certainly act within the family unit, and females engage in activities with an impact beyond the family unit and that involve the control of persons, for example by distribution of information that influences other families' social position.

Clearly, the specification of a definition of status that is appropriate to the traditional Muslim context is a problem.

In the meantime, in an attempt to avoid some of the problems with status already mentioned, I will discuss the "position" or "ranked position", based on the amount of respect and deference accorded them by others, of both males and females in a large Moroccan village in which I resided for over three years. I will consider the males' positions in the male realm in which they primarily function, and those of the females in the female realm since, for the village people discussed here, these are two almost totally separate realms of existence, delineated by household walls: the world of women and the world of men. Females exist in the indoor, household-based world of women, while their fathers, brothers, and husbands exist mostly outside that realm, in the world of men. Men do appear in the female-filled home to eat and sleep, but spend most of their time outside it, with other men.

My justification for considering female position within the female realm and male within the male is that this is how the members of the society do it. A female's position is considered and evaluated relative to those of other females: she is not compared to males, and the same is true for males vis-à-vis females. Rogers (1975) feels this is a valid position to take with regard to peasant societies in general.

This approach also gives us a chance to ask some of the questions Beck (1974) suggests are important in developing theoretical perspectives on the position of women, such as whether there is a hierarchy among women, and what would be the bases of a hierarchical order. In addition, we can compare the hierarchies and their bases for males and females in traditional Moroccan society. If we find, as is suggested later, variation in the hierarchies, in their bases and in the possibility of changing one's position in the hierarchy, then we have certainly increased our understanding of Muslim society beyond the traditional view, which regards women merely as childbearing subordinates to men.

The people described here are residents of a very large, agriculturally based central Moroccan village. One would certainly not call these women modern, although neither are they typical of very isolated rural women. Their lifestyle has been somewhat influenced by their proximity to a town of 26,000. Many have seen television, most visit the larger towns occasionally, and a few do wage labor; but basically they are still traditional Moroccan women. They have been much less touched by modernization than have their husbands. Their traditional condition is stressed in distinction to women in a more modern situation, for whom many of the statements later will not be valid. It is suggested that while this study was carried out in Morocco, these people are in many ways similar to rural Muslims throughout the Middle East and North Africa, so that these findings would not reflect patterns unique to Morocco.

When one examines what determines a person's position in the hierarchy of either the male or female realm in rural Morocco, several factors emerge. The presence or absence of these factors and their degree of importance varies for males and females, as illustrated in table 1 below.

TABLE 1
Factors in Determining Person's Position in Male or Female Realm

Status of Family	Character or Morality	Manipulation of Information	Economic Assets	Informal Access to Formal Pol. Power	Position in Life Cycle	Magic	Religiosity
Female ✔	+	+	✔	0	+	+	✔
Male ✔	+	+	+	+	✔	✔	✔

+   Important in determining one's position.
✔   Considered in determining one's position.
0   Not considered in determining one's position.

It is clear that certain factors have the same degree of importance in determining a male's or female's position; these include family status (deriving mainly from the degree of access to political and/or religious power), personal character, the manipulation of information and religiosity. However, certain factors (economic assets and access to formal political power) are very important for males but not for females, while others (position in life cycle and magic) are more important for females than for males. In one case (access to formal political power) a factor considered for one sex is not involved at all in the determination of the status of the other sex.

A closer examination of these factors will reveal precisely what each one involves; in several cases even though one factor is equally important for males and females, its content will be found to vary.

The first factor in table 1, the status of a person's family in the village, is perhaps the most similar factor for males and females. It is considered, but is not especially important, in determining one's position. This can be seen with respect to the *shorfa*, or members of the saintly lineage, the descendants of the saint who founded the village around A.D. 1670. Although descent is traced through the male line, *shorfa* often intermarry, and there are currently over 300 male and female *shorfa* living in the village. Of these *shorfa*, a few are important people locally, but most are just ordinary villagers. Rather than automatically giving them a special position in the village, their family status as *shorfa* is a resource that they can use. Thus one local woman was a *sherifa* but generally scorned by other women for her sharp tongue, bad disposition, and two divorces, while her mother, also a *sherifa*, was respected for her good advice and general wisdom. The situation is the same for males: being a *sherif* is considered, but certainly does not determine one's position locally.

The next two factors in table 1, one's character or morality and one's manipulation of information, are important in determining both male and female position in their respective realms. In spite of this apparent similarity, however, we find differences in the content of the factors for the two sexes.

Although the attributes of a pleasing character, including kindness, verbal skill, and a good sense of humor, are similar for men and women, what constitutes a moral man is different from what constitutes a moral woman. A respectable or moral man is *nishan* or honest (literally, "straight") in his interactions, supports his family well, and does not gamble or drink or go to prostitutes *too* often. A respectable woman promotes the welfare of her family as a good wife and mother, is an excellent and thrifty housekeeper (*hadga*), and keeps her family's honor pure by never interacting with strange men, staying inside, and not spreading the affairs of the family around the village. One gossips, of course, but about *others,* while keeping family problems out of the public realm.

Whether or not one works reflects on one's character or morality, but in different ways for men and women. A man must work to support his family if he is to be considered of good character. For a woman to work outside the home, however, usually reflects badly on her character. If a woman must support herself and her children (because of divorce, for example), she frequently turns to field labor as the most readily available work. Although she may be grudgingly admired because she is managing to survive on her own, her position always is lowered because she is putting herself on view in the public realm where she can be seen by unrelated males. A more extreme example of this is the prostitute. Although this is a much more lucrative way to support oneself than field labor, few women turn to it because of the degrading effect it has on one's own and one's family's status.

Manipulation of information is also important for both men and women. Gossip is a major means of women's manipulation of information, and their social standing is raised both by their greater access to and clever use of this information. Men, too, find manipulation of information important, but with the significant difference that the information dealt with by men and women is not the same. In the men's world, it involves men, their work, their leisure time and occasionally their families, while in the women's world, it involves mainly women, their families, and their activities in this realm. These topics may appear trivial until one recalls the import of female honor in the Muslim world.

The honor of the women of a family usually concerns younger women and is very important to the position of the family as a whole. A young woman is capable of discrediting the entire family by a dishonorable act, such as becoming pregnant while unmarried or having an affair after marriage. One might expect that a woman would use this capability, or at least threaten to use it, in disputes with male kin in an attempt to influence decisions in her favor. In fact this was never observed, probably because not only the family suffers the dishonor; the female offender suffers the most. While gross infractions of honor were not observed, minor violations of the behavior required for the ideal of female honor were ready grist for the gossip mill. Thus a woman in the street in midafternoon makes it clear she is on her way to see the doctor to allay other suspicions. A local girl who lived in another town while supposedly working for the electric company damaged the honor of her otherwise reputable father by her dishonorable associations with men. These infractions of the honor code become known to local people, male and female, primarily through the network of the women's world and its contact with the men's world through husbands.

We further see the importance of women's manipulation of information in the activities and revered position of the bath mistresses. Two local women hold the rather high-status job of mistress of the *hamman* (public bath) during women's hours. Their importance derives not from possession of an independent income so much as from their position at a center for female communication: the baths. Women do visit frequently with friends and neighbors, but the public baths and the well are the two places where large numbers of women frequently gather and exchange information. While no women are *always* present at the well, the bath mistress is at the *hamman* during the whole time it is open, and so has access to most of the information relayed there. She can control other women by her use of this information; a mention that one's daughter seems to chat a lot with the butcher's assistant while she is buying meat may seriously impede her chances for a good marriage, especially if the mention is made in the *hamman,* where a woman seeking a bride for her son might inquire about a girl she did not know. The seamstress-teacher (*ma'llma*) is another job open to females through which they can manipulate their status. Once again they have access to information by dint of their contact and conversation with their numerous female customers.

The next two factors in table 1, a person's economic assets and informal access to formal political power, are of greater importance for males.

While economic assets are very important in male status, they are less so for females. Even though a male and female in the same family will have the same ranking on this scale, that is, they will both be rated rich or poor depending on the man's resources, this factor carries less weight for a woman in her world than for a man in his. An occasional woman will have control of economic resources independently of her husband; but this is rare, and also it has less influence on her position than it would if she were a male. While a woman may work in cases of necessity and thus increase her economic assets, this does not enhance her position but rather lowers it due to the already mentioned reflection on her character. Thus a rich male is generally placed high within the male hierarchy, while a rich female's position varies depending on other characteristics. The well-off wife of the head of the saintly lineage was lower in the female hierarchy than a poorer woman who possessed a good character and much verbal skill with which to manipulate information.

Informal access to formal political power in terms of established governmental offices is an important factor in determining a male's position, but is not considered with regard to a female. Only a few village males occupy formal political positions, and in fact these local positions confer very little power. Instead, a man's position in the male hierarchy is raised with greater informal access to formal political power. For example, a local man, a worker with no political office, was a friend of the police chief in the nearby town. He could use this contact to control other people and/or for economic gain. Thus he could be influential in getting a friend out of jail, or for a fee might see that one's car license was processed quickly, all through his informal contacts with the police chief. Women, on the other hand, did not function in the realm of access to formal political power; no one tried to get to know the chief's wife, for example, and even had they, she would not have had much input to the chief's political decisions, which were considered outside her realm.

One's position in the life cycle and the use of magic are just the reverse, that is, important factors for women's positions and less so for men. In the local view, a woman's life cycle contains more gradations than that of a man. A male by virtue of his age is either basically immature and not a full participant in society, or mature and fully eligible to participate. Since most full participants in the men's realm are mature males, this factor has relatively little influence on their general rank.

Women, however, may be teenage girls, new brides, young mothers, older mothers with several children, or mothers-in-law controlling also their sons' families; their behavior and rank will vary accordingly. The phases of the life cycle each involve a type of role model: a new bride is expected to be shy and demure and seldom to speak, while a postmenopausal woman can be, and often is, raucous and bawdy, even in her newly permitted interactions with men. While a new bride does not dare address her father-in-law, her new mother-in-law may make jokes, even of a sexual nature, with him and his friends.

Access to and use of magic is also more important for women than it is for men. While both men and women have contact with the supernatural, for men this contact is usually through the channel of their religion, orthodox Islam. There are a few local male religious teachers (*fqi-s*) who deal in magic also, but generally magic outside orthodox Islam is the realm of the women. Many women know a little magic on their own, but they frequently consult a specialist. In my area such a woman was called a *sahra* (a sorceress) and was greatly feared by men. Women too feared her, but they also had access to her, so could exercise a degree of control, at least in the form of counterspells. Men seldom, if ever, contact these women; rather, they avoid them. This magic consists basically of spells and potions used either to revive a husband's interest, to terminate his affection for another woman, or to get rid of a female competitor, and is thus used extensively as an indirect means of control of men as necessary to the stability of the family. Whether or not magic works directly was not assessed (though several of the potions used are basically herbal poisons), but the threat of its use seems very effective and constrains the actions of men and other women toward women.

The final factor in table 1 is a person's religiosity. It is a minor factor, considered for both males and females, but a very small percentage of the villagers are considered extremely religious. In fact, only a few of the very old men, who are concerned about death and the afterlife, pray regularly at the mosque and are respected for their religiosity; an even smaller number of old women pray regularly.

With all these differences in the factors contributing to a man's position in his realm as opposed to a woman's position in hers, it is obvious that a woman's position will not be based solely on that of her father, brother, or husband, and that we increase our understanding by examining both realms carefully.

In addition to the content of the above factors, we can also consider to what degree they can be manipulated by males and by females. I suggest that women in general find it easier to raise their position relative to their own group than do men. Women's character, use of information, and access to magic are all basically under their own control and can, if used properly, raise their position among women. Certain aspects of the male's position are also individually achieved, but an important one, economic status, is very difficult to manipulate. This is not due so much to a rigid class character of the society as to current economic conditions, which make it very difficult for the average villager to improve his economic situation. For women, however, the economic aspect of their position is less important than other factors over which they have some control.

An example of female manipulation of status is seen in the loosely defined work/leisure groups to which most women belong. A group of neighbors usually spend their afternoons together on one or another woman's roof, doing household chores and simultaneously discussing the recent developments in the women's world. In these groups one woman assumes a dominant position so that her view prevails, or she is the one who suggests and organizes a luncheon together, even though there is no special occasion to celebrate. Other women in the group also are more or less dominant, so each has her own particular status rank, which carries over into other situations to some degree. As already stated, factors such as a husband's economic status and one's life cycle position enter into this, so it is seldom that one will find a poor, newlywed bride as an assertive group leader. However, a poor younger woman who is quick and clever with words and has a good sense of humor has a higher rank in the group than an older woman from the highly respected saintly lineage who is not very good with words, and, furthermore, has some access to magic. Actually, while access to magic does influence one's position, it is difficult to judge in exactly what manner. Women frequently utilize magic, as already noted, to revive a husband's lagging interest or to decrease his interest in another woman, so in those situations they value the access to magic. However, women with access to magic can also work evil spells on women (a woman may want to render her co-wife sterile), and so are also feared rather than unilaterally respected.

In addition to the female's situation being more under her own control than is that of the male, one can suggest two other aspects of the Muslim female's life that may confer advantages compared with those of males. Women may acquire a certain adaptibility in the changes experienced during their life cycles, from secure adolescent among known kin, to new bride beleaguered by her mother-in-law and other new relatives, to moderately secure mother, to domineering mother-in-law. Also, after being a new bride, a woman's situation usually improves (it can't get much worse!), so women are both accustomed to change and basically optimistic about its outcome. Men do not have the experience of and flexibility derived from reaction to dramatic life cycle changes; change for them means confrontation with the modern world and with new ways of doing things, which can make them feel insecure and inadequate. A second advantage may derive from the fact that women still live in the traditional world, one in which it is within nearly every woman's grasp to be the culture's ideal female—that is, a respectable wife and mother, with clear rules given to guide that behavior. Muslim males, in more direct contact with the modernizing world, lack clear guidelines concerning their behavior; rather they must discover them—and worry what their peers will think—as they go along.

This is not to suggest that women's position in Morocco could or should be ranked above that of men, but merely to demonstrate that, by considering both male and female realms carefully, we come a long way beyond the stereotype of the meek and subordinate Muslim female.

Bibliography

Beck, Lois Grant
    1974 "Theoretical Perspectives on the Position of Women in Iran."
    Paper presented at the Annual Meeting of the Middle East Studies
    Association, at Boston, Mass.

Linton, Ralph
    1936 "Status and Role." Originally in *The Way of Man*;
    reprinted in *Theories of Society*. Edited by Talcott Parsons et al.,
    New York: The Free Press, 1961:202-8.

Rogers, Susan Carol
    1975 "Female Forms of Power and the Myth of Male Dominance:
    A Model of Female/Male Interaction in Peasant Society."
    American Ethnologist vol. 2, no. 4, pp. 727-756.

Rosenfeld, Henry
    1968 "Change, Barriers to Change and Contradictions in the
    Arab Village Family." *American Anthropologist* 70:732-52.

Sanday, Peggy
    1974 "Female Status in the Public Domain." In *Woman, Culture
    and Society*. Edited by Michelle Rosaldo and Louise Lamphere.
    Stanford: Stanford University Press.

The Social and Political Roles of Arab Women: A Study in Conflict

NANCY ADAMS SHILLING

Managing Director, Inter-Crescent Publishing and Information Corp.

Introduction

In approaching my topic from my particular perspective as a political scientist specializing in Arab politics and, particularly, in the political roles of contemporary Arab women, I am confronted by three problems, which this essay will consider.

First, there is the still unresolved question of how to conceptualize the social and political concerns about women that we wish to study. Is it, in fact, appropriate to conceptualize them from the "minority" perspective? Is there a "women's perspective" that has been neglected heretofore by male researchers and male decisionmakers? If so, what is this perspective conceptually? Does it help us to explain some of the social concerns, such as development, on which much research on the Arab world currently focuses?

Second, what are the methodological problems of both conceptualization and field research that the social scientist confronts in doing current data studies, and, specifically, in doing such research in the contemporary Arab world?

Third, this essay will examine some of the methodological

problems I encountered in conceptualizing the roles of Arab women vis-à-vis modernization and development in the contemporary Arab world, and in attempting to collect data with which to test my hypotheses.

I will approach the problems of conceptualization and method more or less directly, with some illustrations drawn from the Arab experience. I will also set forth my model for studying Arab women and development and refer, *inter alia,* to the methodological problems encountered in attempting to develop these concepts.

The data included herein with respect to Arab women are drawn largely from my manuscript of a book on Arab women, using Arabic and European language sources, that has been my main research concern for the past three years. That book, and thus this essay, includes impressionistic data gathered over twenty years of experience with the Arab world, including prolonged periods of residence and travel there, as well as the usual survey data and secondary source material, such as it is, and case study material on particular groups of Arab women.

The Majority-Minority Perspective

Although Arab women are probably a slight majority of the population,[1] they represent a *political* minority in terms of almost total powerlessness. There are virtually no women in positions of *real* power in Arab countries; women lack channels for input into the policymaking process; their policy priorities are not considered by national governments in devising development goals;[2] there are very few champions of women's-policy priorities among Arab decisionmakers; and women are not considered by society as a whole to have any legitimate political role, except to reaffirm, support, or legitimize actions determined by and taken by men.[3] To the extent that Arab women have, through militancy, injected their priorities and demands into the political process, they have been viewed as an unrepresentative minority in conflict with the legitimacy of the status quo. Both the ruling groups and society as a whole have in the recent past denounced women's activism on behalf of their own voice in political decisionmaking as contrary to religious and community values;[4] sanctions have been taken against them by the community, and antifeminist activities have been sponsored by those in political authority.[5] Even in those countries where official ideology supports women's right to political participation, this right is honored more in the breach than in practice.[6]

Although survey data are lacking to substantiate the assertion, there is ample impressionistic data to suggest that Arab women, of the middle class in particular, but recently a few among the lower class as well, perceive themselves to be a political minority.[7]

They have responded to this perception of their position as minorities elsewhere in the world have done: with rage and frustration that so far have been more frequently directed against themselves than against society.[8]

Arab women as a whole have not yet arrived at the point of collective awareness of their position and of their collective ability to bring about change through unified action. They do not yet have a consensus upon the desirability of change in their position or what form such change should or might take. They are not yet, then, politically modern in the sense that politically modern persons consider themselves able to influence the course of events.[9] But as more and more Arab women become educated, as is presently happening, and more and more of them become employed outside the home, either by choice or through economic necessity produced by inflationary economies, we can expect their political consciousness to change as well.

If Arab women follow the pattern of women in other societies, they will begin to develop a collective awareness of their deprived position vis-à-vis their society as a whole, and to mobilize, on a mass as well as an elite level, to change their politically inferior status. The fact that some legislative change in women's status has been produced for ideological reasons by most Arab states does not change the fact of continued deprivation, in fact, of both legal standing, through nonenforcement of existing law, and of political power, for Arab women.[10] Giving women the vote, as most Arab states have now done, is a meaningless gesture in societies where political power rests, and is exercised largely outside the framework of the electoral process. The notion of "one woman, one vote" is a liberalizing one only in societies where the franchise is a meaningful way of selecting leaders and determining policy.

If our analysis of the actual and potential position of Arab women is correct, the study of Arab women as a political minority, in reality and in their own self-perceptions, is a meaningful and useful way of looking at the subject. The literature on political minorities in other settings can then be helpful in assisting us to develop working hypotheses about the actual and potential political behavior of Arab women, and in formulating relevant field data survey projects. From this perspective, we may be able to explain some types of political behavior in the Arab world more realistically, and predict more accurately probable outcomes of a variety of policy initiatives vis-à-vis developments that characterize Arab society in the 1970s.

Methodological Problems

A number of methodological problems immediately present themselves in attempting to study Arab women in contemporary context. Many of these problems are common to the study of women in other contexts as well, as previous literature and seminars on the general topic of women have demonstrated.[11] However, some of these problems take on somewhat different dimensions or are placed in sharper focus in the Arab context.

One category of problems that we confront are the definitional, and therefore, to some extent, conceptual, such as the appropriate definition of *liberation, modernization, development* in the Arab cultural context, or even the question of whether or not the framework of *political system* is an appropriate one when studying a cohesive culture that encompasses a number of political systems.

A second set of problems are the technical ones, relating to the gathering and interpretation of information in and about the Arab world, including the problems connected with survey research, data collection, and language.

Problems of Definition: Why "Arab Women"?

There are those who argue that one cannot study Arab women — that one must study Moroccan or Algerian or Egyptian women — as though the political barriers represented by the creation of a number of sovereign states in the Arab world after World Wars I and II created in a previously homogeneous and politically unified culture area the same kinds of profound historical differences that developed over centuries among the nation-states of Europe.

Clearly, the variables that one is attempting to isolate and the dimensions that are being studied bear upon the question of the size of the scale in which any study should be conducted. There are arguments that could be made, for example, for studying only southern women, or black women in cities over 100,000, or New England women, in the United States; but no one would argue that in developing certain kinds of macrotheory about women in North America, the category of "American women" is never valid. This is because we basically accept the premise that American women, of whatever color, educational background, place of residence, and economic level still have in common a certain kind of socialization, certain disadvantages, political, economic and social, arising out of and being manifested in a common political culture, and that the remedies for these disadvantages, insofar as they are subject to legislative, judicial, and political remedy, will probably have to be national in scope.[12]

If one understands Arab culture realistically, one will recognize that, particularly with regard to women — their social and political roles, their disadvantages and the remedies for these — the same argument applies.

First, almost all legislation directly applicable to women is Islamic legislation, derived from the Qur'ān and the *sunnah* of the Prophet Muhammad and merely incorporated in the civil codes of the individual Arab states when they were created by the European powers after the two world wars.

Second, not only are the laws universal in Arab culture, but the political culture from which these laws spring and which is defined in some detail in the Qur'ān and Muslim political literature forms the basis of virtually all Arab political organization and decisionmaking processes; the value system that applies in Arab society is the value system of a long-standing Arab-Muslim society that was unified for hundreds of years under a variety of empires, some of them autonomous and all of them Muslim, and that has only very recently been fragmented by outsiders.

Third, the policy concerns of women themselves are virtually always transnational — Palestine, Arab nationalism, neutralism, anticolonialism, much more frequent themes at women's conferences than local or so-called national concerns. Moreover, the more specifically women's concerns — population control, education, health care, and so forth — are almost always approached by women themselves on a transnational basis. The question, for example, would be not what do women do about increasing educational opportunities for 'Irāqī women, but for Arab women; the question of coeducation versus separate education is not a distinct question in each Arab country, but is generally approached in a transnational context. Even legislative reform in one country tends to be treated as a transnational issue, although the specific reform may be legislated in a single country. Arab women, and Arab society as a whole, are quite conscious of the fact that legislative change in the controversial area of women's rights in one Arab country will almost certainly set a precedent for all of the others.

Since independence, interest groups in the Arab world, including women's groups, have tended to become more rather than less transnational. Almost all significant decisionmaking forums chosen by representative groups of women in Arab countries tend to be transnational in focus and participation. The enforced fragmentation of interest groups imposed during the co onial era has been replaced by a significant degree of cohesion by women as "Arab women," recognizing the commonality of their cultural value systems, political systems, laws, and, therefore, problems as women.

In studying the Arab world from many perspectives, not merely that of women, the territorial delimitation of "culture area" is vastly more useful than that of "national state" or "political system," unless the latter is given a transnational significance corresponding with the Arab culture area. Not only has the cohesiveness of the Arab world as a culture area been reinforced in recent years by a proliferation of transnational bodies, including women's organizations, but development planning and the formulation of priorities for the area tend to be increasingly regional. This reflects, of course, in part, the uneven distribution of oil wealth in the area; but the very willingness of the oil-rich states to contribute to the development of the poorer Arab states suggests the probability of closer policy coordination and even more transnational cooperation in the coming years. Thus, for our purposes, which involve assessing the role of women in development, the adoption of the "Arab culture area" as the territorial scope of our analysis seems most appropriate, if not essential.

We are not, of course, trying to argue that microstudies confined to a single Arab country or region are not valid and useful. Indeed, they are most necessary and essential as sources of vital data and as inputs into macrotheory of the kind that we are trying to create.

One could even argue that, in culture areas where scant survey evidence has heretofore been collected, there is a good case to be made that a broader approach may produce greater initial payoff than a limited one, particularly as regards our ability to conceptualize about the status, roles, problems, and participation of Arab women in national and transnational frameworks. The broader conceptualization may also encourage the collection of data from a number of different settings that make detailed comparative analysis later possible (Frey 1970:197).

Problems of Definition: "Arab Women's Liberation"

Western social scientists approaching the study of women in other culture areas may exhibit a cultural bias if they define *liberation* for Arab women as it has been defined by the American or European women's movements. In reading the literature, sparse as it is, that touches on this question vis-à-vis Arab women,[13] one finds frequently the assumption implicit or explicit, that Arab women's liberation is or *should be* oriented toward the same goals that have characterized women's liberation movements in the West, and that it should happen in more or less the same order, beginning with the struggle for voting rights.

Through study of the legal status of Arab women, by which, according to Muslim law and tradition (Tībī 1968:68-79), they were and still are considered the property of someone else throughout their lives, passing from father to husband without legal standing of their own, social scientists may logically assume that one of the basic priorities of Arab women *must* be to liberate themselves from this legally subordinate position. But along with this subordinate legal status go a series of interlocking privileges for the woman, reponsibilities for the man and protections from the society that make woman's role often seem to her a desirable one, especially since it is still almost universally reinforced by a society whose values she accepts as valid. It is entirely conceivable, then, and has been demonstrated to be the case in practice, that the Arab woman may have no conception of herself as requiring or desiring "liberation" at all, that the price she would have to pay for it is too high, or, at least, that she would not voluntarily opt for the sort of liberation that the Westerner thinks appropriate.

Only a few Arab women have yet internalized goals of "liberation" in any context, and they are a distinct minority, largely of elite women, now and for the foreseeable future. But even these few have not necessarily internalized the kind of self-image that represents the goal of women's liberation or of human liberation in the West. Individualism is not a value on which most Arab women place a high priority. Quite the contrary, they are often bemused by the Western preoccupation with individualism, or even vehemently opposed to it. They want to retain as much as possible the communal, extended family aspects and supports of their traditional society, while eliminating its worst abuses, such as easy divorce for men and virtually none for women, and forced marriage.

The struggle to obtain the vote was one of the dominant themes in Western political development, and therefore also in the first stage of the women's movements in the West. Thus great stress is placed by social scientists in studies of Arab women on their having achieved or failed to achieve the right to vote. In fact, one casual measure in the literature of the 1950s, none other having been available at the time, to test the "advancement" of the women's movements in Arab countries, centered around how long and how successfully they had struggled for the right to vote. But in societies in which individualism is not a valued characteristic and in which the political culture strongly reinforces the notion that politics is not the concern of women, obtaining the right to vote for women is often an irrelevant exercise. Moreover, in many Arab countries, at this stage in their political development, at least, voting as a means of either making policy or of leadership choices is a rare occurrence. Thus, the struggle hardly seems worth the game either to the masses of women, for whom it goes against their values and concerns, or to the limited elite, who recognize it rightly as an exercise in futility.[14]

While the ballot box may have drastically changed the position of American blacks in the 1960s, this could only happen in a society in which voting in some way influences policy or personnel decisions of government and in which the voters can recognize the relationship between their individual acts and national public policy outcomes.

Since political communication to and among women in Arab countries is negligible; since their own degree of personal political modernity (Sherrill, 1969) and therefore their ability to perceive the relationship between the abstract act of voting and any impact on their own lives or the lives of those around them is limited; and since voting, in fact, seldom does have any significant impact on public policy, to stress voting as a priority goal for Arab women is an exercise in irrelevance.

Western social scientists recognize the necessity in at least some Arab countries for population control as a prerequisite, not only of development, but of not falling farther and farther behind in the effort to achieve economic well-being for the masses. They therefore stress as a goal for women and as an incentive for liberation of Arab women, the activist role that they can then presumably play in the national struggle for effective population control.

One finds the literature on Arab women full of references to the important role that women have to play in this area,[15] and that, usually implicitly, the particular writer believes they will automatically play if liberated. But, within the framework of Arab popular culture, which strongly supports the production of large numbers of children on religious grounds, and in which men are considered virile in relation to the number of children that they sire, the degree of "liberation" that would be required to persuade women to accept and practice, let alone actively to foster and campaign for, effective population control is at least a generation away.

Meanwhile, little enthusiasm for population control can be found among lower-class Arab women, at least as long as it requires overt action. That is, women when questioned about how many children they would like to have may name a figure somewhat lower than that desired by Arab men;[16] but when it comes to practice, few lower-class women will risk the displeasure, possible physical abuse, and/or divorce that may be visited upon them by irate husbands should they introduce any idea so controversial as birth control or family planning.

In the short run, at least, the priorities of Arab women for which they may be willing to mobilize are not necessarily those that seem most vital to outside observers. Limitation of polygamy, forced marriage, and easy divorce for the man with total custody of the children and no requirement to support his former wife, even if she has no income or job skills, have so far proved of greater interest to women's groups than have national development priorities.

Technical Problems: Language

Social scientists have long recognized the crucial role that language plays in obtaining valid results in field surveys of the sort that are needed in order to study the attitudes of the masses of Arab women vis-à-vis development goals of the 1970s.

Where studies of Latin American women are concerned, virtually every field researcher and director possesses a command of Spanish sufficient to permit effective field work. While the project director may use field interviewers who are native to the environment for political reasons and to facilitate the gathering of data, the principal researcher is usually in a position to check at first hand the translations of the data survey instrument and the responses to it in the original language.

Very few social scientists working in the Arab world, with the notable exception of the anthropologists, possess the language facility, in both classical and colloquial Arabic, written and spoken, to be able to check translations or to validate findings themselves in the original language. And since Arabic is an extremely rich language in which several words may exist to express a single English concept, a thoroughly bilingual researcher capable of making an accurate translation from the concepts of one language to the other is a prerequisite to obtaining valid results. Language is a particular problem in mass data studies, especially when they deal with relatively subjective questions of value and attitude, where nuances of language play a crucial role. The lack of bilingual, trained social scientists has been and continues to be a barrier to rapid accumulation of data on the Arab world, and particularly on Arab women, where for cultural reasons the interviewers and researchers must usually be women.

Technical Problems: Field Survey Research

The ideal field data study maximizes the satisfaction of participants and respondents, minimizes any inherent threats to them, and is viewed by the host population as legitimate.

It is extremely difficult, if not impossible, for data surveys in the Arab world, particularly on a sensitive topic like that of the status, attitudes, and political behavior of women, to come close to meeting these criteria.

If even the project supervisors, let alone the field survey staff, are non-Arab, there is the strong possibility of national chauvinism coloring even the formulation of the questions; there is the problem of language, already mentioned; there is the likelihood of callousness by foreign researchers, or simply lack of awareness of local sensitivities in an alien culture;[17] and there is the danger of either engaging in, or appearing to be engaged in, espionage or espionage-related data collection.

If, on the other hand, the directors and field staff are Arabs, there are the problems of local research competence and training, lack of familiarity with the disciplinary literature, and overspecialization in the particularity of the culture being studied; there is the possibility of political paranoia and hypersensitivity to both national government reaction and foreign response to the data being collected. Local power struggles between data collectors and local leaders who want to bend the study to their own purposes but who are also quick to denounce it if the results are unfavorable or disapproved by the national government also place obstacles in the way of objective and thorough data collection. There is the problem of ideological, class, religious, and/or educational biases on the part of both interviewers and interviewees that may also distort the results. The lack of adequate sampling aids — census data, records, maps, street guides, street names, phone books — often renders the random sampling technique that forms the basis of so much field survey research in the West difficult or impossible.

Also on a practical level, there are additional problems of comparability of data from one setting to another, if one is working on nonurban areas, in addition to the usual ones of size of the community, distance from the city, occupational divisions of the population, the accessibility of a paved road in or near the village, and so forth.

Whether the village is Christian (and, if so, of what sect or sects) or Muslim, or mixed; whether or not it has a large expatriate population; whether it was traditionally a religious center for the area, and thus provided Islāmic education for generations of villagers; whether it was an administrative center of the Ottoman Empire and therefore subject over a long period to foreign influence; whether it was a place of easy or forced resettlement of Bedū on the land within the past few generations — these and many other factors, both culturally and historically determined, must be added to the usual variables to be considered in selecting representative sampling areas. Because not all of these culturally determined variables are readily discernable to the social scientist, they may not appear significant enough to mention; many otherwise well-conceived data studies have gone astray.[18] It is usually better in the Arab world not to begin testing a hypothesis with a data survey. In such situations, survey techniques are most appropriately employed after considerable impressionistic and case study data has been collected (Frey 1970:258).

Survey research, far from being a familiar or understood practice in the Arab world, even among the middle class, is viewed with suspicion and hostility by the masses, who suspect that it may be a disguised government ploy for ferreting out disloyal citizens, raising tax bases, and other, to them, nefarious purposes, for such has been their general experience with government over the generations. Thus even when native trained female interviewers are used for survey research, results are likely to be distorted by the hostility and suspicion of the respondents on the one hand; and on the other, by a desire to please the interviewer and meet her expectations, a dominant characteristic in Arab culture. Further, a recently acquired national chauvinism in many Arab countries, coupled with a sense of inferiority to the West, often impels even illiterate respondents to reply to questions with answers that will not reveal what they perceive as their cultural weaknesses vis-à-vis the West, particularly to the interviewer who, if not actually Western by birth, is Western in the respondent's mind by virtue of dress, attitudes, and mere presence in the role of interviewer.

Moreover, there is the ideological problem in the more authoritarian military regimes — that the interviewees will try to reinforce government objectives, whether through fear of punishment, hope of reward, or political socialization, by telling the interviewer what they believe the government wants them to say in order to appear "modern," ideologically correct or, minimally, to be politically safe.

From the side of the interviewer, too, a significant distortion is likely to occur, perhaps less consciously than that sometimes contributed by the field subjects, but nonetheless distorting the

statistical results. Because of either social origins or accultura-
tion in the course of attaining the skills required to do field
survey work, the interviewer in the Arab world tends to be not
only middle class but often militantly so. That is, the interviewer tends to hold aggressively middle class values that she
may project onto her field subjects, thus imposing a kind of
middle-class filter on the material that she gathers.

This problem of the middle-class filter is evident not only in
field survey research but in other kinds of information gathering about Arab women. If one asks the most available infor-
mants, i.e., the middle-class activists who, for the most part,
populate Arab women's organizations, about the goals, values,
and practices of Arab women, they will almost invariably give
you a response that is typical of themselves and their class — the
urban, educated, middle-class woman. But the respondent's
frame of reference tends to cast the reply in universal terms,
i.e., encompassing all Arab women, even though the content
of the reply is only descriptive of the small minority to which
she belongs. And she is usually not aware of this discrepancy.
Only if pressed to make the distinction between herself and
the masses of Arab women may the middle-class woman
recognize the possibility of differences and, even then, she is
often reluctant to do so; the need for solidarity and support
behind them often makes the visible, militant leadership of
Arab women project onto others the values that they
themselves have only recently acquired and often fragilely
hold.

Since field survey interviewers tend to be drawn from this
same limited pool of relatively educated Arab women, there is
little doubt that their bias *in favor of* their own values can easily distort the results of survey research, no matter how great the
precautions taken against such distortion.

Another probable source of distortion arises from the communal nature of Arab societies, in which status derives from
one's religious identification, and minority communities live in
relative isolation from each other and from the Muslim community as a whole. Within the Muslim community itself there

are distinctions drawn between Shī'ite and Sunnī Muslims and among adherents of different schools of Islāmic jurisprudence, and all of these distinctions involve invidious comparisons by the dominant group vis-à-vis the less powerful.

Sending a Christian to interview Muslim women or a Sunnī to interview Shī'ī women in an area where the Sunnī are domi- nant and the Shī'ī a depressed community would tend to pro- duce the same kinds of distortions as sending a racist to gather objective data on poor blacks in the rural South.

In the United States, because the pool of potential field survey personnel on which we have to draw is so many times larger than in the Arab world, we can usually find relatively appropriate candidates and train them to some degree of ob- jectivity. The same possibility does not often exist as yet in the Arab world, which may be one reason why so little field survey research is carried out and why the results of what does take place are often suspect. The pool of trained interviewers is ex- tremely small and tends to be heavily weighted toward Chris- tians, who traditionally take greater advantage of educational opportunities than did the dominant Muslim community. If one accepts that field survey workers interviewing lower-class Arab women must be of the same sex, then the pool of eligible interviewers becomes smaller still and the opportunity or even possibility of screening for communal as well as cultural and class bias becomes limited. And the kinds of biases that have become entrenched in the culture over centuries are unlikely to be much affected by a short period of retraining.

If male interviewers or interpreters are used at any stage in connection with field studies of women, another set of biases is likely to be added to those mentioned above. Even trained male social scientists in the Arab world are likely to assume and even to maintain in the face of contrary evidence that "Arab women love their role" and to interpret that role favorably to their own and society's interest in maintaining the traditional male-female relationship.

More often than not, what I call the "pedestal theory,"[19] which Arab men entertain about the status of Arab women, is advanced by even the most educated to explain away the need for significant change in women's condition or even for any serious attention to the possibility of the need for reform where Arab women are concerned.

For male interviewers there is also the problem of access. Most traditional Arab women are not permitted to meet strange men (not close family members) anywhere or for any reason, except in the presence of their husbands. Where data surveys have been taken among Arab women at which the husbands were present, the latter have taken over and responded on behalf of their wives, a distortion that might altogether invalidate the results of many surveys. Thus if male interviewers are used, the pool of available respondents, and thus their representativeness in societies where most women are still secluded, becomes highly questionable.

Finally, in terms of the ability to do comparative research in the Arab world among different classes of women, or women from different areas, or even, for whatever utility it may have, among Muslim women from different national states, the problem of comparability of existing data arises.

Since record keeping and data collection are not as yet very advanced in most Arab countries, and the Arabs who are responsible for its collection are the first to admit this, it is usually not possible to obtain comparable data from a variety of settings; much of the existing data is not of great assistance to the social scientist wanting to do comparative analysis; the existing literature using data that is available to us in English is, for the most part, at least ten years old and often possesses no applicable conceptual framework, or indeed, any at all; the literature in Arabic on women is for the most part data-free, polemic, apologetic, or platitudinous, without even an attempt at conceptualization, although it is sometimes heavily ideological, especially in recent years and in certain Arab countries.[20] While there are a few fine analyses based largely on impressionistic data and the personal experience of the writers,[21] these analyses need updating, reinforcement or debunking through data studies and field surveys.

A single synthesis of available data and its analysis in terms of some conceptual framework that raises significant questions and provides the fragmentary answers presently available, or points out the lacunae with respect to the study of Arab women, remains to be written.

While the past two or three years, in particular, have seen a new flowering of interest in, and work on, Arab women by social scientists, most of this work, with the exception of some done by anthropologists, remains largely unavailable and unintegrated into any overall conceptual framework. Interesting and potentially productive conceptualizations of Arab women or certain categories of Arab women that have been produced largely out of impressionistic literature and/or the personal experience of the writers require data verification. And data verification by field survey techniques is limited both by political considerations in many, if not most, Arab countries and by the various inhibitions to field survey research already described.

Because of the political limitations imposed by the international and domestic political situation in the Arab world in recent years, major foundation subsidies have not generally been available to field survey researchers in the Arab world. Thus, the state of our knowledge or our ability to verify models with data derived from field studies has remained relatively stagnant over the past decade. Few social scientists have in recent years attempted to work in such an inhospitable environment.

But the need for such research is evident, both in terms of its potential contribution to policy formulation and, perhaps, simply because "it is there"—intellectual curiosity for those of us interested in the Arab world demands satisfaction.

Technical Problems: Existing Data

Data on Arab women, particularly for recent years, is extremely limited and fragmentary, much of it based on second- and third-hand impressions rather than on direct field contact with Arab women. Subject matter of existing data studies tends to be concentrated in the areas of health and family planning and to be very sparse indeed when it comes to women's values, attitudes, and participation in social and political affairs.

On the other hand, what data exist with respect to general indicators, like education of women, topics of women's conversation, interests, self-perceptions, attitudes, and the like permit the political scientist familiar with Arab culture to extrapolate by extension to formulate working hypotheses with respect to women's role in modernization and development, actual and potential.

One of the significant problems with respect to data that we have to confront deals with the fact that most works in English by social scientists that touch on the role of Arab women at all, and they are few enough, tend to draw exclusively upon other Western language sources, to rely upon each other as sources for their "conclusions." Thus a very narrow, ethnocentrically oriented base of opinion about Arab women constitutes the bulk of the literature currently available on the subject. Most of the early studies, really little more than impressionistic assertions about Arab women, were done by men with little or no access to the subjects of their study or by Westernized Arabs alienated from their own mass societies. These writers felt it necessary to be apologists for their culture or at the very least to emphasize only the positive aspects of it.[22] Thus, most of the assertions about the values, attitudes, and participation of Arab women in society have tended to focus upon the values and behavior of an extremely limited stratum of urban, elite women, without admitting this limitation. For example, one finds the statement, "Arab women have mobilized actively and effectively on behalf of their own emancipation" (Woodsmall 1956:56). This statement is so patently absurd to anyone familiar with Arab culture that one must assume that the writer either was totally ignorant of the facts or that he intended to say, "Some urban, elite women have organized effectively in support of causes, like independence and anticolonialism, already supported by men." To assert the first statement at a time when 98 percent of Arab women were not even aware that they might need or desire emancipation, were not mobilized in any way at all on behalf of it or any other feminist cause, and might very well have refused to cooperate in such activities had they been confronted by the opportunity do so is clearly to mislead the reader seriously.

But such unsubstantiated generalizations by a few writers in the 1950s have been widely adopted by contemporary social scientists, who often enough are themselves unfamiliar with the Arab context per se and are using presumably reliable secondary sources to illustrate a point. It is only recently that trained social scientists who have the advantage (for this kind of research) of being women, have gained access to a variety of women in different settings throughout the Arab world, and using appropriate language and research skills and familiarity with Arab culture, have begun to produce valid data and analysis with respect to the post-World War II roles of Arab women.[23]

The Research Problem: The Social and Political Roles of Arab Women

The research problem with which this essay is concerned, on which I have been working since 1973 and which forms the conceptual basis of my forthcoming book on the modern Arab woman, is the question of woman's role in development. Existing discussions of Arab development over the next decade or two widely assume that women will mobilize on behalf of and contribute to the goals of existing development plans. The literature is full of assertions that it is vital to further development that women be educated and trained so that they can play a crucial role, perhaps a unique one, in introducing new programs of birth control, improved nutrition and hygiene, infant and maternal care, and a wide variety of other socially oriented development plans that are the priority development goals of most Arab governments for the 1970s. It is usually simply assumed that there is a cause and effect relationship between educating women and their adoption of officially sanctioned roles and, moreover, their successful pursuit of such goals.

I find in Arab history and contemporary culture serious reason to question this set of assumptions and to raise questions about the inevitability of women playing the contributive roles assigned them by others.

For purposes of my analysis, I take "development" to be what official policy says it is, and focus on the aspect of it that spells out a series of policy goals that for social reasons require women's direct acquiescence and/or participation in order to be implemented effectively or at all—such as those just identified. I leave to others to further define development and modernization in the abstract,[24] and I focus my attention on current and probable responses of Arab women to whatever is defined as development or modernization in the context in which they function.

One qualification should be raised here, however, bearing on the content of the process of modernization. This is a question that Arab society as a whole and Arab governments in particular have, for the most part, yet to confront. Can modernization be achieved in the economic and material sectors of the society while leaving the value system and traditional practices and relationships intact? Can the Arab world have both advanced technology and high standards of living and still keep intact the extended family, the pattern of marriage as an economic and political alliance between groups without regard to personal feelings, and the communal nature of social organization and control? For the most part, this philosophical problem has been little confronted in the Arab world, either in the literature or in practice. When we apply this notion to Arab women, the relevant question to ask is whether it is realistic to expect that they can be widely mobilized in support of specific programs that are of significance to *governments* without also being socialized in ways that will lead them to demand other changes that may not be acceptable to the governments at all. Mobilizing women for any purpose is, in the currently fashionable phrase, likely to raise their consciousness, both individually and collectively, so that they begin to perceive their position as a deprived one vis-à-vis men and to mobilize for individual legal rights—the right to work, the right to divorce and to custody of their children, the right to education, and the right to be a full legal person instead of a chattel, which is what the Arab woman has traditionally been by law.

Thus mobilizing Arab women for any purpose at all may cause them to formulate their own power blocs and set their own priorities in terms of what they are willing to be mobilized for. And women's priorities are not inevitably those of Arab governments—in fact, one may suggest, on the basis of the largely impressionistic data so far available, that at least initially women are likely *not* to be concerned about issues that concern Arab governments in the 1970s. Not that they will be *unconcerned* about issues of birth control and improved nutrition, but that they are likely to be, in this first politicized generation, more concerned with their own condition; this may lead them to agitate more for individual rights than for social programs. Moreover, the logic of a successful birth control program is that somehow men must be persuaded or forced to accept it. So long as women are chattels of men and can be cast aside easily and without recourse on the part of the wife, most Arab wives would be foolhardy in the extreme to agitate for birth control programs until either the values of the society change to support such a program, in which case their agitation and organization is either unnecessary or marginal, or until they are in a position to protect themselves legally and economically, and to retain some rights to their children, if their agitation and mobilization remove them from the protection of their husbands in a society in which there is little or no protection for the woman who has no husband to defend her.

So far, the only successful participation by women in the policymaking or policy implementation process has been in areas where the goals of their agitation were either irrelevant to the decisionmaking process, were also supported by men who encouraged women's participation for their own reasons, or were achieved through the intercession of a man or men, usually in powerful positions who, by their own experience and philosophy, had already adopted values or goals that happened to coincide with some of the goals of women. Great success in direct pressure upon the political process has often been ascribed to the Lebanese women's movement for having "won" the unqualified right to vote for Lebanese women in 1953; while it is true that Lebanese women obtained the franchise in that year, I cannot ascribe their success to agitation by women's groups. I know of no instance in the Arab world in which a woman's organization successfully mounted an independent campaign to win a controversial goal and achieved success through pressures upon the political process.[25]

Even if the efforts by Arab governments to involve women in their development programs were accompanied by an effective program of politicization, which is generally not the case, it is doubtful that the intermediate step of women developing their own self-awareness and reflecting this awareness back to national institutions as an independent process of interest formulation and articulation can be avoided.

Considering the disadvantages under which Arab women live and the failure of social and political institutions to resolve or even to confront seriously these disadvantages over the last 50 or 276 years (the figure some historians give as the time span of modernization efforts in the Arab world[26]), one can expect that Arab women's priorities, in terms of their relationship to power centers and the nature and focus of their confrontations with power, may well be quite different from those that currently inspire their male contemporaries. While ultimately the mode of relationship between Arab women and development planners may become collaboration, in the short run it is more likely to be one of confrontation and conflict, with women's priorities competing with national priorities for the limited funds, emphasis, and support available from existing power centers.

In terms of the majority-minority analysis that is under question here as an appropriate analytical focus for the study of Arab women, one is reminded in political, social, and psychological terms, if not in numbers, of the black experience in the United States.

Blacks did not generally (limited elite movements to the contrary notwithstanding) confront the power structure on a continuing basis with demands or even assertions of their existence as a distinct interest group, or of their right to participate in power as a minority. From the end of reconstruction until the founding of the NAACP in 1910, there was really no ongoing black voice mobilizing support from the mass population within its own community and arousing consciousness of its minority position. The same has been true, and to some extent is still true, of Arab women. Until recently the only voices raised on behalf of women as a deprived minority have come from a small elite, largely middle and upper middle class, with little audience but itself, with little or no influence upon power or policy, and thus with negligible impact upon either potential followers or the society as a whole. Like black Americans of the postreconstruction years, Arab women today are not only powerless, but also often unaware of or comfortable in their powerlessness; they seldom participate in the economic or social rewards that the system has to offer and are unable to affect the existing power structure in any significant way. "They know their place" when referring to American blacks and "they support the Islāmic way of life"[27] are equivalent myths serving as rationalizations by nonminority groups for maintaining the legal, political, and economic status quo. "They are happy with their lot," justified by the lack of massive overt evidence to the contrary, typified both complacent American thinking about black Americans as late as the 1950s, as well as Arab men's thinking about Arab women in the 1970s.

Of course, one can argue that analysis of Arab women as a political minority is not relevant so long as they do not perceive themselves as a minority, but the processes of education, value change, and political socialization that have been put in motion either willy-nilly or deliberately by Arab governments and interest groups over the past fifty years vis-à-vis women have all combined to spread ever more widely the Arab woman's view of herself as a deprived, powerless, and ineffectual member of society.[28]

While it does not necessarily follow from the analogy being developed between Arab women and black Americans that Arab women will pursue the militant tactics of job action, rioting, and other forms of political violence that have been a part of black Americans' efforts to obtain a share of institutional and policymaking power, this is not necessarily an indication of a real difference, either in the condition of the two groups or in their perceptions of their position. It is rather a question of the difference of timing (Arab women's consciousness level today approximates that of black Americans in the 1930s) and of culture, particularly political culture. It is also a question of what is required in order to produce change and bring about participation for the disadvantaged minority.

Black Americans confronted a well-institutionalized political system, with a recognizable and legitimate political elite and a broad consensus upon the values of the political culture and the kinds of policies that those institutions and that culture should and would sponsor. Handing a share in power over to a political minority that was also a racial minority with a history of slavery and subordination was not a value that the political culture embraced. In order to achieve a share of power, confrontation politics were eventually necessary.

But in the Arab world, there is a very low level of institutionalization of national power and a similarly low level of legitimacy of national leadership and policy. If Arab women, mobilizing on behalf of legal and policy goals in the near

future, can overcome the sanctions of traditional Islāmic practice and belief with respect to women, they may be able to have
a much stronger and more durable impact on national policy
organs more quickly than American blacks could. There are
far more possibilities of political alliances for them in a society
in a state of rapid change; their ability to influence policy will
result in part from the declining power and influence of the
traditional religious establishment.

In order to hypothesize about what roles women are likely to
play in the process of development and how they are likely to
use any access they gain to the power structure in Arab society,
we must know something of the traditional roles and status of
Arab women.

In terms of personal status, the traditional Arab
woman—and this still means the average woman today, in
practice, if not in law—had no legal standing except such as
was specifically laid down by the Qur'ān, which together with
its referents, the *sunnah* and *hadīth* of the Prophet Muhammad,[29] and the interpretations placed upon these three
primary sources by the learned members of the Muslim community in the early centuries of Islām, constituted, and still
constitute, the sole sources of Islāmic jurisprudence. According
to this law, the Arab woman is basically a chattel, the property
of her father, initially, and later of her husband, to dispose of
as they will. While she may, under Qur'ānic law, inherit half
the share of a brother, and pass that share to her heirs at her
own discretion, she has no independent right to education,
work, travel, divorce, financial support in the case of divorce,
choice of husband, postponement of marriage to a later age, or
custody of her children beyond the age of seven, or even visita-
tion rights to them, in the event of divorce.[30]

On the other hand, although not sanctioned by either the
Qur'ān or all schools of Islāmic jurisprudence to the same
degree, men in traditional Arab society may dispose of their
daughters, sisters, or wives more or less as suits them. The male
guardian may marry his daughter or sister to whomever he

chooses; he may deny her opportunities for education and employment; once married, the woman may be divorced easily and with no financial obligation on the part of the husband to support her; the husband retains absolute and total custody of children over the age of seven and may, and often does, deny his former wife all opportunity ever to see them again; if a wife leaves her husband in some Arab countries, including Egypt, the police power of the state may be and is used to force her to return to him, even though the cause of her leaving may have been grievous physical abuse of herself and her children. Until recently in all Muslim countries the husband had the right to take second, third, and fourth wives, thereby, perhaps, depriving his first wife and her children of a significant share of his estate; he still has this right in many states.

Moreoever, since responsibility to guard family honor rests with the nearest male relative of a woman, who is the embodiment of that honor, and since women are still widely considered to be "weak, lascivious creatures who cannot resist temptation and who are unfit for participation in public life,"[31] the man's most sacred duty is to see that his honor (*'ird*) is not blemished by the conduct of any woman under his control. If the woman violates the code, however unwillingly, the man must compensate for her dishonor through blood revenge or public reparations appropriate to the code.

Thus only five years ago a case made the headlines in Lebanon, supposedly the most advanced of the Arab countries, in which a father slit his daughter's throat on the public street because she had been abducted and raped by three village youths. Since none of the three would marry her, an act the code would have considered just recompense, and since the event had become public knowledge, the father was forced to kill his daughter publicly to restore the family honor. In another case only two years ago in Kuwait, a well-known politician was murdered by political opponents. His mistress was also from a prominent family. The families of the two hushed up the political scandal, and the murderers went free, in order to avoid making the matter public, for in that case the girl would have had to be slain. An Arab proverb goes, "If you are going to sin, sin in secret" and so it is with the honor code. One need not retrieve the family honor unless it has been publicly besmirched or the news of the dishonor has been publicly discussed; if it has, the man must retrieve it, no matter what the penalty demanded by the code.

Most of the customs surrounding the current status of Arab women are not the direct result of Qur'ānic prescription or Islāmic legal practice. The Qur'ān actually improved the status of women over what it was in pre-Islāmic times, and there is a substantial body of evidence that women were under no disadvantage, either spiritual or temporal, in the early days of Islām.[32] But popular Islām has come to view women as unfit for public responsibility. This view, rather than the Qur'ānic one, has come to be the operative concept that circumscribes woman's role in the male-dominant tradition of the contemporary Arab world. In fact, the code of honor and the legal status of women are the societal embodiments of the currently operative Muslim (as opposed to Islāmic) philosophy and value system.[33]

The corollary of the view that women are emotional, irrational creatures, not to be trusted to play a positive role in public affairs, is that the proper role of women is limited to child bearing and keeping house. Thus, Arab society so far exhibits very little sense of guilt about the fact that Islāmic law relegates woman to the status of a chattel or denies her equal rights with men in any sphere.

The average Muslim woman still tends to share the dominant view of men about women's abilities and proper roles, although some change in this respect on the part of women can be found in the limited attitude studies that have been done in recent years.[34] For example, in one Sudānese study that was done by the government prior to building a new housing project for the poor, men and women were queried about which of five "luxuries" they would most like to have in their new homes, assuming that only one could be made available. The five choices were a bathroom, an earthenware storeroom for water jugs, a pantry, a veranda, or a high wall between the houses so that the women of the family could not be seen by outsiders. The women variously chose any one of the first four amenities, in about equal proportions; the men almost unanimously chose the high wall (A. S. al-Shāhī, "Politics and the Role of Women in a Shaiqīya Constituency, 1968," *Sūdān Society,* 1969, pp. 33-35). If this study is at all representative — and it is too little evidence from which to draw firm conclusions — while women's attitudes are changing, men's are not.

In some countries, such as Egypt in the 1940s and Algeria in the 1950s, women have been active in the independence movements, where their participation has been welcomed by men as a means both of legitimizing the movement in foreign eyes and providing additional guerrilla fighters or support forces. But once the revolutionary objective was attained, Egyptian and Algerian women found their opportunities very much circumscribed, with strong societal pressure for them to return to the home and assume their former status and roles.

Arab women no longer need struggle for their rights using assumed names, so as not to disgrace their families, as was necessary for Egyptian women in the 1940s. But neither can they expect vigorous enforcement, or often any enforcement at all, of their rights to education, employment, legal equality, protection against forced or early marriage, easy divorce, and loss of their children, even in those countries, few though they are, that have legislatively changed the status of women.

The pace of change with respect to women's actual status in the Arab world makes a snail appear to be a streaker. A commission on the status of women created in Egypt in 1929 studied the problems of women and came out with a report recommending no change at all, on the grounds that such change would go contrary to public opinion. By 1949, although the commission continued to exist and meet, there had been no significant change in Egypt, either through legislative reform or through education of public opinion by efforts of the commission. In that year, the government created a new body, composed of twelve members, eight of them over seventy years of age and most of them conservative members of the Egyptian religious establishment. Only one woman was on the commission. This body unaccountably did not begin its work until 1962, a thirteen-year lead time, and had reached no conclusions by 1966. In 1967, when the government informed the commission that it would act if they did not, the commission produced in three days what it had been unable to produce in 38 years — 400 articles of "reform" of the status of women, which basically left Egyptian women's position unchanged and, instead of emphasizing their rights, stressed throughout the "obligations" of women, as understood by popular Islām in Egypt of the 1960s. *al-Ahrām*, the official government newspaper, criticized the work of the commission as retrogressive, and the government subsequently revised women's status by decree, but the decrees have by and large not been enforced.

The one Arab country in which women's rights have been both legislated and widely enforced is Tunisia, where the vehicle for both legal reform and enforcement has been the leadership of President Habib Bourgiba, himself a firm believer in the intrinsic relationship between feminism and development, at least for countries of limited resources and in need of rapid change.

There are many and obvious differences between the two countries — analyzed at length in my forthcoming paper on this subject[35] — that made possible reforms in Tunisia and not in Egypt. The purpose of mentioning these illustrations here is merely to point out that, for whatever reasons, most Arab countries have not yet made significant change in the traditional status of women, although they recognize woman's crucial role in certain aspects of the development programs of the 1970s and desire and need woman's contributions to these programs.

We can find logical support for the possibility that when women do achieve legal emancipation, or are emancipated by national governments bent on enlisting their services in the cause of development, (1) such emancipation may be achieved only at the price of abandonment of traditional values and lifestyles and may engender significant new kinds of social conflicts; and (2) that such emancipation may work counter to, or at least not in conjunction with, the development priorities established by Arab governments for the 1970s. Most Arab governments want to make citizens of their populations, male and female; that is, they desire to transform them into autonomous voluntary participants in programs of social change. They widely recognize that such a role cannot be played by ignorant, veiled, secluded women. Their national ideologies support liberation of women. Arab governments have, in most cases, legislated some political rights for women, like the right to vote and hold office, in the expectation that these will be sufficient to produce the kind of political support from women that will lend legitimacy to programs of national development. Since few elections are held, since they almost never determine actual power relationships, and since a woman candidate has little chance of being elected, it costs Arab governments very little to legislate change in women's status in this area. Essentially, they hope to buy women's support at a cheap price, without disturbing the essential aspects of male domination of society and thereby creating social controversy. But for most Arab women, voting rights, even if they could have an impact on power, would be meaningless without legal, psychological, and value changes that have yet to occur.

In the few studies done so far about women's voting patterns in the Arab world, the women have either (1) not voted at all; (2) permitted their husbands to vote a second time in the same election, in their wives' names, on the grounds that voting is, after all, a man's responsibility;[36] or (3) voted for the most conservative and antifeminist candidates (ibid., pp. 33-36).

The pressures of husbands and male relatives, of their communities, of popular religion, their own educations and socialization, all of which proclaim female activism and even political participation as unfeminine and antireligious, and which prescribe submission to male-dominant values, noninvolvement in the community, and apathy in social affairs as the appropriate attitudes for women, have not yet been counterbalanced in any significant way by imperatives of national ideology, legislative change, education, political socialization, or any other factor of change in women themselves. Ideology has occasionally brought about transformation of laws in the Arab world with respect to women; it has less often enforced these new laws; it has yet to transform values.

On the basis of the limited data now available and of the foregoing analysis, I have developed a number of tentative hypotheses relating to the actual and potential role in the immediate future of Arab women in development. I am in the process of attempting to locate or gather data that may prove to substantiate or negate these hypotheses.

Hypothesis I

While most Arab elites are firmly committed in theory to the legal and social emancipation of Arab women, they do not pursue these goals vigorously. Given the prevailing values of Arab society, governments would have little chance of success in accomplishing even modest change in women's status, and such change as could be accomplished might have to be bought at the risk of escalating levels of political conflict. This is a risk that Arab governments are not prepared to take, given the tenuous holds most have upon power and the already manifold disruptive issues that the process of economic and political development inevitably bring. Moreover, since the modernizing governments usually in power have overthrown traditionalists in the recent past, these new governments are unwilling to present their opponents with an issue that might well bring them back to power. In the early stages of nation-building by a modernizing government, priority tends to go to highly visible prestige projects that are noncontroversial or even unifying in the sense that they produce a feeling of emotional community and pride in the nation. Divisive, invisible, or controversial problems, such as significant change for Arab women, tend to become very low priority issues and are likely to remain so for some time, whatever ideological prescriptions may exist to support them. Only a charismatic leader secure in his control of power can afford to risk the social disruption and political consequences that will certainly characterize serious efforts at reforming the status of women. And that is not to say that such a leader, like the late Jamāl 'Abd al-Nāsir, will necessarily attempt such reform. His own outlook and value system may prevent it, or it may prove too controversial for even a charismatic leader to take on. Thus for several reasons, reform in the status of women seems unlikely to emanate from present Arab elites.

Hypothesis II

Where Arab elites do seek to involve women in specific, preordained community efforts at development, through an active program of politicization, they are likely to be creating an additional barrier to the short-term nation-building and development process. It seems unlikely that women will actively and continuously support development goals while they themselves remain nonmodern and legally subject to the sanctions of a traditional legal system that rewards subservience to their immediate families and punishes public initiative by women in community affairs. Arab women are for the most part not permitted to attend political meetings except for those few specially aranged for them, at which only other women are present. In fact, a *fetwā* (legal ruling) from al-Azhar University, the most exalted seat of Islāmic learning in the Arab world, and the last word on the subject of Arab women in politics, says that for women to attend political meetings would be immodest and provide them with a temptation to promiscuity.[37] Given this prevailing social attitude, it is little wonder that even the educated women of Kuwait refused to use their organizational efforts to lobby for political rights, when to do so would arouse their husbands' ire and brand them as immodest in the eyes of their society. Thus, on the one hand, women are likely to remain traditional in their outlooks and therefore unlikely actively to support development programs, including birth control, that go against traditional values. Where Arab elites, on the other hand, succeed in socializing women to adopt modern outlooks, the inevitable raising of women's consciousness about themselves that is an intrinsic part of this process is likely to cause women to develop their own priorities in relation to societal change. It is very likely that modernist Arab women will mobilize in support of the very controversial changes that governments wish to avoid, rather than use their energies to promote government-ordained programs.

Hypothesis III

Urbanization in the Arab world does not seem to set in force the process of individual change that might raise women's consciousness and motivate them to struggle for their own rights and to become an effective interest group on their own behalf. Since urbanization has been characteristic of the more populous Arab states for centuries and has occurred gradually over a long period of time, it does not have the same impact in terms of societal disruption and therefore creation of openness to rapid change that much of the literature on urbanization suggests. One does not find in Arab cities nearly as much of the disorientation and need for adaptation, and thus availability to new social and political movements and ways of thought, that seem to characterize urbanization elsewhere. In the Arab world for the most part, the city was the focus of all significant economic, political, religious, educational, and cultural life for centuries; thus there has been a continued gradual influx into

Arab cities. This gradual influx has been continuously absorb-
ed into already existing family structures and social institutions. The institutional patterns of behavior control that apply
in the villages and on the farms apply almost as firmly in Arab
cities and always have. It is only recently, and then only partially, that the anonymous urban center that frees people from
traditional social controls by virtue of size and anonymity has
begun to appear at all in the Arab world. So far, what evidence
we have suggests that at the lower educational levels, where
most of the current influx is taking place, there occurs no
significant change in educational levels, outlooks, values, or
behavior of Arab women.

Hypothesis IV

Women's organizations have so far not proved effective instruments for changing legislative outcomes or influencing national policy. They have not yet been able to become mass
mobilizing organizations, but remain urban middle- and
upper-class elitist, structurally diffused, with little sustained
activist support even from among their own members because
the goals that they have traditionally pursued, such as voting
rights, have not spoken to the most pressing needs of the masses
of Arab women. Women's organizations have also not been
able to arouse sustained support from the community as a
whole, because their goals are at wide variance with prevailing
social norms. Only if their opposition be similarly disadvantaged might women's organizations, in their present forms, hope
for any significant sucess. But since they have arrayed against
them the entire power structure and effective instruments of
social control, they are more likely to fail totally than to succeed even partially. Thus, women are unlikely to be able to
play a role in mobilizing other women toward modern goals or
in setting forth feminist priorities to be incorporated in the
development plans of Arab states in the 1970s. The most that
women's organizations have so far been able to accomplish has

been to find a patron to put one of their proposals before the decisionmaking bodies — usually with no success; to attain irrelevant rights like the right to vote in societies in which all significant political decisions are made entirely outside the electoral process; to support symbolically the legitimacy of male-led political issues and struggles, such as independence and Palestine; and to begin to move tentatively into the area of feminist education — a "freeing from" some traditional restrictions for those women reached by their programs. But the issue of "freeing women for" new obligations, autonomy as individuals, new lifestyles, rights and responsibilities such as responsible citizenship and active mobilization on behalf of development causes, has yet to become a significant part of the activity of women's organizations. While weaknesses in the present distribution and institutionalization of power make it *possible* for women's organizations to play a significant role in changing women's legal and social status, they cannot play this role so long as they remain elitist organizations, functioning chiefly through men and supporting causes that are not of primary importance to their current and prospective members.

Hypothesis V

Prodevelopment, nation-building goals, however, require active participation by women. Since coeducation beyond primary school is heavily frowned upon by Muslim (as opposed to Islāmic) tradition, universal literacy, teacher training for girls, education in domestic arts and, ultimately, availability of women for political socialization and indoctrination in citizenship and development goals can only be attained by widespread training of women as teachers and the establishment of a full-fledged system of women's education by and for women. The same thing is true in medicine, where traditional attitudes preclude the use of male physicians, especially but not only in the areas of obstetrics, gynecology, and pediatrics. If infant and maternal mortality rates are to decline and health standards and conditions to improve, it is necessary to train large numbers of women in medicine, particularly for work in the villages and farms of the Arab world. A limited middle-class elite of women working in the cities will not meet the needs of women for women's services. Nursing, much in demand, is considered a low-status profession, into which middle-class women seldom go. Service professions in which women must meet the public are also frowned upon for "respectable" women, thus depriving development planners in underpopulated countries of a vital source of labor supply. Women clearly are needed to talk to other women about population control, health and hygiene, education and training programs, and a myriad of social ills that either affect women most directly or that women must be primarily instrumental in alleviating.

The development goals of the 1970s in the Arab world are more social than the economically oriented programs of the 1960s. While industrialization and increase in gross national product and other gross economic indicators, diversification of industrial and agricultural production, and other large-scale economic enterprises were stressed in the 1950s and 1960s, development goals of the 1970s stress much more the social problems of population control, family health and hygiene, including mental health, family fragmentation, disorientation and accompanying malaises such as rising crime rates in societies that have previously known very little serious crime, inadequacy of housing, education and welfare services, and public facilities for the indigent, the aged, and other economically marginal groups.

It is now widely recognized that women are an essential part of the support facilities that must be available to governments if they wish to deal successfully with these problems. The emphasis in Arab development has shifted from economic aggregates to individual problems and, with this shift, the role of women becomes central.

This shift in development goals has been accompanied by a

shift in the focus of political issues. In the 1940s and 1950s, the issue was independence and women legitimized the movement by an occasional march on behalf of the goals of their men. In the 1950s, the issue was competition between traditionalists and modernists, with the traditionalists for the most part holding power and the modernists attempting to gain it. To do so, it was necessary to develop ideologies that justified the wresting of power from incumbent elites whose rule was sanctioned by Islāmic doctrine and history. In this struggle, women for the most part played a peripheral role, occasionally being used by one side or the other in a particular confrontation, but seldom playing a crucial and certainly not a continuous role.

In the 1970s, the consolidation of power in the hands of modernizers having already been accomplished in most Arab states, or an acceptable accommodation between traditionalists and modernizers having been arrived at, the chief political issue becomes enactment and implementation of the social reforms that the modernizers of the 1950s and 1960s promised would result for the masses who supported their seizures of power. The success of these reforms is now needed to justify both independence and ideology. And in insuring the success of reforms, in those areas of life that have been traditionally relegated to women — family welfare concerns — the role of Arab women is a significant one.

Current State of the Research

I am currently living in Sharjah, United Arab Emirates, with frequent travel throughout the Arab world. I am attempting through interviews with women at many social and economic levels to gather preliminary information on the basis of which to do a data survey in a number of Arab countries to either substantiate or refute my hypotheses.

I have encountered severe problems in the areas of lack of availability of basic statistical data, a problem of which Arab women's organizations themselves are acutely aware. My immediate project will be to attempt to gather such data for all Arab countries and make it available to Arab women's organizations as well as to further my own research.

I have also encountered great difficulty in finding research assistance competent to conduct this kind of study. The problems of conceptualization and technique discussed in the methodology section of this essay are the problems, in practice, that I have had to confront in attempting to develop a macrotheoretical view of the role of Arab women in development.

Notes

1. Either recent and accurate population statistics are not available for several Arab countries, or a breakdown by sex is not included in the data. Extrapolating from the data available in *The Middle East: A Handbook* (London: Europa Publications, 1973) we can assume that women constitute a slight overall majority of Arab populations.

2. Or at least this is how Arab women seem to perceive it. Women's organizations are not consulted by government planners. Whatever development programs for women appear in the plans are those that men have apparently decided women *should* want.

3. This remains true despite the recent formulation of national ideological prescriptions to the contrary.

4. For an exposition of the traditional Muslim view, see Hajji Shaykh Yusuf, "In Defense of the Veil," trans. Charles R. Pittman, in *The Muslim World*, vol. 23, no. 3 (July) 1943 [originally published in Iran in 1926] pp. 203-12; and Sayyid Qutb [Kotb], *Social Justice in Islam*, trans. John B. Hardie, (Washington, D.C.: American Council of Learned Societies, 1953), pp. 49-54.

5. In response to the 'Iraqi women's campaign for the franchise, the orthodox Muslim hierarchy responded with a "week of virtue" to counteract it. See Ruth F. Woodsmall, *Study of the Role of Women in Lebanon, Egypt, 'Iraq, Jordan and Syria, 1954-55*, (Woodstock,: Elm Tree Press, 1956), p. 50. See also the *Kuwait Times* and other local newspaper coverage of the reaction of conservative religious groups to women's demands that the national legislature consider revisions in the *Shari'ah with respect to women's status and in the civil code to give women voting rights (December 1973 and January 1974)*.

6. See, for example, David C. Gordon, *Women of Algeria: An Essay on Change*, (Cambridge, Mass.: Harvard University Press, 1968); N. Tomiche, "The Position of Women in the United Arab Republic," *Journal of Contemporary History*, vol. 3, no. 3, (July) 1968, esp. p. 140; and F. Lewis, "No Revolution for the Woman of Algiers," *New York Times Magazine*, Oct. 29, 1967, p. 28ff.

7. See, for example, Aziza Husayn [Hussein], "The Role of Women in Social Reform in Egypt," *Middle East Journal*, 7 (1953): 442-44; Fadela M'Rabet, *Les Algeriennes*, (Paris: Librairie François Maspero, 1967).

8. As pointed out most convincingly in a paper presented by Amal Vinogradov to the National Academy of Science, November 1973, suggesting that her field work in Morocco and Algeria had uncovered an unusually high degree of psychosomatic and mental illness among two groups of women—the very young and those past child-bearing age. Prof. Vinogradov suggested further investigation into this data to try to determine whether there may exist any correlation between frustration over their status in society and mental and physical illness among Arab women. See also Cynthia Nelson, "Changing Roles of Men and Women: Illustrations from Egypt," *Anthropological Quarterly*, vol. 41, no. 2 (April) 1968, p. 71ff.; *Arab Women in Love*, (Beirut: Khayat's, 1969), passim.

9. Kenneth S. Sherrill, "The Attitudes of Modernity," *Comparative Politics*, vol. 1, no. 2 (January) 1969, pp. 184-210. In this connection, it might also be interesting to consider the possible application of Donald L. Horowitz's theory to Arab women in relation to their potential impact on national policy; "Three Dimensions of Ethnic Politics," *World Politics*, vol. 23, no. 2 (January) 1971, pp. 232-44.

10. One is strongly reminded of the parallel between Arab women's position today and that of black Americans prior to 1954. Whatever legal rights they might have had were seldom enforced and through both lack of awareness of their own potential power and legislative efforts to restrain them from exercising that power black Americans, with the exception of a few unrepresentative members of the black elite, had virtually no imput into the policymaking process, no voice in power, and no ongoing protection of even such legal rights as they possessed.

11. See, for example, *Preliminary Paper on Integration of Women in Development*, (United Nations, Social Development Division, February 1972).

12. See Carolyn Bird, *Born Female: The High Cost of Keeping Women Down* (New York: David McKay, 1970) and, for further extensive bibliographical references of useful works dealing with American women as a whole, Sue-Ellen Jacobs, *Women in Perspective: A Guide for Cross-Cultural Studies*, (Urbana, Ill.: University of Illinois Press, 1974), pp. 107-17.

13. See, for example, Raphael Patai, *Inside the Arab Mind*, and Michael W. Kamell, *The Middle East: A Humanistic Approach*, (Andrews Publishing Co., 1973).

14. According to numerous interviews held by the writer with members of elite women's groups in Lebanon, Kuwait, Egypt, Saudi Arabia, Iraq, and the Arab Gulf States over a nineteen year period from 1959 to 1978.

15. For example, "The Role of Women in Development" (Arabic), *Majallat al-mar'ah*, June 15, 1970, pp. 22-26.

16. James M. Gillespie and Gordon W. Allport, *Youth's Outlook on the Future, A Cross National Study*, Doubleday Papers in Psychology (New York: Doubleday, 1955, table 2, p. 54.) There was also, however, a strong tendency to fatalism among female respondents who, after naming the number of children they might consider desirable would often append the statement that they would happily accept as many "as God wills."

17. Even competent Arabists are often familiar only with the middle- and upper-class urban Arab values and life-styles.

18. For example, the Woodsmall *Study of the Role of Women* presents a highly misleading picture of the status of Arab women at the time, since all respondents were members of the extremely small educated urban elite, and most of them were apparently Christian. Thus, the "data" reflected by Woodsmall and her conclusions about "Arab women" are, in fact, the self-perceptions of a limited elite of Christian, educated urban women who want to view themselves as modern, à la the West.

19. I refer of course to the cliché about "placing women on a pedestal." Arab men defend the disadvantages from which Arab women suffer by arguing that it is a small price to pay for the privileges and protections that Arab men give to their women. And while one can certainly find much romanticization of woman by Arab men in their poetry and conversation, the day-to-day life of Arab women and the protections offered to them by society in the event of misfortune — such as divorce, or in the event that their desires and goals run counter to those of the men in their lives — are minimal and their disadvantages much more real than any actual privileges or protections that are provided on a day-to-day basis.

It is interesting to note in this connection that the position of the ordinary Arab women today is very much like that of women in medieval Europe. Romanticized in fantasy by men, they had no freedom, autonomy, or rights in practice. It is also interesting to note that several historians of the Arab world believe that Europe derived its notions of medieval chivalry from contact with Arab civilizations. See, for example, R. A. Nicholson, *A Literary History of the Arabs* (Cambridge: Cambridge University Press, 1956), pp. 88-90.

20. The pedestal theory enjoys great vogue in Libya as rationalization for an ultra-conservative and traditional Islamic ideology based on popular rather than orthodox Islam, which requires "keeping women in their place" as a religious imperative. The place is then defined as an advantageous one in which to be kept to legitimize the ideology and eliminate the need for reform. Libyan feminists disagree and have spent years in exile or in prison under the rule of Muammar Ghaddafai.

21. For example, Morroe Berger, *The Arab World Today* (New York: Doubleday, 1964), and Sania Hamadi [Hamady] *Temperament and Character of the Arabs* (New York: Twayne, 1960).

22. In the 1950s, "positive" usually meant those aspects that most closely approximated a Western model. See, for example, Najla 'Izz al-Din, [Izzedin] *The Arab World: Past, Present and Future* (Chicago: Henry Regnery, 1953).

23. Among the many competent studies that have recently appeared is that of Kay Boals, *A Comparative Study of the Development of Political Consciousness*, presented to the 1972 American Political Science Association meeting, Washington D.C., Sept. 5, 1972, panel on "Women and Political Change in Developing Areas."

24. In addition to Sherrill, "Attitudes of Modernity," one may cite the work of Daniel Lerner, *The Passing of Traditional Society*, (Glencoe, Ill.: The Free Press, 1958); David E. Apter, *The Politics of Modernization*, (Chicago: University of Chicago Press, 1965); Manfred Halpern, *The Politics of Social Change in the Middle East and North Africa*, (Princeton: Princeton University Press, 1963); and S. N. Eisenstadt in most of his writings, including "Breakdowns of Modernization," *Economic Development and Cultural Change* 12 (July 1964): 345-67.

25. As I explain in my forthcoming article on "The Role of Women in policy Formulation and Their Impact on the Electoral Process in the Contemporary Arab World."

26. The Napoleonic invasion of Egypt in 1798 is given by most Arab historians as the starting point of modernization of the Arab world.

27. This is an extremely conservative view, espoused by such writers as Qutb, *Social Justice in Islam*, and Hajji Shaykh Yusuf, "In Defense of the Veils." On the other hand, the vast majority of Arab intellectuals have long argued for reform in the status of women, on Islamic as well as practical grounds. Qasim Amin (d. 1908) in *Tahrir al-mar'ah*, al-Qahirah: Maktabat al-Turqi (*The Emancipation of Women* 1899), and *al-mar'at al-jadidah*, al-Qahirah: Muhammad Zaki al-Din (*The New Woman*, 1908) led a procession of reformers who tried to convince their fellow Arabs of the necessity of reform for women.

28. See, for example, Peter C. Dodd, "Youth and Women's Emancipation in the United Arab Republic," *Middle East Journal*, vol. 22, no. 2, (Spring 1968), p. 160ff.

29. *Sunnah* and *hadith* — the actions and sayings of the Prophet Muhammad.

30. For a general survey of woman's position in the *shari'ah*, see J. N. D. Anderson, *Islamic Law in the Modern World*, (New York: New York University Press, 1959), chap. 1. For a comparative analysis, see Josephine F. Milburn, *Cross National Comparisons of Women's Legal Status*, (American Political Science Association, 1973). See also J. N. D. Anderson, "The Role of Personal Status in Social Development in Islamic countries," *Comparative Studies in Society and History*, vol. 13, no. 1, (January, 1971), pp. 16-31; A. M. M. Salman, "Polygamy and the Status of Women in Islamic Society" *Majallat al-Azhar*, 33i, 1961, 17-24; 'Abd al-Hamid Ibrahim Muhammad, *al-mar'ah fi al-islam* [Women in Islam], al-Qahirah: al-Dar al-qawmiyyah lil taba'ah wa al-nashr, 1963.

31. Yusuf, "In Defense of the Veil," pp. 103-5. See also Peter O. Dodd, "Family Honor and the Forces of Change in Arab Society," *International Journal of Middle Eastern Studies* 4, (1973): 40-54.

32. Qur'an IV, 3, 23, 26-27, 123; 3:193, 16:99; 23:35. See also Nabia Abbott, "Woman and the State in Early Islam," *Journal of Near Eastern Studies* 1 (January 1942): 107.

33. Cf., Wilfred C. Smith, *Islam in Modern History*, (Princeton: Princeton University Press, 1957), pp. 3-40, on further distinctions between Islam and Muslims.

34. See, for example, Ibrahim 'Abdullah Muhyi, "Women in the Arab Middle East," *Journal of Social Issues* 3 (1959): 56f; Kazim Daghestani, "The Evolution of the Muslim Family in the Middle Eastern Countries," *International Social Science Bulletin* 5, (1953): 685; Levon Melikian and E. Terry Prothro, "Sexual Behavior of University Students in the Arab Near East," *Journal of Abnormal and Social Psychology*, vol. 49, no. 1, (January 1954, p. 60ff; Gordon K. Hirabayashi and May Ishaq, "Social Change in Jordan: A Quantitative Approach in a Non-Census Area," *American Journal of Sociology*, vol. 64, no. 1, (July 1958), p. 38ff; William J. Goode, *World Revolution and Family Patterns*, (London: Collier-Macmillan, 1963, and E. T. Prothro and L. N. Diab, *Changing Family Patterns in the Arab East*, (Beirut, Lebanon: American University of Beirut, 1974).

35. "Some Implications for Policy Formulation and Institutional Change of the Status of Women in the Contemporary Arab World," forthcoming.

36. *Agence France Presse*, as reported in *Le Jour*, Feb. 7, 1967; see also al-Shahi, "Saiqiya Constituency," p. 33.

37. This interpretation was given in a *fetwa'* (legal ruling) laid down by al-Azhar's

'ulama' in 1952; the *fetwa* quoted in the Qur'an (XXIII, 33) to justify the *'ulama'*s position, interpreting the verse to say that woman's primary duty is to guard her honor and reputation. Thus, women must be kept away from temptation themselves or from being a source of temptation to others. Participation in public affairs, the *'ulama'* continued, runs counter to this injunction.

Bibliography

Abbot, Nabīa
   1942 "Women and the State in Early Islam." *Journal of Near Eastern Studies* 1 (January).

'Abd al-Ḥamīd Ibrahīm Muḥammad
   1963 *al-Mar'ah fī al-islām (Women in Islam)*, al-Qāhirah: al-Dār al-qawmīyyah lil tab'ah wa'l-nashr.

Amīn, Qasim
   1908 *al-Mar'at al-jadīdah*, al-Qāhirah: Muḥammad Zakī al-Dīn *(The New Woman)*.

   1899 *Tahrīr al-mar'ah*, al-Qāhirah: Maktabat al-Turqi *(The Emancipation of Women)*.

Anderson, J. N. D.
   1959 *Islamic Law in the Modern World.* New York: New York University Press.

   1971 "The Role of Personal Status in Social Developments in Islamic Countries." *Comparative Studies in Society and History*, vol. 13, no. 1 (January), pp. 16-31.

Apter, David E.
   1965 *The Politics of Modernization.* Chicago: University of Chicago Press.

Arab Women in Love
   1969 Beirut: Khayat's.

Berger, Morroe
   1964 *The Arab World Today.* New York: Doubleday.

Bird, Carolyn
   1970 *Born Female: The High Cost of Keeping Women Down.* New York: David McKay.

Boals, Kay
   1972 "A Comparative Study of the Development of Political Consciousness." Paper presented to the American Political Science Association. Washington, D.C., Sept. 5, 1972, Panel on "Women and Political Change in Developing Areas."

Daghestānī, Kāzim
1953 "The Evolution of the Muslim Family in the Middle Eastern Countries." *International Social Science Bulletin* 5.

Dodd, Peter C.
1942 "Family Honor and the Forces of Change in Arab Society." *International Journal of Middle Eastern Studies* 4.

1968 "Youth and Women's Emancipation in the United Arab Republic." *Middle East Journal*, vol. 22, no. 2 (Spring).

Eisenstadt, S. N.
1964 "Breakdowns of Modernization." *Economic Development and Cultural Change* 12 (July).

Frey, Frederick W.
1970 "Cross Cultural Survey Research in Political Science." In *The Methodology of Comparative Research.*, edited by Robert T. Holt and John E. Turner. New York: The Free Press.

Gillespie, James M., and Allport, Gordon W.
1955 *Youth's Outlook on the Future, A Cross National Study.* Doubleday Papers in Psychology, New York: Doubleday.

Goode, William J.
1963 *World Revolution and Family Patterns*, London: Collier-Macmillan.

Gordon, David C.
1968 *Women of Algeria: An Essay on Change*, Cambridge, Mass.: Harvard University Press.

Halpern, Manfred
1963 *The Politics of Social Change in the Middle East and North Africa*, Princeton: Princeton University Press.

Hamādī (Hamady), Sania
1960 *Temperament and Character of the Arabs*, New York: Twayne.

Hirabayāshī, Gordon K., and Ishāq, May
1958 "Social Change in Jordan: A Quantitative Approach in a non-Census Area." *American Journal of Sociology*, vol. 64, no. 1 (July).

Horowitz, Donald L.
1971 "Three Dimensions of Ethnic Politics," *World Politics*, vol. 23, no. 2 (January).

Ḥusayn (Hussein), Azīza
1953 "The Role of Women in Social Reform in Egypt," *Middle East Journal* 7.

'Izz al-Dīn (Izzedin), Najla
1953 *The Arab World: Past, Present and Future.* Chicago: Henry Regnery.

Jacobs, Sue-Ellen
    1974 *Women in Perspective: A Guide for Cross-Cultural Studies.*
    Urbana, Illinois: University of Illinois Press.

Kamell, Michael W.
    1973 *The Middle East: A Humanistic Approach.* Andrews
    Publishing Co.

Lerner, Daniel
    1958 *The Passing of Traditional Society,* Glencoe, Illinois: The Free
    Press.

Lewis, F.
    1967 "No Revolution for the Woman of Algiers." *New York Times
    Magazine,* October 29.

Melikian, Levon, and Prothro, E. Terry
    1954 "Sexual Behavior of University Students in the Arab Near
    East." *Journal of Abnormal and Social Psychology,* vol. 49, no. 1
    (January).

The Middle East: A Handbook
    1973 London: Europa Publications, Ltd.

Milburn, Josephine F.
    1973 *Cross National Comparisons of Women's Legal Status.*
    American Political Science Association.

M'rabet, Fadela
    1967 *Les Algeriennes,* Paris: Librarie François Maspero.

Muhyī, 'Abdullāh
    1959 "Women in the Arab Middle East." *Journal of Social Issues* 3.

Nelson, Cynthia
    1968 "Changing Roles of Men and Women: Illustrations from
    Egypt," *Anthropological Quarterly,* vol. 41, no. 2, (April).

Nicholson, R.A.
    1956 *A Literary History of the Arabs.* Cambridge: Cambridge University Press.

"Preliminary Paper on Integration of Women in Development"
    1972 Social Development Division of the United Nations, February.

Prothro, E. T., and Diab, L. N.
    1974 *Changing Family Patterns in the Arab East,* Beirut, Lebanon:
    American University of Beirut.

Qutb (Kotb), Sayyid
    1953 *Social Justice in Islam.* Translated by John B. Hardie.
    Washington, D.C.: American Council of Learned Societies.

"The Role of Women in Development" (Arabic text)
    1970 *Majallat al-Mar'ah,* June 15.

Salman, A. M. M.
    1961 "Polygamy and the Status of Women in Islamic Society." *Majallat al-Azhar*, 331.

al-Shāhī, A. S.
    1969 "Politics and the Role of Women in a Saiqīya Constituency, 1968." *Sūdān Society.*

Sherrill, Kenneth S.
    1969 "The Attitudes of Modernity." *Comparative Politics*, vol. 1, no. 2 (January).

Smith, Wilfred C.
    1957 *Islam in Modern History.* Princeton: Princeton University Press. Press.

Tibī
    1968 "The Problem of the Emancipation of Women in the Modern Arab Society" (Arabic text). *al-Tabīah*, vol. 4, no. 11.

Tomiche, N.
    1968 "The Position of Women in the United Arab Republic." *Journal of Contemporary History*, vol. 3, no. 3 (July).

Woodsmall, Ruth F.
    1956 *Study of the Role of Women in Lebanon, Egypt, 'Iraq, Jordan and Syria, 1955-55.* Woodstock, Vermont: Elm Tree Press.

Yusuf, Hajji Shaykh
    1943 "In Defense of the Veil." Translated by Charles R. Pittman, *Muslim World*, vol. 23, no. 3 (July).

Access to Property and the Status of Women in Islam

CARROLL McC. PASTNER

University of Vermont

Introduction

Social scientists and feminists of both Marxist and non-Marxist persuasion have in various ways addressed themselves to the interrelatedness of feminine status and the control or lack of control over property. This essay examines the relationship between female access to property and the status of women in Islam. The term *status* refers here to that which applies to the domestic sector of society. While it is understood that female status in the public domain is certainly affected by domestic status (and vice versa), this does not mean a priori that one is the replication of the other. In order to clarify this distinction in terms of Muslim women, concentration will be placed on the transmission of property of women in the context of the institutions of marriage and the family. Two particular aspects of feminine domestic status to be considered are the differences marking (1) the receipt of property through either the contraction of marriage or patrimonial inheritance and (2) the receipt of either movable or immovable property.

It will be noted that this essay deals with two separate levels of analysis, the jurisprudent and the ethnographic, with a bias toward the latter which is consistent with the training of its author. The approach of the anthropologist is one in which law is investigated in terms of how it affects the day-to-day lives of individuals in specific types of situations; hence, it examines variations in the degree to which legalistic ideals are met. By focussing on the interplay betweeen law and social custom, not only the manifest but the latent functions of law are revealed; in this case, demonstrating how access to property and feminine status help mutually to define one another. Laws pertaining to property constitute only one component in the delineation of feminine status, but at least indirectly reflect social structural and ideological factors that serve to mold feminine status.

The procedure of this essay is as follows: After elucidating several terminological points, a consideration will be given to traditional Islamic precepts as they apply to property rights for women. Emphasis will be placed not on the specifics of the various law schools but on the general attitude of Islam toward women and property. Then there follows an outline of examples of the actual dispensation, or abrogation, of female property rights, largely in traditional, but still contemporary, Muslim settings. The interest here is not so much whether individuals do or do not live up to religious and legislative ideals, but how they behave in terms of localized, consistent means of coping with particular kinds of situations — means that include accommodations to norms and ideals that emanate from wider-than-local contexts. Of particular concern in the presentation of examples will be the functions of property in the structuring of natal and conjugal relationships for women. Last, the modernizing context will be examined in order to suggest how economic changes in the public sector affect property access and feminine domestic status.[1] One of the conclusions drawn is that nuclear familism alone need not drastically alter domestic status, but that female employment in the public sector, a potential result of such family status, significantly alters the access of Muslim women to property and suggests more pertinent changes in domestic status.

Bridewealth, Dowry, and Indirect
Dowry: Terminological Considerations

While focussing only parenthetically on Islam, Goody and Tambiah (1973) have recently put forth a theoretical treatment of marriage presentations that provides a useful framework for the present discussion. Clearing up terminological points at this juncture will facilitate the ensuing consideration of Islamic property codes as they affect women. Particularly helpful is the distinction drawn by Goody and Tambiah between types of presentations all too often confused in both the anthropological and nonanthropological literature. To summarize their conclusions, there are major economic and social structural differences between (1) *bridewealth* (sometimes called brideprice), (2) *dowry* (sometimes called trousseau) and (3) *indirect dowry* (sometimes called dower or even brideprice). While bridewealth represents a transaction from the groom's kin to the bride's kin, providing a circulating societal fund most often used by the bride's brothers for their own bridewealth, both dowry and indirect dowry ideally establish familial or conjugal, not circulating, funds (ibid, pp. 1-2). More specifically, dowry is a form of premortem inheritance to the bride from her parents, while indirect dowry consists of gifts from the groom and his kin to the bride, with her father or guardian oftentimes playing the role of middleman.

One major difference between the three modes of property transmission is that the transfer of property to women (through either dowry or inheritance) is linked with "bilateral ideology" (ibid, p. 17), while bridewealth most often, but not always, occurs in a unilineal context. Further, dowry is associated with intensive agriculture and complex forms of social stratification (ibid, pp. 51-52). The same authors also emphasize the differences between movable and immovable wealth in terms of such property transfers. Dowry in movables in the Hindu case, for example, can play a vital role in the expression of status relations between wife givers and wife receivers.

Turning to the specific case of Islam, several points suggested by Goody and Tambiah's discussion emerge as particularly relevant. One is the distinction between premortem and postmortem inheritance by women. To phrase the question in one form, to what extent and under what circumstances does dowry serve as a substitute for postmortem female inheritance? Secondly, in the presence of indirect dowry, to what extent and under what circumstances is this marriage presentation matched up with dowry in the course of marriage negotiations, and what effect does this have on the nature of the subsequent alliance? As will be demonstrated, the movable/immovable distinction in property suggests one clue in the treatment of both these questions.

Islam and Women's Rights to Property: The Role of Traditional Religious Authority

Despite variations between the major schools of Islamic law, it is possible to outline the general tenor manifested by Islamic property laws in regard to women. Thus, it has been noted that Islam pays more attention to female rights than do a number of other codified law systems. Muslim women are explicitly accorded rights to property gained through both marriage and inheritance. While it is true that female inheritance rights are not mathematically equal to those of men and that the acting out of the letter of the law must be documented rather than assumed, it is nonetheless a fact that such rights are granted in de jure fashion to women under the terms of religious authority.

Let us first consider property that is transmitted to women in the contraction of marriage. It is generally believed that in pre-Islamic Arabia there was (in Goody and Tambiah's terms) bridewealth known as *mahr* paid by the groom and his kin to the girl's kinsmen and, secondarily, an indirect dowry (*sadāk*) paid to the girl. By the time of Mohammed, *mahr* and *sadāk* appear to have become amalgamated and were to be paid directly to the girl, thereby weakening the significance of *mahr* as a "purchase price" (Gibb 1953: 314). Whatever may have been actually relevant by the advent of Mohammed, the Qur'ān (Sura 4:24) demands a bridal gift in order to legitimize marriage. Subsequent theories laid down by Islamic jurists further justify the need for such a gift, even if it does not involve anything of great value (Gibb 1953: 314). In fact, the Sharī'a sets no maximum or minimum for indirect dowry (that is, *mahr*), and the amounts set by the law schools vary according to economic and social conditions relevant to the areas in which the specific schools prevail (ibid.)[2] In general, however, the amount of the bridal gift is left to bargaining between the families of the bride and groom, with emphasis placed on the social position of the bride.

While the legitimacy of indirect dowry is substantiated by religious authority, no specific mention is made of dowry, either in the Qur'ān or in subsequent reinterpretations and justifications. Rather, emphasis is placed on indirect dowry, with consideration given to both donors and recipients. Thus, the Qur'ān justifies the authority of men over women in terms of the property brought by men into marriage (Sura 4:38), and simultaneously recognizes the convenience and profit afforded men if their wives should waive their right to *mahr* (Sura 4:3). As to women, while the husband has managerial rights over *mahr*, it is to remain the wife's property with full rights of disposal. Expressions of concern for female economic security are evidenced in the stipulations set out in terms of the payment of *mahr*. That is, while it is customary in a number of settings (to be described) to pay part of the *mahr* at the time of marriage and postpone (or waive) the rest, the remainder must be paid if the woman is divorced and cohabitation has taken place (Gibb 1953:315). By the same token, one of the several traditional means by which a woman can gain a divorce is to prove nonpayment of the deferred portion of the bridal gift agreed upon in the marriage contract (Charnay 1971:64).

Religious authority not only accords property rights to women as participants in the contraction of marriage but also provides access to property for women through inheritance (*mīrāth*). The complexity of Islamic inheritance laws need not be stressed, paticularly if we were to take into account fundamental differences between Sunni and Shiite codes. Let us, however, consider the general outline of female rights. While female inheritance seems to have been the custom in pre-Islamic Mecca but not Medina (Rodinson 1971: 232), the Prophet established rules of inheritance that universally stipulated that a woman is to receive one-half the share of her male counterpart. Therefore, since Islamic inheritance is partible, everyone is according to the Qur'ān guaranteed his or her share. By means of laws that set fixed shares for specific persons and categories of persons, Islam, in fact, serves to modify what would otherwise be a system of purely agnatic succession (Schacht 1966: 171). This works for both men and women, since husbands and wives, as affines, can inherit from one another.[3] Widows in Sunni codes receive one-quarter or one-eighth, depending on whether they inherit with or without children or filial grandchildren. With regard to agnates, virtually every contingency is anticipated in religious law, as demonstrated in the establishment of the exact size of female shares. Thus, a daughter receives one-half a share, unless there are two or more daughters, in which case they together get two-thirds of a share. Son's daughters, full sisters and half sisters, as potential heirs of smaller shares, are subject to the same kinds of rules. Beyond the primary category of "people of fixed shares" (quota-heirs), provisions are also made for more distant agnates. The extension of agnation can be partly viewed as a means of protecting female relatives in cases in which they had not otherwise received a share (father's sister, for example), "although they are less privileged than the corresponding males" (ibid., p. 172).

Several points emerge in a general consideration of female

inheritance. One is that inheritance law, a branch of family law, has a religious character and is thought to have "always been one of the chapters of Muslim law most carefully observed in practice" (Gibb 1953: 388). It was just noted that religious authority makes an effort to provide economic security to both agnatic and, to a lesser extent, affinal kinswomen. By the same token, women are not equal heirs. While there are strong cultural justifications offered for this inequality, men receive twice as much as women in all categories. Secondly, despite its religious aura, codified law is not always adhered to in actual practice. A major reason for this gap between theory and practice lies in the overall character of Islamic inheritance as it applies to both sexes. As a partible system, problems of fragmentation are logically acute, this being particularly true in the context of traditional agrarianism, but less so in the contexts of pastoral nomadism and industrialism because of the differences between movable and immovable wealth. Thus, in terms of agricultural property, sisters appear to be more apt to benefit from inheritance if jointly maintained land is not subdivided at the death of the father. But a second consideration is exogamy: if a sister marries out of the kin unit or village, she is less apt to receive inheritance in the form of land, although she may be compensated by movable property. Hence, the distinction between forms of property is particularly relevant to a consideration of the circumstances under which women receive patrimonial wealth. In turn, whether or not the spirit or the actual letter of the law is upheld provides helpful indicators of the domestic status of women.

Empirical Realities of Bridewealth, Dowry, and Indirect Dowry

On the level of revealed codified law, Islam has made an effort to eliminate bridewealth and all that this institution implies in economic and social terms by replacing it with indirect dowry in the form of gifts from the groom and his kin to the bride. Nonetheless, the economic and social implications of bridewealth can remain intact under certain sets of circumstances. Thus, a customary reliance on bridewealth may be continued, despite Islamicization in other areas of social life, because the unilineal tenor of the society is such that bridewealth continues to be functionally more appropriate than indirect dowry. One example among many is found in the case of the Swat Pathans described by Fredrik Barth (1965: 36-137). In this intensely patrilineal context, contrary to the Hanafi law code imposed by the state of Pakistan into which Swat had, until recently, been incorporated as a semiautonomous kingdom, *mahr* functions as bridwealth, not indirect dowry, in sums up to £500 pounds. It should be emphasized that in this instance authority over women is transferred completely from the father to the husband, a point that will gain further significance when the relationship between natal and conjugal rights over women in other settings is examined.

It should not be assumed, however, that the continuance of bridewealth in Islamic settings is simply a defiance of religious authority in contexts in which bridewealth is structurally more appropriate. Due to contingencies inherent in the way indirect dowry systems function generally, this marriage presentation can take on some of the characteristics of bridewealth independently of the presence of strong unilineal tendencies. In Islam, the bride is represented by a marriage guardian,[4] her father or nearest agnatic equivalent, who has the opportunity to alienate property that, according to religious authority, is to be redistributed to the bride. One complication is that, in some instances, it is customary for the guardian to use part of the *mahr* to furnish the bride with clothing, household equipment, and the like. Such a custom could be regarded as a "disguised" form of dowry since it does constitute a gift to the bride from her guardian, but one that, in fact, does not come directly out of his pocket. In spite of this custom, followed in some parts, of redirecting a portion of the indirect dowry as a kind of dowry, features built in to the system of indirect dowry also make possible the siphoning of portions of *mahr*, or even all of *mahr*, to the economic advantage of the marriage guardian. Several examples will serve to illustrate the feasibility of this practice. Among the marsh dwellers of the Iraqi Euphrates Delta, what is described as "brideprice," paid in cash but sometimes also in cattle and furniture, is usually kept by the bride's father, although he is expected to supply his daughter with household equipment amounting to about one-third of the "brideprice" (Salim 1962: 60). A more intricate, but revealing, example is provided by Henry Rosenfeld in the context of Israeli Arab villages (1974). Here, *sdāq raqbatha* represents a portion (from 30 to 50 percent) of the *mahr* that is redistributed to the bride by her father and brothers. Rosenfeld interprets this as a form of compensation to daughters/sisters that provides a means of "saving face," since brothers frequently use their sisters' indirect dowries to gain their own brides. In this instance, indirect dowry is economically and socially transformed into bridewealth by means of the manipulation of women by their kinsmen.[5]

Variations in terms of the dispensation of indirect dowry in the Islamic context exist not only cross-culturally, but intraculturally as well. Among the Kurds, for example, in the urban milieu the bride's family spends up to one-half of the *mahr* on wedding expenses and jewelry for the bride, while this is not true in villages (Hansen 1961: 125). In central Turkey, the procedures vary from village to village, indicating that variations do not stem solely from the contrast between urban and rural settings. In some Turkish villages, the groom's father gives the bride gold ornaments, but these may have been borrowed and then restored to their owner after the wedding. In such instances, the dowry (or trousseau) from the bride's father to the bride is not "disguised" since it is not covered by the indirect dowry. In other villages, part of the cash indirect dowry is used for dowry items. Here, indirect dowry is regarded as a quid pro quo for such items given to the bride from her family (Stirling 1965: 186).

Serving to complicate the ways in which indirect dowry is redistributed is the aforementioned practice of prompt and deferred portions. Examples from Palestinian and Lebanese villages of such a practice are found in, respectively, Granqvist (1931) and Fuller (1963); in the Egyptian village context in Ammar (1954), and in the Egyptian urban setting, Moshen (1974). An example from a non-Arab context is Korson's description of *mehr* (*mahr*) in contemporary urban Pakistan (1973). As a form of indirect dowry, *mehr* is a cash gift from the husband to the wife, part of which can be deferred, but payable at divorce or the death of the husband. The size of *mehr* correlates directly with the socioeconomic status of the bride and constitutes an essential element of the marriage contract. A second marriage presentation in urban Pakistan is *jahez*, a dowry of clothing, jewelry, and household goods given to the bride by her family and friends. The institution of *jahez* represents a true dowry, not a "disguised" one redistributed from indirect dowry. Accordingly, the size of the dowry is an important point in betrothal negotiations, resulting in families of bridegrooms seeking girls with large dowries (ibid., p. 143).

In order to elucidate the role played by indirect dowry in the provision of economic security for women, emphasis should be placed on a characteristic pertaining to property in the Islamic legal context that will have a good deal of relevance to our later discussion of marital alliance formation: the nature of conjugal property. There is a strong deemphasis on such property in codified Islam; marriage does not explicitly produce community property. Thus, as already indicated, *mahr* is defined as the property of the wife. It would seem, however, that, pragmatically speaking, there must be a fine line in terms of certain items of "prompt" *mahr*, such as household equipment and clothing; and it must also be reiterated that managerial rights on the part of the husband can serve to blur the lines between what can be regarded as either individual or conjugal property. In the presence of a customary deferred portion of indirect dowry, the question of female access becomes more complex. In a well-established union the remainder is ordinarily never paid, and at separation and divorce, when the remainder should, according to religious authority, be paid, this holds true only under certain conditions. First, as previously noted, cohabitation must have taken place. Second, the deferred portion is not forthcoming if divorce is the result of the wife's adultery, childlessness, or unwarranted repudiation of the husband. In such cases the wife may even have to return that portion of *mahr* paid at the time of marriage.[6] Third, a strong tendency throughout Muslim areas to pay deferred *mahr* in cash means that it will not be forthcoming if, in fact, the funds do not exist. Thus, it can be concluded that the access of women to property through *mahr* is not, under all circumstances, a fully guaranteed eventuality. On the other hand, other characteristics of deferred *mahr* that can serve as a form of security for the wife should not be overlooked. Where the deferred portion is purposely set high, the financial threat to men can be such that they are dissuaded from repudiating their wives too quickly for reasons that might easily be proved unsubstantial.[7] The role of indirect dowry as a deterrent to divorce should not, by any means, be overlooked.

With regard to dowry, property is much more securely in the hands of the wife than is indirect dowry. It is difficult for men to alienate their wives' dowries even though dowry may function as de facto conjugal property in an unsevered union.

Rights in Natal Kinship: Inheritance by Women

There are three categories of inheritance applicable to Muslim women. These are patrimonial inheritance, affinal inheritance (inheritance by widows), and uterine inheritance.

The last category pertains particularly to dowry, since dowry items, including jewelry, usually pass from mothers to daughters, either at the time of marriage in the form of dowry or else through postmortem inheritance at the death of the mother. Inheritance by widows has previously been mentioned, and sometimes substitutes for deferred *mahr* at the death of the husband (cf. Karim 1963), although this can create problems with other potential heirs. Further on, the role of the widow, not as an heiress, but as an estate trustee, will be considered.

At this point, however, particular attention must be paid to the issue of patrimonial inheritance. It has already been indicated that daughters and sisters may be denied inheritance in order to prevent the alienation of property and that this motivation is especially relevant to the agrarian economic context where problems of fragmentation are acute. There are a number of ways to prevent a daughter from inheriting land, including leaving her share with her brothers in order to prevent alienation by her husband, compensating her with bridal gifts at marriage, and signing land over to her brothers if it is formally registered (Baer 1964: 39). To take one example, in court cases involving female demands for rightful shares of land in Pakistani Punjab, most often occurring when relations between brothers and sisters are strained, brothers may attempt to show that their sisters had already received their "fair share" in the form of dowry.[8]

Of crucial significance to the disposal of female inheritance rights is the degree to which the establishment of a conjugal relationship acts to diminish rights and obligations between a woman and her natal kin. Among the aforementioned Swat Pathans, bridewealth functions to sever a woman from her natal kin from whom she gains no protection after marriage. Women here do not inherit patrimony; nor are they compensated by dowries (Barth 1965). In other settings, however, the situation is quite different: women retain natal kin rights after marriage and have a more definite lien on patrimony.

Nonetheless, this does not necessarily mean that property is forthcoming. Women may forfeit their rights to property in order to ensure continued protection and security for themselves and their offspring in the context of natal kinship. Such is the case among seminomadic goat and sheep herders in the western desert of Egypt where the male rationale for "side-stepping" Qur'ānic law is that women are not capable of caring for the livestock and rights to land-use that comprise items of inheritance (Moshen 1967: 165).

Rosenfeld's analysis of what he calls "masked reciprocity" in an Arab village illustrates very well how women's rights in natal kinship affect the outcome of their property rights. Gifts from fathers and brothers to daughters and sisters on ceremonial occasions are interpreted by Rosenfeld as forms of "masked gift-giving" serving as compensations for the female forfeiture of property rights. While these gifts are not consciously recognized as such by men, they not only symbolize a male "indebtedness" to women for their act of forfeiture but also substantiate a married woman's continued protected position in her family of origin (Rosenfeld 1974; and Rosenfeld 1960: 66-70).

Serving to complicate the issue of kinship and female inheritance is an ideological emphasis on kin endogamy relevant to a number of settings under consideration in this essay. While differences exist in terms of the degree to which actual kin endogamy occurs, the general nature of the value orientation emphasizes the superiority of in-marriage. Some attempts to explain the most extreme form of endogamous values, the preference for marriage with the patrilateral parallel cousin (FBD), have emphasized the role that such endogamy plays in the preservation of patrimony in the agnatic unit (e.g., Westermarck 1914, Granqvist 1931, Baer 1964). But this explanation is insufficient, given that endogamy need not involve biological parallel cousin relationships and that, in fact, inheritance by women is generally inconsistent. Thus, even in areas where the preference is highly emphasized, actual FBD marriage can represent for the ethnographer a small proportion of marriages (cf. Ayoub 1959: 266-75). A more recent attempt to explain FBD marriage puts forth the hypothesis that the preference for such unions is a metaphorical statement "which expresses an ideal about all of the relationships which a marriage should engender between affines" (Keyser 1974: 293). An important corollary to this hypothesis is that women in such social systems do not lose membership in their natal families, this being made clear in the preference for FBD marraige. "Perhaps the most convenient way of seeing marriage in the Middle East is to call it an investment involving goods and people which are both continually tended" (ibid., p. 307).

The relationship between endogamous values and the access of men to resources and women is, on the level of theory, complex. Nonetheless, in a number of empirical instances the preferential marriage rule is more consistently carried out than in others and, in the presence of other ideological factors, endogamy fulfills a specific economic function. In one Shi'ite Lebanese village, for example, a very high rate, not only of endogamy in general, but of FBD marriage specifically, serves to maintain property intact in the context of a genealogically defined "stock group" (Peters 1963). Women in this case receive their one-half share of land at the time of marriage, resulting in "intense competition" for women with large holdings and the strict control of marriage due to the threat of property alienation (ibid., p. 187). It should be emphasized, however, that the functioning of endogamy here is dependent on the presence of patrilineal descent groups, not bilateral kin groups, in which transfers of property occur easily under most conditions of even fairly close kin endogamy, due to the presence of multiple ancestors. Hence, it cannot be concluded that endogamy always results in the preservation of intact patrimony; it only does so under certain social structural and economic conditions. At the same time, however, it should be kept in mind that an ideological stress on generalized endogamy in other settings, whether or not such unions are consistently contracted, says very important things about marriage that go beyond economic considerations.

Last, while more will be said about this further on, at least some mention should be made at this point of the implications of female inheritance in terms of female status. To what extent does such access to property afford independent status to women? One of the more consistent sets of circumstances under which women do inherit patrimony is in the absence of male siblings (e.g., Eglar 1960). However, this appears to be a way to ensure security to a woman in the absence of male guardians and/or to guarantee that patrimonial property is held intact. Thus, for example, in the Arab village described by Rosenfeld, in the absence of brothers, a sister marries a close cousin with her share of property maintained by her (agnatically related) husband (Rosenfeld 1960: 67). Rosenfeld asserts that women otherwise rarely receive property grants from their fathers and that, if they do, this is an indication of ascribed, not independent, status for the woman; that is, she is enjoying her father's status. "The man loses nothing in the process, rather he gains, for she reflects his higher status" (Rosenfeld 1974: 163).

Women and Property: The Contraction of Marital Alliances

Now that some of the central issues regarding female access to property in the Muslim context have been touched on, keeping in mind the interplay between male and conjugal kinship, attention can now be focussed on some more specific aspects of the relationship between female property and the contraction of marriage.

First, to follow through on the topic of endogamy, it should be indicated that *mahr* is ordinarily lowered, or made negligible, in cases of close kin endogamy and exchange marriage.[9]

Mahr is also lowered for divorcées and widows and, logically, eliminated in the case of levirate. The ideological reason behind the arrangement of kin endogamous unions, despite a lesser economic gain in terms of marriage presentations, is that such unions are considered more "honorable," representing a valued kind of affinal relationship, not only for the couple, but for their families. Exogamous (that is, "less honorable") marriages require larger indirect dowries. In these terms indirect dowry can be viewed as a form of compensation in the contraction of what are otherwise, in the presence of an ideological stress on kin endogamy, less valued unions. Thus, there are two ways in which families can maintain interests in their daughters after marriage. In the case of kin endogamy, this is achieved structurally by the intersection of affinal and natal ties. With regard to exogamy, the degree to which the families, and not just the couple, maintain interests in a marriage is partly related to the amount of property transferred at marriage. In a cross-cultural statistical treatment of the relationship between wealth transfer and restrictions on sexual relations during betrothal, it was shown that, "Where the wealth transferred is great, the commitment appears to develop mainly among the kin of the betrothed couple as the families become enmeshed in the economics of the marriage, and the couple is usually allowed less sexual contact so that family economic interests can be served" (Rosenblatt 1969: 326). With its well-known insistence on female virginity at marriage, the Muslim case is one in which the interests of kin are maintained in marital unions, not only for economic reasons, but for ideological ones as well, with a stress on the perpetuation of female, and thus, family honor.

Nonetheless, ideological concerns should not be overemphasized in the face of economic interests. Of especial significance is, not only the amount, but the kind of property transferred at marriage. To illustrate this point, as well as other pertinent ones, particular attention to one specific example can be paid. Vanessa Maher has recently investigated the relationship between property transfers and marital stability in contemporary Morocco (Maher 1974). She contrasts divorce rates between rural villagers and aspiring urban bourgeoisie, and indicates that the kind of property transferred at marriage has to do with differences in these rates. In the town, where there is a lower divorce rate, a woman brings into marriage a dowry in movable assets that represents her one-half share of inheritance and is subsequently matched up with an indirect dowry in betrothal negotiations. Under these circumstances, marriage becomes a type of business alliance. At the same time, "conjugal isolation" is created by the cutting off of the wife from her own kin and by her economic dependence on her husband stemming from her seclusion and hence inability to work outside the home. In the villages, conversely, the divorce rate is very high. Both men and women inherit mainly in land, resulting in the maintenance of natal kin rights and obligations in the context of common interests in landed property. Simultaneously, marriage presentations between villagers are negligible, with no pooling of conjugal capital as in the town setting. And since the deferred portion of indirect dowry is customarily low and seldom materializes due to a lack of ready cash, divorce results neither in capital withdrawal for men nor loss of status and security for women since these are retained in the context of natal kinship.

On the basis of this material, it can be concluded that the movable/immovable distinction in property, not only the amount of property, is relevant to the nature of marital unions, since it can affect the degree to which natal kin ties are retained. While it was noted earlier in this essay that women may forfeit their inheritance rights to land in order to substantiate other rights in natal kinship, Maher's data show that if female inheritance in communally held land does take place, the resulting retention of mutual interests in property can detract from the establishment of "conjugal isolation." This observation is consistent with a more general anthropological view of the inverse relationship between the stability of the marital union and the degree to which women retain natal kin ties (cf. Lewis 1965).

Different implications arise when female inheritance in immovable property is substituted by premortem inheritance in movable wealth in the form of dowry. One complication that should be mentioned is that the institution of dowry in some parts of the Muslim world may represent a cultural borrowing from a non-Islamic source. In parts of eastern Bangladesh, for example, there previously had been no dowry, but only indirect dowry, although recently there has grown a tendency among merchant and educated middle classes to demand presents from the bride's family, reputedly the result of influence by Hindu custom (Karim 1963:311-12). In other Muslim areas dowry does not represent a cultural borrowing, and pertinent to the discussion here is the pooling of indirect dowry and dowry in movable assets to create affinal alliances. Political and "business" alliances of this sort among well-to-do families in urban areas throughout the Muslim world certainly do take place, although the degree to which this fosters economic independence for women would seem negligible if the conjugal property is managed by the husband. By the same token, we should not confuse the Muslim institution of dowry with dowry systems in other culture areas. That is, parallels cannot readily be assumed with, for example, areas of agrarian non-Muslim Mediterranean Europe, where dowry in land can provide a very real source of economic power for women in the conjugal relationship.[10] As will be suggested, basic structural differences between types of family organization help explain why this is less apt to hold true in the traditional context of the social system within the Muslim culture area.

Given that indirect dowries and dowries can be matched up for purposes of capital accumulation and the formation of economic marital alliances, to what extent do hopes of gaining wealth through a wife's postmortem inheritance enter into marriage choices on the part of a potential groom and his family? In a kin endogamous union, this would be part of a more complex economic consideration. Otherwise, the general impression is that such calculations are not culturally appropriate. Stirling indicates in a rural Turkish setting that it is considered "undignified" for a man to interfere in his wife's claim to patrimony; the ideal is that men derive land not from their wives and mothers, but from their male agnates (Stirling 1965:30-31). In the Arab Sudan, Barclay maintains that while husbands can gain de facto control over their wives' land by taking advantage of their male status and their wives' illiteracy, this is not considered the best way for men to acquire land (Barclay 1964:32-33).

De Facto Control of
Property by Women:
The Traditional Context

At various points in this paper it has been suggested that differences between female access to property and the actual control of property must be recognized; access in no way necessarily implies control, just as female "influence" does not necessarily connote true female "power." Managerial rights on the part of the father, brother, or husband, provide a major means of detraction from Muslim female rights of property disposal. On the other hand, just as it is true that Muslim women can and do inherit land, it is possible, under certain circumstances, to speak of actual property control by women. Barbara Aswad (1967:139-52) provides a good example of such control. In a land-owning lineage community on the Turkish-Syrian border, widows of polygynous unions who are members of the patrilineage and have immature sons can control property until their sons mature. Some of these women "have exercised substantial direct economic and political influence substituting for men" (ibid., p. 144). Elder unmarried sisters with immature brothers can sometimes play the same kind of role. But, it should be pointed out that, as in the previously noted custom of inheritance by sisters in the absence of brothers, the ability of women to control property is dependent upon very circumscribed conditions. In Aswad's example female controllers of property are primarily restricted to widows in polygynous unions who had married endogamously and subsequently never remarry. In-marrying or childless widows are never granted such responsibilities. The primary motivation is more in terms of keeping intact jointly owned lineage property than the exercise of female abilities to effectively manage property. Aswad also indicates that, in the case of land control by urban women in the same geographical vicinity, such women are either relatives or from other aristocratic families, again illustrating the ascribed character of female economic status (ibid., p. 151).

In the final analysis, as long as the traditional context is under consideration, economic control by women is certainly feasible, but appears largely the result of specific de facto circumstances. Just how often situations of female control have more generally arisen in the past or continue to arise cannot be documented, but remains an interesting question. In any case, a number of variables pertinent to female status in the domestic sphere relate to the question of possible female control over property. Louise Sweet maintains that no Middle Eastern community makes it impossible for women to achieve control of property but "that there is no general movement to secure sole control of property is not surprising" (Sweet 1974). According to Sweet, this is because of the enormous "interior power" women hold in the traditional Middle Eastern household. Without in any way diminishing the point that women may certainly wield "interior power," this observation should, in structural terms, be seen in the same perspective as the aforementioned role of female forfeiture of property as a means of substantiating other rights in natal kinship. That is, the available room for female maneuvering remains in the domestic context of society and must be defined in terms of relationships women have with specific males.

What, however, might be said about the relationship between property and female status in the modernizing context? More specifically, in what ways has social change served to alter the traditional relationship between women's access to property and their status in the domestic domain?

Changes in Female Access to Property: The Modernizing Context

The emphasis in this essay has thus far been placed not entirely but for the most part on traditional Muslim settings characterized by largely preindustrial forms of socioeconomic organization. While it should be stressed that for many Muslim women these contexts remain wholly relevant, the relation between property and female status under modernizing conditions must also be considered.

To begin with, however, it is necessary to distinguish Islamicization and, in some instances, Arabization, from modernization, industrialization, and westernization. These acculturative processes are by no means identical, and any number of them may be occurring simultaneously. Thus, westernization can be "overtly technological and economic (and) only surreptitiously ideological" while Islamicization is "primarily ideological and symbolic" (Barclay 1965:43). An example of Arabization has already been encountered in this essay. In Maher's Moroccan example there is a greater retention of Berber customs in villages, whereas, in the town, aspiring male bourgeoisie attempt to prove their Islamic citizenship and assimilation into Arab culture by, among others, secluding their women in purdah (Maher 1974). In terms of female rights to property, Islamicization can either limit previous forms of culturally defined access or open up new avenues of access to property for women. Among the pastoral nomadic Fulani of Niger, for example, it is the men, influenced by the prestige of Islam, who provide the initiative by allowing women to inherit in the line of paternal descent (Dupire 1971:90). In terms of marriage presentations, Goody indicates that, since it is regarded as unprestigious, bridewealth is deemphasized in Muslim areas of sub-Saharan Africa, with the result that more is invested in wedding expenses and dowries (Goody and Tambiah 1973:14).

Apart from the Islamicization of social systems of varying cultural background to which new religious precepts must be adjusted, how has Islam itself reacted to changing social conditions in the traditionally Muslim world? While in the area of public life much of Islamic law has been replaced for some time by secular codes, personal status and family law, those branches of most concern to women, are often continued as traditionally applied, if not formally then at least in spirit. Unlike traditional law, which sets moral standards for society, current reforms in family and personal status law have, for the most part, followed rather than brought about social change, and all attempts at modernism have been confronted by both religious traditionalists and advocates of women's rights. While several of the specifics of modern legislation are dealt with in the appendices of this essay, a few observations about reformism can be made at this point.

It should not be assumed that modernist Islamic or civil intervention in the areas of law concerned with women is only a recent development. A modest beginning for reform legislation was made in 1917 with the Ottoman Law of Family Rights, which clarified the terms under which women could gain a divorce. Developments in Anglo-Muslim law included the Shariat Act of 1937 in India, which was aimed at correcting the fact that Muslim women were being excluded from inheritance although, interestingly, the act did not apply to agricultural land (Schacht 1966:96). After independence the Punjab Muslim Personal Law Application Act of 1948 in

Pakistan made Shariat laws applicable to land, although this by no means ended the exclusion of women from such inheritance.

A number of examples from the Arab context of more recent legislation illustrate the point that current law, be it defined as either religious or secular, can constitute in certain respects a reaffirmation or modification, rather than a cancellation, of orthodox precepts. Hence, Sharī'a courts were abolished in Egypt in 1956 but, while personal status and family law cases are now heard in civil courts, they are still judged according to Sharī'a (Moshen 1974:39). In Tunisia, marriage contracts and the disposal of *mahr* were placed under the jurisdiction of civil courts in 1955, ensuring, for one thing, that women have rights of disposal over *mahr*,[11] a right already accorded by the Qur'ān. A similar reaffirmation of religiously defined rights has transpired in Lebanon, where husbands and wives are permitted under civil law to maintain separate estates, with full female rights of disposal over personal property.[12] Civil law in Lebanon has also relegitimized the custom of deferred *mahr* as a form of insurance for the divorced woman.[13]

But what of Turkey, which provides a historically quite different case? Here is the one example of a Muslim country that, as part of an overall effort to secularize and westernize its society, chose wholly to replace Shariate law with civil law, and in doing so anticipated changes in domestic life that had not yet taken place. The Turkish experience might provide some general clues to future developments in other Muslim countries that have not yet fully secularized their personal status and family laws but have made, or will make, efforts along these lines. With the adoption of a family code based on the Swiss model, Turkish women in 1926 gained, among other things, equal rights to property and inheritance. Stirling's experience in rural central Turkey in the 1950s, however, was that the inheritance rights of daughters were very inconsistently maintained, and that the provisions of State law were not generally being applied except when it proved convenient to men (Stirling 1965:122). Nonetheless, there are indications that female rights to property are now being increasingly recognized in Turkey. In a recent survey of ethnographic reports, and on the basis of his own work in 1969-70, Magnarella, by differentiating between agrarian and nonagrarian economies, illustrates the significance of the movable/immovable property distinction in terms of female inheritance. Among agricultural villagers he finds a variety of means being used to fulfill obligations to daughters, with a stress on "need and practicality, rather than equality" (Magnarella 1973; and 1974:112). Such means include the provision of dowries and the payment of inheritance shares in income and other forms of immovable property. However, not only do townsmen seem more aware of their daughters' rights than do villagers, the nature of property is the nonagrarian context—that is, wages and salaries rather than land—makes the equitable division of property, at least in economic terms, more feasible (Magnarella 1973:112).

Overall changes in economic structure, on the basis of the Turkish material at least, evidently affect the access of women to traditional forms of property. One ancillary factor is that education can serve to alter both the form of female access to property as well as attitudes about traditional forms. In a recent questionnaire survey of middle-class male and female graduate students in Karachi and Lahore, Korson found that 40 percent of the respondents felt that both *mehr* (indirect dowry) and *jahez* (dowry) should be discontinued, and that married couples should seek economic independence from their parents (Korson 1973:146). It might reasonably be assumed that in less conservative Muslim societies than Pakistan such views would be held by a larger percentage of a similar sample population. Another important role of education is to make women more aware of their existing rights and thus allow them to translate theory into practice or, conversely, seek to change the theory where it is found lacking.

Coupled with increasing participation in secular education is the fact that opportunities have opened up in a number of sectors of Muslim societies for women to work outside the home in public, nonagricultural realms. While the actual present inclusion of women in the nondomestic economy should not be taken for granted (as will be discussed), it is still true that in introducing a totally new form of property access for women, such employment, where applicable, has important potential affects on the nature of conjugal relationships. At the very least, in betrothal negotiations, a woman's education and access to employment can provide criteria supplementing those related to her family's wealth and social position. A number of other considerations apply to the effects on conjugal relationships of female participation in the public labor force. It has been noted that in Islam and in most modernist interpretations there is a stress on the right of individual control over property by both husbands and wives. Under these legal conditions, to what extent do men fear their wives working outside the home and becoming economically independent? By the same token, how does female employment affect traditionally defined responsibilities of the husband to support his wife? These are complicated questions for which there are no data that can be generalized. However, in a survey of business women and clerical workers in Turkey, where secular law emphasizes conjugal property, 80 percent of female earnings in the sample were added to the family budget (Nerim Abadan 1967:96). There are potential effects of female employment on severed unions as well, illustrated in changing patterns in the economics of divorce. In Tunisia, for example, in a redefinition of the terms of alimony, wage-earning divorcées under modern legislation can be made to contribute to the upbringing of their children (Chamay 1971:65).

One way to approach the question of how changes in female access to property affect domestic status is to look at the manner in which control over economic resources alters the format of household decisionmaking. Some recent analyses have suggested that the strategies available to women in general for affecting such decisionmaking are dependent on the structure of the domestic unit. Thus, Louise Lamphere (1974) has posited that where domestic and political spheres are separated and extended family structures are found, with power and authority revolving around a hierarchy of males, women focus on "political" goals; that is, they attempt to influence men with authority. But in nuclear family structures that by definition eliminate the male hierarchy, women can have an effective voice in domestic decisions if they themselves have control over their own economic resources. In these terms it could be hypothesized that in modernizing Muslim contexts female strategies become less "political" and more "economic" if, in fact, extended family structures are being replaced and women are being employed in the public sector.

In the light of Lamphere's argument, however, might not it also be concluded that traditional Muslim dowries play a similar role of providing "economic" female strategies, given that women have de jure control over their dowries? Perhaps to some degree this is so, although Maher's Moroccan data cited above indicate that dowries can, in fact, result in a very high degree of economic dependence on the husband. In addition, it should not be overlooked that, even in the context of social change, dowries can still serve to bolster the prestige of a girl's family through "conspicuous consumption" and to affect business and political alliances between elite families.[14]

Female employment in the public sector, on the other hand, introduces a totally new variable with respect to the relationship between female property and domestic status. Potential changes in the area of conjugal decisionmaking have already been noted. Natal kin ties would also be influenced, in that the feasibility of female employment would deemphasize traditional obligations to support unmarried, divorced, and widowed kinswomen. If the reasons for forfeiting patrimonial inheritance no longer exist—that is, to ensure other rights in natal kinship—then it would also be expected that women would increasingly make good their claims to patrimony. That property is movable in nonagrarian sectors makes this more feasible. By extension, female inheritance of patrimony implies significant changes in marriage prestations. In this regard it might be asked to what extent dowry continues to serve as a substitute for female inheritance or, conversely, to what extent the provision of a daughter's education substitutes for either dowry or inheritance.

Changes even in predominantly agrarian sectors should not be overlooked. In the Arab village he has studied, Rosenfeld indicates that the groom can build a room or house as part of the marriage agreement, often serving to lessen or do away with *mahr*. In addition, social change has resulted in more educational and occupational distinctions between women. Not only has there been a decrease in gift-giving between married women and their natal kin, but a woman's "sense of individuality and self-importance, derived from her kin, family-lineage name" has also decreased (Rosenfeld 1974:162).

While it can be concluded that female employment in the public sector and increasing educational opportunities for women are powerful instigators of change in terms of the topic under consideration in this paper, several words of caution are necessary. Taking a more careful view is in keeping with recent attempts by a number of analysts to reassess theories of modernization in nonwestern societies. Thus, Elise Boulding (1972) has concluded that there is no statistical correlation between degrees of industrialization and female rates of participation in the labor force, and that "modernization per se does not increase participatory competence of women in society." She specifically cites Middle Eastern traditional and modern urban centers in also stating a negative correlation between urbanization and female participation in the public sector. Other observers have as well questioned western models of modernization in the area of family structure. In a recent analysis of biases in theories that equate modernization with urbanization, M. A. Qadeer has shown that in the South Asian case "family structure has not undergone the kind of change normally associated with urbanization" (Qadeer 1974:269). That is, the replacement of extended or joint family structures by nuclear familism is not widespread, and is not even an exclusive characteristic of urban areas. Qadeer's contention that an emphasis on nuclear familism is primarily a middle class phenomenon in the South Asian example (ibid., p. 270) may have implications for the Muslim case if it can be assumed that a reexamination of models of modernization is also called for here. Several of Boulding's points also merit attention.

Actual opportunities for female employment are severely limited in most Muslim societies by the institution of purdah. Even under circumstances in which purdah is not formally practiced, the mentality of purdah and all that it implies in terms of moral and ideological concerns can still be pervasive. In Pakistan, for example, even highly educated women may not be permitted by their families to work at all or, if they are, constraints are placed on suitable forms of employment.[15] Limitations of female "participatory competence" also emanate from considerations of social class. Pertinent here is the extent to which middle-class female employment is limited by the fact that aspirations to middle-class status in Muslim societies are frequently accompanied by the status-enhancing practice of the seclusion of women. What this suggests, of course, is that a priori assumptions cannot be made about the degree to which social change has served to alter the domestic status of women with regard to property access. Nuclear familism, ordinarily considered in the company of industrialization and modernization, must not only be reconsidered in terms of its occurrence, but in and of itself may not necessarily provide a wholly reliable indicator of change unless it provides the financial impetus for the wife to work outside the home.

For one, the maintenance of nuclear family residence, often a pragmatic necessity in urban areas, need not imply the eradication of extended family norms. In corollary fashion, change in male economic status need not be accompanied by change in female status; sexual roles may remain as compartmentalized as in the traditional context. This is illustrated by a recent study of a rapidly industrializing setting 18 miles south of Cairo. Formerly agriculturalists, men now work in nearby factories but return home every evening to assume the role of "head of the household: as the chief decision-maker, disciplinarian, and value-transmitter."[16] One wonders to what extent this form of male adaptation to social change that reinforces the traditional sexual division of labor would be found in other settings.[17]

In this vein, modernization for many occupants of Muslim societies seems to imply the loss of a former complementarity between the domestic roles of men and women. In her assessment of the female condition in contemporary Egypt, Moshen maintains that both male and female conservatism apply, but that female equality in public life has been more readily accepted than in family life.[18] That female as well as male attitudes prove ambivalent should come as no surprise; women may fear the erosion of the "power" maintained by them in the context of traditional extended family households. As for men, twenty years ago an Egyptian educator expressed what can be construed as a by no means extinct attitude in his assertion that female education can result in women "neglecting" their husbands and "trying to lead an independent life." He went on to explicate an increased divorce rate in Egypt as partly the result of "the emancipation of women which detracts from the idea of cooperation which is one of the essential requirements of happy family relations" (Nahas 1965:245).

Conclusion

A range of societies from Morocco to Pakistan has been considered in this essay, and while Iran, Algeria, India, Indonesia, and other Muslim countries and Islamically influenced societies have purposely been neglected, one might still conclude that some questionable methodological ground has been treaded on. Seminal differences in cultural background, in

history, and in more recent political events are certainly pertinent to the examples presented here. Differences also stem
from variations in the development of contemporary legal
codes; thus, Near Eastern modernism should be distinguished
from what has transpired in Pakistan with its background in
Anglo-Muslim law. Nevertheless, a comparative stance can be
methodologically justified on two major counts. First, despite
the myriad of contemporary Muslim societies, there is a
backdrop of homogeneity originating not only in the totality of
the Muslim experience but in terms of past similar solutions to
ecologically and politically oriented problems that are
reflected in socioeconomic organization and ideology.[19] Thus,
the patrilineal, patrilocal, extended family with its corollary
ideological means of coping with the presence of female
members is the most elemental component of the substratum
of traditional society within the areas cited in this essay. Other
sources of homogeneity stem from common experiences in the
face of industrialization and modernization that include potential changes in family structure that must be met by alternative
ideological means of coping with (still inevitable) female
members.

While some Muslim societies are economically more modernized than others and their civil governments have to varying
degrees intruded on traditional religious precepts, in any contemporary Muslim society there are at least some
socioeconomic sectors in which the nature of the relationship of
women to property is undergoing important change. Keeping
in mind the necessity for caution in the assessment of the outcome of modernization in terms of family structure and the
sexual division of labor, the feasibility of change in the division
of labor does mean that women's property can become the
residual of not only ascribed but achieved statuses as well.
Under these circumstances *mahr* and dowry become increasingly less relevant to the conjugal relationship as it is contracted, as it functions, and as it dissolves through death or
divorce. For most women in Muslim societies, however, this is

not true. The access of women to property remains dependent upon ascribed statuses maintained in natal and conjugal domestic units.

It is within the domestic domain of society that Islam has paternalistically accorded specific property rights to daughters and wives with the explicit aim of providing them with moral and economic security. But what of contemporary legislation in this regard? For those Muslim societies of modernist orientation that take traditional law as an inspiration to secular legislation (unlike Turkey, which has rejected the legalistic ideal of Islam), the task is complex, depending in part on the extent to which social change has already served to alter the domestic roles of women. In assessing the future of family and status law reform, one of the foremost Western students of Islamic law has made this conclusion:

There are manifest signs today of (a) radical and progressive spirit in some quarters, while there are also signs of a much more conservative and even retrogressive spirit elsewhere. It would be a bold man who would venture any positive assertion as to which attitude will prevail. (Anderson 1971:31)

These societies must cope with the by no means unique nor simplistic task of reflecting diverse realities of social life in legislation. Since, in the strict sense, traditional Islamic law does not grow out of society but is imposed on society by divine ordination, it has always had to face a gap between theory and practice. In the attempt to adapt divine law to changing social circumstances, secularized law is still confronted with such a gap. What is applicable to the upper-middle-class woman in Cairo or her counterpart in Karachi does not, in terms of property access, pertain to their sisters in the thousands of villages beyond the urban sphere.

Notes

1. See Peggy R. Sanday, "Toward a Theory of the Status of Women," *American Anthropologist* 75 (1973): 1,682-1,700, who indicates why female participation in traditional economic production in the areas under scrutiny in this essay does not provide sufficient conditions for the development of an economic status for women.

2. A few Hadiths, however, tried to show that the amount must be neither too high nor too low.

3. Among Shiites, for example, heirs are divided into those "by relationship" and those "for special reasons" (such as husband and wife).

4. Only the Hanafis and Shiites recognize marriage concluded by a woman without a *wali* (marriage guardian).

5. "The fact is, that in this society where property rights exist and serve as the backbone to the male controlled "patriarchal" household, it is the father and brother who have exploited the potential for manipulation of the woman and who gain from her bride price," Rosenfeld 1974:156.

6. I am basing this description on data derived from my own work in Pakistani Baluchistan, but it holds for other areas as well, and has to do with what are regarded as the mutual rights and obligations contingent on marriage.

7. On the oasis I studied, this threat was perceived as a real one. A local adage has it that "this is why you try to remain at peace with your wife; for the sake of a hundred date trees."

8. Zekiye Eglar, *A Punjabai Village in Pakistan* (New York: Columbia University Press, 1960), pp. 186-77. Here, as in many instances elsewhere, if daughters inherit land in the absence of male siblings, the land passes to her male agnates at her death.

9. See, for example, Granqvist, *Palestine Village*; Salim, *Euphrates Delta*; Louise Sweet, *Tell Toquaan: A Syrian Village*, (Ann Arbor: University of Michigan Press, 1960); Fredrick Barth, "Father's Brothers Daughter Marriage in Kurdistan," *Southwestern Journal of Anthropology* 10, (1954):164-71.

10. See, for the Greek example, Ernestine Friedl, "The Position of Women: Appearance and Reality," *Anthropological Quarterly*, vol. 40, no. 3, (1967), pp. 97-108.

11. Raphael Patai, ed., *Women in the Modern World*, (New York:Free Press, 1967), p. 114. It should be noted that at the same time, Tunisian women were also accorded greater equality with regard to monogamy and divorce.

12. Ibid., p. 115. Note that such rights are not available to women in a number of non-Muslim societies.

13. Ibid., p. 113. Interestingly, this " new custom" is followed only rarely in Saudi Arabia, usually when a Saudi marries a woman from a more westernized country such as Lebanon.

14. In 1967 and again in 1976 the Government of Pakistan passed the Control of Jahez Law in an attempt to limit the "conspicuous consumption" tenor of dowry, but at the same time to ensure that women retain exclusive control over their dowries.

15. J. Henry Korson, "Career Constraints Among Women Graduate Students in a Developing Society," *Journal of Comparative Family Studies*, vol. 1, no. 1 (1970); Hanna Papanek, "Purdah in Pakistan: Seclusion and Modern Occupations for Women," *Journal of Marriage and the Family*, August 1971; see also Lee L. Bean, "Utilization of Human Resources: The Case of Women in Pakistan," *International Labour Review* vol. 97, no. 4, (1968), pp. 391-410. The proportion of "economically

active" women in Pakistan was 14.5% at the time of Bean's analysis, with 68.3% of this total classified as unpaid family labor.

16. Hani Fakhouri, *Kafr El-Alow: An Egyptian Village in Transition*, (New York: Holt, Rhinehart and Winston, 1972), p. 40. It should be noted that the retention of the traditional male role in the household is regarded by Fakhouri as one of the positive results of industrialization in this particular setting.

17. For a quite different view which shows how conjugal relationships have changed in a formerly agricultural but now industrializing Turkish case, see Paul J. Magnarella, "Conjugal Role Relationships in a Modernizing Turkish Town," *International Journal of Sociology of the Family*, vol. 2, no. 2, (1972), pp. 179-92.

18. Moshen 1974: p. 38; see recent comment by Jihan Sadat, wife of the president of Egypt in the context of securing rights for Egyptian women: "Of course, we have some people who are not willing, some of the religious people. I'm not trying to catch up with European women. I know our traditions and customs. I believe in equal participation and equal pay for women. But I believe at the same time the husband must be the head of the family." Associated Press Wire Service, Feb. 19, 1975.

19. See Jane Schneider, "Of Vigilance and Virgins: Honor, Shame and Access to Resources in Mediterranean Europe," *Ethnology*, vol. 10, no. 1 (1971); Richard T. Antoun, "On the Modesty of Women in Arab Muslim Villages," *American Anthropologist*, vol. 70. no. 4, (1968), pp. 671-97 and Antoun's Reply to M. Abu-Zhara's comment on preceding paper in *American Anthropologist*, vol. 72, no. 5, (1970), pp. 1,088-92.

Appendix 1
Major Legislative Reform In Family And Personal Status Law in Arab Countries And Pakistan

I. *Chronology*
    1917   Ottoman Law of Family Rights

Egypt:
    1920,   1923, 1929: Reforms in marriage and divorce
    1943:   Law of Intestate Succession
    1946:   The Law of Testamentary Dispositions
    1946:   The Law of Provisions of Waqf

Jordan:
    1951:   Replacement of Ottoman Law of Family Rights; included Egyptian reforms.

Syria:
    1953:   The law of Personal Status

Tunisia:
   1956:   The Law of Personal Status
   1959:   Supplement
   These represent the most radical reforms to date in Arab
   countries.

Morocco:
   1958:   The Code of Personal Status

Iraq:
   1959:   The Law of Personal Status
   1963:   Amendment (repeal of more radical elements of 1959
   law)

India and Pakistan:
   1939:   Dissolution of Muslim Marriages Act
   1961:   The Muslim Family Laws Ordinance

II.   *Major Changes* (Cf. Anderson 1971, pp. 16-31)

   A.*Judicial Divorce at Request of Wife:*
      Most of these reforms are based on rights originally granted
      by traditional authority.
      In Morocco, a woman can claim a judicial divorce if her
      husband's second marriage has "harmed her;" otherwise,
      breach of contract must be proven.
      In Pakistan, grounds of "incompatibility" are permitted in
      a woman's claim to divorce, but she must repay the *mahr.*
      In Tunisia, despite other major reforms in divorce, under
      certain circumstances, wives can still get a divorce if they pay
      compensation.

   B.*Limitations on Unilateral Repudiation by the Husband:*
      In Syria, Tunisia and Morocco the husband can be made to
      pay financial compensation at the order of the court, serving
      to restrain his right of repudiation.

   C.*Limitations on Child Marriage, Forced Marriage, and
   Polygamy:*
      Only in Tunisia is polygamy invalid per se. Elsewhere, men
      have to prove their viable financial position; otherwise, par-
      ties may be liable to criminal sanction, but the union is still
      valid per se.

D. *Question of idda, Paternity, Custody, and Guardianship:*
   Divorcées and widows can no longer demand maintenance for an *'idda* of excessive duration.
   No major changes in custody and guardianship of children.

E. *Law of Testate and Intestate Succession:*
   More emphasis on the nuclear family, at the expense of agnatic heirs (see appendix 2).
   Use of the doctrine of the "return" (*radd*) can mean that a solitary daughter will receive as much as a solitary son would have by means of cutting off collateral agnatic heirs. In Tunisia, the wife is entitled to take the *radd*.

F. *Awqāf Law:*
   Family *awqāf* abolished in Syria, Tunisia, and Egypt, thereby eliminating a traditional means of depriving spouses and children of property.

III. *Other Relevant Changes:*

A. Of great potential is a wider acceptance of the Hanbali view that husbands are bound by stipulations set at marriage, such as agreements not to take a second wife and to permit the wife to work after marriage.

B. In Egypt and Tunisia, civil and religious courts have been unified, although Moshen (1974) notes that in Egypt this does not prevent rulings according to Shariate. Nonetheless, a decrease in the use of *qādī* courts for family and personal status cases could have a cumulative effect if one assumes that civil judges are less conservative than *qādīs*.

Appendix 2

In *Succession in the Muslim Family* (Cambridge: Cambridge University Press, 1971), N. J. Coulson argues that changes in the nature of family life in Muslim societies are now reflected in reforms in family law that show "a progressive improvement in the legal status of women." He sees an emphasis on the nuclear family that accords a more effective and responsible position for women. To document this view he looks at the succession of orphaned grandchildren as an example of a greater stress on lineal descendants to the exclusion of collateral kin.

But it is not entirely clear that the motivation behind such a reform is, in all cases, the improvement of the status of women per se, although, in fact, it may have that effect. In Pakistan, radical changes in succession laws were made in order to improve the position of orphaned grandchildren, but with the result that a daughter is much worse off than a granddaughter, since a son's grandchild receives twice as much as the deceased's own daughter (Coulson, p. 155). Coulson's summary of six cases of reform, indicating the size of shares accorded to daughter, daughter's son and agnatic cousin, is as follows, (p. 157).

	Syria Morocco	Iraq	Egypt	Pakistan	Tunisia
Daughter	1/2	All	1/3	1/3	2/3
Daughter's son	—	—	1/3	1/3	1/3
Agnatic cousin	1/2	—	1/3	1/3	—

Bibliography

Abadan, Nerim
   1967   "Turkey," in *Women in the Modern World,* Edited by Raphael Patai. New York: Free Press.

Anderson, J. N. D.
   1971   "The Role of Personal Statutes in Social Development in Islamic Countries." *Comparative Studies in Society and History,* vol. 13, no. 1.

Antoun, Richard T.
   1968   "On the Modesty of Women in Arab Muslim Villages." *American Anthropologist*, vol. 20, no. 4.

   1970   Reply to M. Abu-Zhara's comment on preceding paper. Ibid., vol. 72, no. 5.

Aswad, Barbara
   1967   "Key and Peripheral Roles of Noble Women in a Middle Eastern Plains Village." *Anthropological Quarterly*, vol. 40, no. 3.

Ayoub, Millicent
   1959   "Parallel Cousin Marriage and Endogamy: A Study in Sociometry." *Southwestern Journal of Anthropology*, vol. 15, no. 3.

Baer, Gabriel
   1964   *Population and Society in the Arab East*. London: Routledge and Kegan Paul.

Barclay, Harold B.
   1965   "Some Aspects of the Secularization Process in the Arab Sudan." *Human Organization*, vol. 24, no. 1.

   1964   *Buurri al Lamaab: A Suburban Village in the Sudan*. Ithaca: Cornell University Press.

Barth, Fredrik
   1965   *Political Leadership Among Swat Pathans*. London: Athlone Press.

   1954   "Father's Brother's Daughter Marriage in Kurdistan." *Southwestern Journal of Anthropology*, vol. 10, no. 2.

Bean, Lee L.
   1968   "Utilization of Human Resources: The Case of Women in Pakistan." *International Labour Review*, vol. 97, no. 4.

Boulding, Elise
   1972   "Women as Role Models in Industrializing Societies: A Macro-System Model of Socialization for Civic Competence," in *Cross-National Family Research*. Edited by M. B. Sussman and B. E. Cogswell. Leiden: E. J. Brill.

Charnay, Jean-Paul
   1971   *Islamic Culture and Socio-Economic Change*. Leiden: E. J. Brill, 1971.

Couson, N. J.
   1971   *Succession in the Muslim Family*. Cambridge: Cambridge University Press.

Dupire, Marguerite
   1971   "The Position of Women in a Pastoral Society," in *Women of Tropical Africa*. Edited by Denise Paulme. Berkeley: University of California Press.

Eglar, Zekiye
1960 *A Punjabi Village in Pakistan*. New York: Columbia University
       Press.

Fakhouri, Hani
1972 *Kafr El-Alow: An Egyptian Village in Transition*. New York: Holt,
       ·Rhinehart and Winston.

Friedl, Ernestine
1967 "The Position of Women: Appearance and Reality," *Anthropolog-
       ical Quarterly*, vol. 40, no. 3.

Fuller, Anne
1963 *Buarij: Portrait of a Lebanese Muslim Village*. Cambridge:
       Harvard University Press.

Gibb, H. A. R., and Kramers, J. H., eds.
1953 *Shorter Encyclopedia of Islam*. Leiden: E. J. Brill.

Goody, Jac, and Tambiah, S. J.
1973 *Bridewealth and Dowry*. Cambridge: Cambridge University Press.

Granqvist, Hilma
1931 *Marriage Conditions in a Palestinian Village*. Helsinki: Commenta-
       tiones Humanarum Societas Scientarium.

Hamed, Ammar
1954 *Growing Up in an Egyptian Village*. London: Routledge and
       Kegan Paul.

Hansen, H. H.
1961 *The Kurdish Woman's Life*. Copenhagen: National Museet.

Karim, A. K. Nazmul
1963 "Changing Patterns of an East Pakistan Family," in *Women in the
       New Asia*. Edited by Barbara Ward. Paris: UNESCO.

Keyser, James
1974 "The Middle Eastern Case: Is There a Marriage Rule?" *Ethnology*,
       vol. 42, no. 3.

Korson, J. Henry
1973 "Some Aspects of Social Change in the Muslim Family in West
       Pakistan," in *Contributions to Asian Studies*. Edited by K.
       Ishwaran. Leiden: E. J. Brill, 1973.

1970 "Career Constraints Among Women Graduate Students in a
       Developing Society," *Journal of Comparative Family Studies*,
       vol. 1, no. 1.

Lamphere, Louise
1974 "Strategies, Cooperation and Conflict Among Women in Domestic
       Groups," in *Woman, Culture and Society*. Edited by M. Z.
       Rosaldo and L. Lamphere. Stanford: Stanford University
       Press.

Levy, Reuben
    1962   *The Social Structure of Islam*. Cambridge: Cambridge University
            Press.

Lewis, I. M.
    1965   "Problems in the Comparative Study of Unilineal Descent," in
            The Relevance of Models for Social Anthropology. Edited by
            M. Banton. London: Tavistock.

Magnarella, Paul J.
    1974   *Tradition and Change in a Turkish Town*. New York: John Wiley
            and Sons.

    1973   "The Reception of Swiss Family Law in Turkey." *Anthropological
            Quarterly*, vol. 46, no. 2.

    1972   "Conjugal Role Relationships in a Modernizing Turkish Town."
            International Journal of Sociology of the Family, vol. 2, no. 2.

Maher, Vanessa
    1974   "Divorce and Property in the Middle Atlas of Morocco." *Man*, vol.
            9, no. 1.

Moshen, Safia K.
    1967   "The Legal Status of Women Among Awled 'Ali." *Anthropological
            Quarterly*, vol. 40, no. 3.

    1974   "The Egyptian Woman: Between Modernity and Tradition," in
            Many Sisters. Edited by Carolyn J. Matthiasson. New York:
            Free Press.

Nahas, M. K.
    1965   "The Family in the Arab World," in *Peoples and Cultures of the
            Middle East*. Edited by A. Shiloh. New York: Random House.
            (Article first published in 1954.)

Papanek, Hanna
    1973   "Purdah: Separate Worlds and Symbolic Shelter." *Compara-
            tive Studies in Society and History*, vol. 15, no. 3.

    1971   "Purdah in Pakistan: Seclusion and Modern Occupations for
            Women," *Journal of Marriage and the Family*, August.

Patai, Raphael, ed.
    1967   *Women in the Modern World*. New York: Free Press.

Peters, Emrys
    1963   "Aspects of Rank and Status Among Muslims in a Lebanese
            Village," in *Mediterranean Countrymen*. Edited by J. Pitt-
            Rivers. Paris: Mouton and Co., 1963.

Qadeer, M. A.
    1974   "Do Cities 'Modernize' the Developing Countries? An Examination
            of the South Asian Experience." *Comparative Studies in
            Society and History*, vol. 16, no. 3.

Rodinson, Maxime
1971   *Mohammed*. New York: Pantheon.

Rosenblatt, Fugita
1969   "Wealth Transfers and Restrictions on Sexual Relations During Betrothal." *Ethnology*, vol. 8, no. 3.

Rosenfeld, Henry
1974   "Non-hierarchical, Hierarchical and Masked Reciprocity in an Arab Village." *Anthropological Quarterly*, vol. 47, no. 1.

1960   "On Determinants of the Status of Arab Village Women." *Man*, vol. 60.

Salim, S. M.
1962   *Marsh Dwellers of the Euphrates Delta*. London: Athlone Press.

Sanday, Peggy R.
1973   "Toward a Theory of the Status of Women." *American Anthropologist*, vol. 75, no. 5.

Schacht, Joseph
1966   *An Introduction to Islamic Law*. London: Oxford University Press.

Schneider, Jane
1971   "Of Vigilance and Virgins: Honor, Shame and Access to Resources in Mediterranean Europe." *Ethnology*, vol. 10, no. 1.

Stirling, Paul
1965   *Turkish 'Village*. New York: Science Editions.

Sweet, Louise
1974   "In Reality: Some Middle Eastern Women," in *Many Sisters*. Edited by Carolyn Matthiasson. New York: Free Press.

1960   *Tell Toqaan: A Syrian Village*. Ann Arbor: University of Michigan Press.

Westermarck, Edward
1914   *Marriage Ceremonies in Morocco*. London: Macmillan and Co.

Ritual Status of Muslim Women in Rural India

LINA M. FRUZZETTI
Brown University

This essay begins with an analysis of Indian society. First, it deals with the question of Hindus and Muslims in the context of Indian society; second, with the question of values in the organization and the structure of Hindu and Muslim societies; and third, with the historic interaction and association of the two communities. Finally, it deals with the question of values, associated and contrasted, related and yet antagonistic.

Historically the Muslims in India were the rulers, but around the late eighteenth century they lost their political dominance. The loss of power and the sociopolitical change gave rise to the formation of two distinct societies from the "point of view of ultimate values," or "the reunion of men divided into two groups," each group with its own distinct ideological features understood within the Indian environment (Dumont 1974:211). "A non-Hindu group cannot be regarded as a society by itself, however strongly its own values push it in this direction" (ibid: 210). The above four points should remind the reader of the peculiar aspect of the Muslim society in India: it is a minority group living within a Hindu majority in a secular state.

This essay will then consider the above points only insofar as they help to illustrate the "Bengaliness" of the Muslim society under consideration. On the other hand, the focus of the essay will be on ritual and the ensuing status indigenously conceived and manifested in a system of stratification by the women in a rural town of West Bengal. Both concepts, "ritual" and "status," are considered to be outside the pale of Islamic teaching by the Muslims in the town, who consider their society as being of a "quite special type which we are scarcely in a position to characterize, except by saying that, lying beneath the ultimate or Islamic values are other ultimate values presupposed by actual behavior" (Dumont 1974:211).

Special acknowledgment is given to the Foreign Area Fellowship Program and the American Institute of Indian Studies, whose generous grants made this research possible. The author would like to thank Ms. Sharon Cronan for her editorial assistance and Akos Ostor for his criticisms and helpful suggestions.

On first consideration, the concept of "status" appears to derive largely from the notion of the pure and the impure, especially since the idiom in which status is cast is closely related to the Bengali Hindu. Nonetheless, there is a fundamental difference in the achievement of status by both communities. Unlike the Hindus, the Muslims in India do not conceive of the separation of status from power. The opposition of the impure to the pure, as the underlying principle, is the basis of the caste system; the status of the high and the low castes can only be achieved by birth. For the Hindus, status is divorced from both economic and political power.[1] Do the Muslims then have a caste system that parallels that of the Hindus? In this essay I will argue that the Muslims do not have a caste system. The classical division of the Muslims into Ashrafs and non-Ashrafs is not the case in rural Bengal.[2] On the other hand, Indian Muslims do have a system of stratification that is both fluid and flexible, and that makes mobility possible within the system. Second, the system of stratification allows for the upward or downward mobility of an individual, an extended family, or a whole locality. Caste mobility for the Hindus (other than a positional change within the group itself) is in itself questionable.

Islam proclaims the equality of all men, before one God; it admits neither hereditary privileges nor professional intermediaries between man and God.[3] Within the Muslim community all people are equal. This is most evident in the celebration of the major Muslim festivals, and in the joint prayers where the community acts as one, in contrast to the separate caste temples of the Hindus. At the Moharram celebration each neighborhood or group of extended families brings about the performance of the festival through their joint cooperation as a single whole. Yet, despite the theoretical equality of all men (and this includes women within the community) one is faced with status differences that are manifested in the daily life of the community. Status difference and standing within the community is also part and parcel of the overall Muslim ideology in rural India. This is the aspect of the Muslim community that I will analyze in this paper. How do differences occur, change or remain; what is the implication of the separation of groups or individuals to the community in Bengal, to both Hindus and Muslims and to Islam in general?

Rural Indian Muslims maintain a dual model of an Islamic society, a society more or less like the "Umma Muslima," which emphasizes the equality of men. The second model of the Muslim society illustrative of the position of women is one that is stratified and in which the criteria used to hierarchize the members into high or low status ranks derive from the everyday experiences of the Muslims as members of a Bengali society and culture. Thus status differentiation for the Muslim correlates to one's economic and political standing as well as one's "religious" standing as it is understood locally. I do not mean that political and economic power are a direct reflection of a high or a low status in the ranking system; on the other hand, the highest ranking families in the town (including two economically lower-class families) simultaneously correlate to a high class level, economically and politically. How then is "status" achieved by the Muslim? What creates rank differentiation among equals in the community of Muslims?

One of the ways that rank is created among Muslim women is through the ritual activities in which they themselves participate. Women's ritual domain spreads from *pir* worship (saint worship) to rituals related to different life-cycle rites. In this women are placed on a high or a low position in the stratification system depending on the performances of certain rituals. In this essay I am not concerned with the female/male dichotomy, nor with the sex role differences in terms of the private and public domains. Nor am I dealing directly with the male/female ranking system, the market versus the house, or the other numerous binary divisions which have been well developed in the literature about women.[4] The essay will attempt to answer the following questions: What kinds of rank do women create through the performance of certain rituals? How is mobility achieved within the system? What is the implication of the rituals and what is their effect upon the generally held Islamic ideology in the town?

On the surface then, the Muslim's notion of high- and low-status caste in Bengali idiom (*niccu/uccu*) seems to parallel that of the Hindu scheme of social gradations and differentiation, though in actual terms the Muslim system is indigenously constructed through the play of "culture" and "religion," the former being Bengali culture and the latter "Din-ul-Islam." Here then is a fundamental difference between the two systems of ranking; for the Hindus, religion (the combination of *artha*, *dharma*, and *karma*) is the overall uniting factor of the caste system, while the opposition of the pure to the impure is the underlying principle of the system. For the Muslims religion (Din-ul-Islam, or the sacred world) prohibits the inequality of persons, even though the local culture

allows for a system of gradation within a society where all
are otherwise considered equals. For the Hindus, the rules
of caste behavior are the rules of religion, while for the
Muslims the rules of behavior can either be regulated by Islam
or can be culturally constructed: that is to say, in Bengali
terms, "The level of ideology (religious ideology) is not
separable from that of action. There are certain beliefs and actions that the Muslims regard as *desher niom* (laws of the land,
laws in the sense that these are referred actions relating to
religion). Together with the prescribed religious injunctions to
Islam, the *desher niom* form a folk religion of Islam unique to
Bengal" (Fruzzetti 1972:3). The blending of the two traditions
is not considered by the Muslims to be contradictory or to conflict with Islamic teachings. On the one level of abstraction
conceived by the Muslims to refer to the Muslim community,
the terms *Bengali* and *Hindu* are coterminus, and are used in-
terchangeably. On the local level, the term *Bengali* is used by
the Muslims to identify themselves as Bengalis, sharing a
similar culture with the Hindu Bengalis.

How then does the system of stratification work, and what
are the criteria used to describe the system? Status differences
amongst Muslims can derive from (1) the occupation of the
male members of each household; (2) the residential locality
(i.e., whether the Muslims live among themselves or with Hindus of low caste); (3) the occupation of the in-marrying
women's brothers and fathers; and (4) from the rituals that
women perform either outside the house or within it. These so-
called rituals are associated with the different life-cycle rituals
and the periodic worship of the saints (both mythical and real)
and with other social rituals. As stated earlier, I am concerned
in this essay with the analysis of women's roles in the rituals and
with the ranking system that results from the performances of
the rituals. This is not to say that Muslims in rural India rank
themselves only in these terms, but here I am simply focussing
on women and on their status within the society of women and
in relation to the society at large. Women's roles in the major

Islamic feasts are almost nonexistent; it is the men who gather in the mosque for the communal prayers, while the women are expected to remain at home. On the other hand, the rituals that we are examining are within the domain of women's actions, where male participation is almost nil (with the occasional exception of the *maulavi*). Not only are specific rituals part of the household activities, but the range of performances goes beyond the house to the shrines of various saints situated on the local river, in the forests, and so forth. The role of these rites in Bengali culture is evident, and yet they are also the criteria used to rank Muslims in a higher- or lower-status differentiation. The Muslim house in secular India in effect becomes "dar-ul-Islam," where the household members and the group of kinsmen share Islamic beliefs and practices. Bengali Muslims do not maintain a strict adherence to the purdah system with its division of the sexes by a symbolic and physical outlay of the house.[5]

The division of the house into a *zenana* and *mardana* (the two parts of the house in which female and male activities take place) is not found in rural Bengal. On the contrary, here one finds a different system, one of "inclusion" and "exclusion" of Muslim women in both public and private spheres. At the major Islamic festivals, women are asked and expected to pray in the house, while the mosque is reserved for male Muslims. Women are excluded from participation in the *mardana*, the arena reserved for males, because it is a matter of social prestige (*izzat*) to seclude one's women, since it brings shame (*sharm*) to the male members for their women to make a public appearance on such occasions. On the one hand then, the exclusion of women from public participation in major Islamic festivals corresponds to the Indian Muslims' conceived ideal of a pure "Islamic Umma," where the house becomes the dar-ul-Islam, and both men and women the preservers of the *din*. On the other hand, a fuller and exclusive participation of women in the *mardana* (public) at the local saint's tombs and at the local rivers and ponds, the abodes of benign and malevolent *pirs* (saints), is made possible because of the nature of local-level Islam, folk Islam that goes beyond the *dar-ul-Islam,* and is understood through the local culture.[6]

The concepts of *izzat* and *sharm* (honor and shame) relate directly to men's and women's activities within the Muslim community with respect to the Umma Muslima. Thus if women's presence at a mosque or at a communal prayer is a loss of a male's *izzat* amongst the male and female kinsmen within the community, women's active and exclusive participation in the ritual performances at the saints' tombs and elsewhere neither affect their status nor represent a loss of *izzat* for their male kin (unless the males themselves participate in the ritual). Women's rituals affect the women themselves; the hierarchy and rank differentiation concern them only. The rank of women in the system of stratification is then determined according to the degree and the manner of worship of these saints. Simply to pay one's respect to the *pir* in itself is not considered as *bi-shar* (harmful or hateful to the religion). To perform elaborate rituals and to treat the *pirs* as divine beings and impute to them special graces and *baraka*[7] is looked down upon by the orthodox Muslims and by the local *maulavi.* Mythical *pirs,* whose attributes, structural positioning, and functions correspond to the Hindu deities and gods, are nonetheless Islamicized, and the ritual recast in an Islamic idiom: the performance begins and ends with a *fatiha* (recitation from the Qur'ān).

On the level of these actions (saint reverence and worship) Muslim women do not differentiate themselves from the Hindus, rather they emphasize their "Bengaliness," both socially and culturally, especially since Hindu women also participate in the same *pir* worship of the saints buried in the town. The case does not follow with the mythical *pirs,* since the Hindus have the equivalent or the counterpart to those *pirs* in their own pantheon. Thus one can say that the Muslims in India face no paradox in living in a secular state. They have constructed a kind of dualistic approach to religious principles in the context of daily living and experience, giving rise to two systems of thought that are interrelated in their minds. A Bengali culture and a Muslim culture exist at the same time without either one of these concepts becoming meaningless. Muslims participate in both spheres even though the boundaries of both are sharply defined in their minds, in their ideology and their practices.[8]

I want to begin looking at these rituals that are often seen as part of folk Islam or popular Islam. Robert and Elizabeth Fernea, in referring to " the patterns of behavior and belief in Middle Eastern villages (or towns or cities)," say, "these worlds are full of holy men and women, shrines, incarnate forces of good and evil, evil eyes, incantations, and ceremonies, all of which help to make up a cosmological outlook in which formal Islam plays an important but by no means exclusive role" (Fernea and Fernea 1972:391). The orthodox *ulama* (religious leaders) cry out against such practices: folk Islam, *pirism*, and so forth are considered as a corrupt form of Islamic life, to which in Bengal many indeed have adhered; but the *ulama* have somehow abstracted it and failed to see that folk Islam gives meaning and significance to the everyday aspects of life within the local culture. For rural Muslim women, *pir* worship and reverence constitute a most important part of their life. It is the women who perform the rites and cook the food offering for the saints; it is they who visit and plead with the saint, intervening on behalf of their brothers, fathers, husbands, or children. The women draw up a contractual agreement with the saint, whereby only after the saint has fulfilled his or her part does the woman then fulfill her promise to the saint. Similarly, the part of the life-cycle rites that women perform occur before and after the formal part of the ritual; the most elaborate life-cycle rites are those surrounding marriage and birth, the two areas of women's greatest concern. Here women are not in any way competing with their male counterparts in the ritual performances. Men do not take part in the *pir* worship, but they do admit the powers of the *pir*. The men share fundamentally in the core of these beliefs, the difference between men and women residing in the behavior that goes beyond the accepted and commonly held belief. Men adhere to the fundamental Islamic principles and emphasize the equality of all men. Women, on the other hand, create arenas of activity within and outside the house through religious practices. Their rituals express their daily concerns: fears of illness, the death of their husbands (the fear of being a widow), barrenness, the coming of the second wife to the house, poverty, and so forth. These concerns and the way women express them through ritual and worship create a division in the society: the divisions of high and low. The localities where the women perform more elaborate rituals to *pirs* sink lower in status than the ones where women do not participate in the rituals.

Reverence to the Pirs

Pir worship is marked by a ritual celebration, often with recital of the *fatiha* and animal sacrifices offered to the *pir*. (Murray 1959; Tara Baig 1958:115). Aziz Ahmad and M. Mujeeb consider the ritual part of *pir* reverence as *bi-shar*, a corrupt form of sufism. I would like to argue here that what is *bi-shar* on one level can impart meaning to actions on another level of the culture.

Devotion to and reverence for the *pir* play an important part in the social and religious organization of the women. Women in distress approach the *pir* for help and comfort. I agree with Gellner's remark that the role of the *Ulama* as spiritual guides does not serve the emotional needs of a large segment of the population (Muslim). As a result, the people turn to "religion not as a form of scholarship and contemplation, but as an alleviation of suffering, as a more drastic alternative to ordinary life. Religion is practised not as a style of life but as escape (from) it" (E. Gellner 1972:7-8). In this sense the saints counteract the role of the *maulavi*, the latter's concern being the formal aspect of the religion.

The devotee of a *pir* draws up a contract with the saint, which involves giving and receiving—gift giving and receiving in itself amongst both Hindus and Muslims plays an important part in their social organization.[9] One offers food, money, prayer, hoping that in return the *pir* will consent to grant them a boon or intercede for them to Allah. Each *pir* is delegated a specific function; thus devotees seek different *pirs* for different favors.[10] In this essay I will be concerned with the mythical *pirs*, and with the *pirs* who lived in the town some 300 years ago. I will not deal with live *pirs*, since there were none in the town during my fieldwork.

Women tend to allude to *pirs* in pairs of opposing personalities, one hot and the other cold in temperament, a female *pir* complements a male *pir*, and so forth. At times (and this seems to be an added feature of *pir* worship) the power of the *pir* corresponds to the Hindu male/female sacred union, to the principle of female power as it complements that of the male power. This is the case especially with the mythical *pirs* Khidr and Olaii Bibi, one the male passive *pir*, the other the awesome, fearful, and very powerful female (at times referred to as a wife), Olaii Bibi. Thus when a pair of *pirs* is discussed, the women contrast the members according to their functions, and subsequently according to their opposing characteristics. Where one of the pair of *pirs* is hot, the other is invariably cold, and where one is benign, the other becomes very fearful. The attributes of the *pirs* are connected to their functions and occupation in the total cosmological context. The *pir* from whom women seek assistance in matters such as child bearing and protection from smallpox and cholera is considered to be a very hot (*gorom*) *pir*. The problems that a devotee puts to the *pir* are difficult, and the requests difficult to answer. The *pir* one approaches for the above kinds of problems is Olaii Bibi (commonly known as Bon Bibi). Her male counterpart, Khidr Shab, is the *pir* of water, the protector of seafaring passengers.[11]

This underlying Hindu element of hot/cold dichotomy, the

principle of Shakti/Prakriti, the female/male divine powers, is also an integral part of the marriage and birth rituals that the Muslims perform. Thus one can find consistency in the saint worship and the life-cycle rituals. The intriguing part of the Muslim society in this case is that, on the abstract Umma level, women do not adhere to the belief in male and female divine powers. Furthermore, their conceptions and notions of the person in relation to his Umma are different.

The Pair of Pirs: Bon Bibi and Khidr Shab

I begin by analyzing the mythical pairs of *pirs*, often alluded to as a husband and wife pair. Bon Bibi is the protectress of the forest: she also protects against cholera and smallpox.[12] Women agree that Bon Bibi's tasks are difficult. At the same time they fear her hot temperament! Today her worship is performed mainly by women, though in the past men did this deep in the forest.

Bon Bibi died a virgin, yet the ritual that the women perform for her is that of a marriage enactment. The women say without much elaboration that the way the ritual is performed (the marriage ceremony) in effect cools her anger. In Bengal, women who died childless or in childbirth and women who died virgins are considered to be very harmful spirits to the living. One must find ways to appease them by performances that would please and pacify them. Water is thrown to the *pir* to cool her, and the marriage ceremony takes place. The ritual for Bon Bibi is done in the mango grove. The myth tells us that before the expansion of the town, the area was a densely populated forest. The forest presently has turned into a mango grove, and is owned by a Brahmin landlord. He yearly opens his garden for the women to perform the ritual for Bon Bibi. The ritual performance takes place around the time of the smallpox and cholera epidemic. The Brahmin landlord has never been known to refuse the women entry to the garden. The actual place where the women congregate to perform the ritual is at the base of a particular mango tree; it is known to the Muslim community as the spot where the *pir* has manifested her powers to the ancestors of these women. Though the tree itself stands on the spot, the women perform the ritual for Olaii Bibi to and around the tree. The tree is the real physical focal point for the ceremonies; it does not represent the *pir* as such, but is worshipped because of the Spirit of Bon Bibi believed to dwell within.

The ritual performance is simple and the only one of its kind. First, the tree is cooled with a few buckets of water drawn from the pond nearby. (Before any major life-cycle ritual begins, the area where the activities will take place is always watered so as to cool and to calm the dust.) Then one of the married women applies oil to the tree, and it is smeared with a mixture of oil and turmeric paste. Turmeric is sacred for the Hindus, while the Muslims stress the medicinal value of it. At marriage functions, the bodies of both the bride and the groom are smeared with turmeric paste. The body of the *pir* is smeared in the same fashion, since the ritual is a marriage enactment. Similarly a red string is tied around the waist of the *pir* (in this case, the mango tree), an act that also takes place at the marriage ceremony.[13] Having tied the red string, the women then apply three or four dots of vermilion paste and turmeric paste to the tree; the application of vermilion parallels the last of the marriage acts (in the marriage ceremony, the groom puts vermilion onto the bride's parted hairline, signifying her married status). The women proceed to cook the food offering for the *pir*, who has her food preferences. Olaii Bibi is also very particular about the cleanliness of the food preparation, unlike Khidr Shab, who makes no specific demands on his devotees. One of the women does the cooking. Three different kinds of fish dishes, sour pickled mangoes, and rice are prepared. One of the women, preferably a widow, will then wash herself in the nearby pond and prepare for the *fatiha*. After the food has been cooked and placed at the foot of the tree, the *maulavi* or the widowed lady reads the *fatiha,* and all of the women wait to partake of the food, which is suffused with the pir's *baraka.* The woman who cooked the food takes a leaf and from each dish puts some of the food into it. She then enters the pond and throws away the leaf together with the food. This food offering is for Khidr Shab, Bon Bibi's "husband." The women now can share in the food, which has become sanctified. Women fear this *pir*: even those women who have given up the worship of the *pir* dare not disbelieve in her powers. For example, as soon as a child gets smallpox, the women make a trip to the abode of the *pir* and perform her worship before approaching a medical doctor. Sometimes a cock is sacrificed for Olaii Bibi, and the sacrificial animal is left behind lying at the foot of the mango tree. In other parts of Bengal the *pir* Olaii is represented by rounded stones similar to those of Sasthi, the Hindu goddess of children.

Even those Muslim women who have given up or abandoned the worship of this *pir*, or the pair of *pirs*, do not forget to offer money to the deity through a third person, or to hire another woman to perform the worship for them.

Khidr Shab (Shab is an honorific title for Muslim males) is an easier *pir* to please; he demands no specific ceremonies to be done for him. A *Fatiha* is often read, and sweets or other food items are offered to him. Usually the food offering is placed in a paper raft and floated on the water. Khidr is often equated with one of the real *pirs* in the town, Kurban Shab. The two *pirs* (the mythical Khidr and Kurban, the real *pir*) are considered to be very benign and gentle, while Olaii and Gorialli Shab (the second *pir*, who died and is buried in the town) are feared because of their hot disposition. These two *pirs* are angered by the presence of impure women and women during their menstrual time. Furthermore, the two *pirs* do not tolerate non-Muslim devotees in their *asthana* (the place where they are buried or worshipped); impure food and so forth angers them to such a point that devotees involved in any of the above mishaps are physically punished. The Muslim women say that in order to ask a favor from these two *pirs*, one must be careful not to anger the *pirs* in the first place. On the other hand, a woman in her "polluted" state (for example, during her menstrual flow or if she has not bathed following sexual intercourse) will in no way anger Khidr Shab nor Kurban Shab, nor would a non-Muslim devotee anger either of the *pirs*. A large number of Kurban Shab's devotees are Hindus; both Hindu and Muslim farmers make their first offering of the harvest to this *pir*. Kurban Shab was known to love molasses, and to this day (some three hundred years later) farmers who are in the molasses business never sell their produce before offering the *pir* the fruit of the first harvest.

Gorialli Shab is the second *pir* who is buried in the town. He died childless, though he was known to love children. Children play and jump around his grave, yet he is not angered. The saint is known to possess devotees, especially if they approach him in an impure state. In the last few years, every Thursday this *pir* possesses the same woman, and through her mouth he answers questions of those who seek favors from him. On his *urus* (death anniversary)[14] this woman is always possessed for the whole day. She cries, laughs, and sings; she speaks Urdu and Hindi languages, which she cannot speak in her normal state. On the *urus* of Gorialli, this woman is often decked with flowers, and the women scent her and treat her like a bride. There is a sexual insinuation between her and the saint in a joking manner, while at times it is seriously argued that the *pir* possesses her because he desires her. In her normal state she is known to have tremendous powers over men, despite her age and physical condition.

For Gorialli Shab, food offering is the major part of the ritual. People offer him a complete meal cooked at home. The food trays are given to the *maulavi* in charge of the *kuburstan* (the place where the saint is buried). He recites a *fatiha* over the food offering, takes half of the food and gives the other half to the devotee. The *pir*'s *baraka* (blessing) is on the food.

Numerous myths surround the *pir*. He is known to appear in

the form of a tiger when he comes to consume the food offered him in the *asthana*. Many have sworn to have seen a tiger come the night of the *pir's urus* and enter the *kuburstan* to eat the food. If the *pir* (Gorialli Shab) sees anyone on that particular day (his *urus*), that one instantly dies. A story goes that once a man lay in wait hidden behind the tree to see the tiger. As soon as the tiger appeared, the tree fell on the man, killing him instantly.

In short, worship of the *pir* is part of the Muslim belief in this rural setting. Reverence is given, food is offered, and a ritual performed for him. (Clay horses and elephants are part of the offerings to the *pir*.) Ideally, the manner in which a person approaches a *pir* for the granting of a favor or a wish should be simple and should involve no formal ritual. A wish can be made at the *pir's* grave or away from it. If the wish is granted to the devotee, he in turn will abide by his contract and fulfill his/her bargain with the *pir*. If the wish is not granted, the devotee is under no obligation to the *pir*. Muslims when visiting the *pirsthan* (the place where the *pir* lives) need only salute (*salam*) the *pir* by raising hands to head. He/she need not bend down to the ground, take the dusk from the grave's floor, or become prostrate before the *pir*. The nature of offering to a *pir* varies from whitewashing the *pirsthan* to giving the *pir* an animal sacrifice, money, flowers, or sweets.

The *urus* of Gorialli and Kurban Shab are celebrated at their respective graves. There is more concern regarding the food offering for Gorialli; each household cooks separately and brings the food offering to the *asthana*. For Kurban Shab the food is cooked by the descendants of the female line of the *pir* at the *asthana*. In each case the *maulavi* reads the *fatiha* and delivers a lecture on one aspect of Islam. The lectures are invariably related to one topic: the necessity for adherence to a pure Islam and for giving up all of the folk aspects of the performance of the religion. In short, the *maulavi* pleads with the Muslims to make the ideal *Umma* into an objectified reality.

Women, when performing their rituals for the *pirs*, do not

conclude with a lecture. On the other hand, they are aware of the relationship of these rituals to the Islamic model of a community, the *Umma* that the *maulavi* asks them to adhere to. Their present performance of elaborate rituals for the *pirs* ranks them lower than those women who do not perform the visit or the rights.

The categories used to demarcate differences in rank among the Muslims within the community are, as I said earlier, cast in Bengali idiom, namely, *niccu/uccu* (low/high with the implications of a ritual purity or impurity attached to the rank). Srinivas has coined the phrase "Sanskritization" to describe attempts by low-ranking Hindus to imitate high-caste life-style in an effort to better their caste standing. Muslim women do not Sanskritize, but they attempt another process, that of Ashrafization. As it is used within the local context, this means the attempt by low-ranking Muslim women to imitate the so-called Ashraf model that corresponds to a Muslim household in the town; this in turn corresponds to that of a Bengali Hindu upper caste. The one upper-class Muslim household in the town (which happens to be the wealthiest family amongst the Muslims, with only two exceptions) maintains a ritual distance from both Hindus and Muslims. For example, they would not interdine with or take their wives from either community. The status of this particular household is so high that orthodox brahmins have accepted cooked food from them, while they maintain a ritual distance from the Hindus as well as the Muslims in the town. Though some of these upper-class Muslim households do not interact with the Muslims in the town (i.e., women do not partake in each other's life-cycle rituals nor in the joint worship of *pirs*), the men on the other hand take part in the occasional communal prayers at the local mosque, where no division among men exists.[15]

Ironically, though the women of the upper-class families have given up the performance of the daily life-cycle rituals and the *pir* worship, they have at the same time accepted Bengali Hindu symbols; i.e., to mark their married status, they wear the iron bangle on their left hand and the vermilion on their parted hairline (both of which distinguish a married from a nonmarried woman in Bengal). In this way these upper-class women identify with Bengali culture and its *adat* (customs), unlike the lower-class Muslim women, who do not follow the same pattern of observances because, as they say, the iron bangle and the vermilion are Hindu in nature. Ashrafization in effect means a closer and a purer life, a life devoid of any non-Islamic element. The higher the status of a Muslim household, the more it will seek social acceptance and recognition by its Hindu equals. Social acceptance by the Hindu would not mean a loss of Muslim identity. Thus, two criteria of "upper-classness" and high status for the Muslims are coterminus. The few Muslim households that are considered to be in the upper-most rank are also independently wealthy in that the men do not work for others but employ others to do their menial labor while they hold lucrative government jobs or own private businesses. The majority of the Muslims in the town are day laborers. They can nevertheless move up in status rank by suddenly acquiring wealth and beginning the Ashrafization process, seeking new acceptance or occasionally moving to a new locality amongst equals. In this sense Muslims are not born into a status; they acquire a high or a low status according to their manner and style of living. That is why one can say that social mobility is possible for a Muslim.

On returning from a two-year absence from the field, I discovered that a whole locality of about twelve households (all consanguineously related) had effected a change in their group standing in relation to other households. First of all, the change was brought about by the prohibition of cousin marriages; second, the women of that locality were professional marriage singers, and they jointly agreed to give up that occupation; third, they stopped the performance of the Bon Bibi ritual. Now the neighborhood women (like the Bengali widows) congregate in one of the houses to hear the Qur'ān recited and interpreted by one of the women. Though the women have in a way bettered their standing through these social changes, they have also affected a change in their rank vis-à-vis the other women. This particular locality supplies fresh vegetables to the local market, and the women used to carry the vegetables to the bazaar; today they have stopped doing so. Nonetheless, their economic standing is still low and, though they do not associate with the lower-ranking women in the town, their Ashrafization process must remain relatively slow, given the fact that they do not have the economic means to receive a higher recognition by equals in both the Muslim and the Hindu communities.

The meaning and significance of women's activities in the life-cycle rites can be analyzed in the same way as that of *pir* worship, especially those rites surrounding birth and marriage ceremonies. There have been attempts to treat life-cycle rites as ends in themselves (Jones), or to consider them only in terms of the Islamic ideology (Cora Vreede-de-Stuers). A cultural study of women in any society is most meaningful when female sex roles are viewed through the life-cycle rituals. But these rites also should be placed into a total cultural context, in this case Bengali culture. Life-cycle rites focus on women's position, role and status in a Bengali Muslim community, either marking the transition from one stage to another or establishing relations among various categories of women (as regards other aspects of the society). The activities of women in the areas of life-cycle rituals and *pir* rituals pose no inconsistencies with the adhered-to ideology. The meaning of these actions within the total context of the local culture and folk Islam gives us a clearer definition of the role of Muslim women in a Bengali society, and of women's sex roles in both the private and public spheres of Bengali society and culture.

Conclusion

Given the nature of the Muslim community, living in a secular state as a minority group, sharing Hindu values, and ranking themselves according to the defined ritual status pose quite different problems to the community as a whole. One can also ask whether Muslim women in other Islamic countries rank themselves in relation to other women within their community through ritual status and differentiation. If so, would ritual differences matter? Would women rank themselves through the division of culture (*adat*) and religion? It is possible to answer the preceding questions through further study and analysis of women in both Islamic and non-Islamic countries; for example, a study of the contrast between Sudanese rural women and Indonesian women might be illuminating.

In studying an Indian Muslim society it is necessary to take into consideration the influences of both Islamic and Hindu cultures; but various aspects of Bengali culture are to be found neither in Islamic nor in Hindu religion, but rather within the total context of the *desher* (country's culture). "This is not to say, however, that Islamic culture (or Hindu culture) has no motivating force in the behavior of people, as it would not be profitable to argue that Christianity is sociologically inconsequential for studies of communities in Europe or America. By the same token it would be as profitless to maintain that social behavior in Muslim communities (or in Hindu society) can only be understood in terms of Qur'ānic verses and the traditions that have grown around them, as it would be to say that Christian European communities can be understood only in conjunction with Biblical texts" (Peters 1968). The emphasis is on the social meaning and significance of the actions, and not on the meaning of traits or behavior within the Islamic tradition per se. To give an example, as we have observed in this essay, *pir*ism or *pir* reverence in Bengal can be meaningful only if it is viewed in terms of Bengali culture. It would be absurd to try to make sense of the hot/cold attributes just as they relate to *pir*s. This does not mean that we should completely dissociate the various subcomponents of Bengali ideologies into Hindu, Muslim, local, regional, and so forth. Rather it is a matter of viewing the relationship between the parts and the whole. The question then is not to ask about the relationship of these holy men to Orthodox Islam, but to relate the organization of *pir* worship to the social and cultural organization of the community.

The similarities and the differences in women's ritual practices are evident within the social context of the rites and the roles performed, with the meaning and purpose of the worship different for each group. Some of these differences are the conceptualization by each group of what the action signifies, the role of the saints in terms of religious ideologies, and the social position of the ritualist (where needed). Women's roles culturally defined in the rite must be seen in the total context of women's activities, sacred and nonsacred, the system of relations made up of all ritual actions, and all other aspects of women's culture in the town.

Notes

1. Mattison Mines, writing on the South Indian Muslims, arrives at conclusions similar to those which I state in this essay. Because Muslims lack an ideology of purity/pollution (in terms of birth), their ideology of purity/pollution and their system of stratification have no integrating ideology to rationalize their social rank, thus making mobility possible (Mines 1972: 339).

2. Sociological studies of Muslim social institutions, and the division of the Muslims into two strata—Ajlaf and Ashrafs—have helped create a distorted view of the Muslims. I. Ahmad, criticizing Ansari's and Z. Ahmad's earlier papers on the Muslim division into two groups, concludes with a similar error. His analysis of the Muslim stratification into "caste analogous," endogamous, hereditary membership and a specific style of life associated with a distinct ritual status in a hierarchical system is far from the real. He insists that the "real units of social stratification are caste analogous, and the day-to-day relationships between different individuals in any local community are determined by their membership in the caste analogue rather than the broad categories" of Ajlaf and Ashrafs (p. 273). Yet we are not told how the so-called Muslim caste system differs in any way from that of the Hindus: For example, how is mobility within the system achieved and what of the ritual status at the major Muslim feasts; what does equality of all men mean at the major feasts, and in the other more mundane social activities of the Muslims within their community and vis-à-vis the society at large?

3. See the work of Vreeda-de-Stuers, 1968.

4. The division of private and public, women's world and men's world, where each sphere is self-contained, is in itself a useless division and a poor guide to the analysis of sex roles in the society. For further discussion of the subject, see the excellent work of Cynthia Nelson, 1974.

5. See, for contrast, the work of Hanna Papanek.

6. Here then the "private" corresponds to the maintenance and the observance of "formal" Islam, and the "public" or *mardana* corresponds to folk Islam, to Bengali culture. In the former domain of activities, the ritual level is prescribed and jointly held, while in the latter, the women are the ritualists and the men are excluded. Thus we have the "private" and the "public" parts of the house loosely defined, while the activities occurring within them are not divided by differences of sex. Female action goes beyond the house, that is to say, beyond the *zenana*.

7. *Baraka* is blessing, divine grace. "The shrines of the most famous *pirs* will necessarily have greater *baraka* than the shrines of a lesser *pir*, but the *mazar* (shrine) of a lesser *pir* might specialize in a special field, and people from great distances might come to that shrine for a particular cure of a disease" (A. K. Nazmul Karim: 34).

8. The *brata*, which is also a petition to a specific deity for a specific favor, is the equivalent of *pir* worship for the Muslims. Both *pir* reverence and observing a *brata* are within the woman's realm of action, the only difference being that, whereas the Muslim women draw a contract with the *pir*, the Hindu women perform worship and make the offering before the boon is granted them by the deity. The relationship of the mythical *pirs* to the Muslim women is similar to that of the *brata*, in that Muslim women do not draw a contract with the mythical *pirs* (as they do with the real *pirs*).

9. The fundamental rule for *wartan bhanji* (a system of gift exchange in the Punjab) is reciprocity: a gift should be returned for a gift, a favor returned for a favor. Over time, through numerous dealings, the giving and the receiving of gifts, people can appraise one another's ways (Eglar: 122). The same ties relate to the saint and the devotee.

10. It is true that *pirs* are not only spiritual guides or leaders. They may also have large land holdings or wealth from donations, enabling them to function as employers or in some cases as political leaders. The *pirs* considered in this essay lack economic and political power. The two saints who are indeed buried in the town settled in the area some 300 years ago. Their power thus lies more in healing and assistance with impossible tasks.

11. *Khidr* means green, evergreen, because every spot on which he steps turns green. He is also known to be as cool as water, his abode.

12. The Hindu equivalent to Bon Bibi (Olaii Bibi) is Sitala. Sometimes the same place is kept for the worship of the two. Sitala means "the cooling one." For both Olaii and Sitala, a devotee first of all cools them with water. Sitala and Olaii are variations of the same goddess/saint; both have the property of being hot (they can cause ailments). Thus it is necessary to cool these two women. "Sitala probably derived from one or more indigenous feminine demons or spirits of diseases who gradually become abstracted into the Hindu pantheon as aspects of Devi, the Mother Goddess, or Sakti, the Female Principle" (Bang: 81, 92, 97).

13. The color red is considered to be auspicious by both Hindus and Muslims. The red string is used at every life-cycle ritual. Red is also the color symbolic of wedlock,

especially for the Hindus. Muslim women do not use red vermilion on their parted hairline except at the marriage day, while Bengali Hindu married women wear red bordered sarees and red vermilion on their parted hairline as long as their husbands are alive.

14. Literal meaning of the word *urus* is wedding, union, because the occasion is the anniversary of the *wisal* or union of the spirit of the saint with Allah, which occurs at death" (Murray 1922-23:136).

15. Islam is understood to be a great brotherhood of believers. No one is barred on account of race, caste, or position. The mosque is the house of God, where everyone, whether rich or poor, king or slave, has equal rights and status.

BIBLIOGRAPHY

Ahmad, Aziz
   1964   *Studies in Islamic Culture in the Indian Environment.* Oxford: Clarendon Press.

Ahmad, Imtiaz
   1966   "The Asharaf-Ajlaf Dichotomy in Muslim Social Structure in India." *Economic and Social History Review,* vol. 3, no. 3.

Ahmad, Zarina
   1962   "Muslim Caste in Uttar Pradesh." *Economic Weekly,* vol. 14, no. 7 (February) pp. 325-36.

Ali, Meer Hassan
   1917   *Observation on the Mussulman's of India: Manners, Customs, Habits and Religious Opinions.* Oxford: Oxford University Press.

Ansari, Caus
   n.d.   "Muslim Caste in Uttar Pradesh: A Study of Culture Contact." *Eastern Anthropologist,* Lucknow, vol. 13, no. 2 (special issue).

Baig, Tara
   1958   *Women of India.* Howrat, India: Glascow Printing Press.

Bang, B. G.
   1973   "Current Concepts of the Small Pox Goddess Sitala in Parts of West Bengal." *Man in India,* vol. 53, no. 1, (January-March).

Dumont, Louis
   1974   *Homo Hierarchicus: The Caste System and Its Implications.* Chicago: University of Chicago Press.

Eglar, Zekiye
   1960   *A Punjabi Village in Pakistan.* New York: Columbia University Press.

Fernea, Robert and Fernea, Elizabeth W.
   1972   "Variation in Religious Observance Among Islamic Women"

in *Scholars, Saints and Sufis.* Edited by N.R. Keddie. Berkeley: University of California Press.

Fruzzetti (Ostor), Lina
1972 "The Idea of a Community among West Bengal Muslims," *South Asian Center, Occasional Papers.* East Lansing: Michigan State University.

Gellner, E.
1972 "Saints and Doctors," in *Scholars, Saints, and Sufis.* Edited by N.R. Keddie. Los Angeles: University of California Press.
1969 *Saints of the Atlas.* Chicago: University of Chicago Press.

Jones, V.R., and L.R. Jones
1961 *Women in Islam.* Lucknow, India: Lucknow Publishing House.

Mathur, K.S.
1964 *Caste and Ritual in a Malwa Village.* Bombay: Asia Publishing House.

Mines, Mattison
1972 "Muslim Social Stratification in India: The Basis for Variation." *South Western Journal of Anthropology,* vol. 28.

Hussain, Mrs. Iqbalunnisa
1940 *Changing India. A Muslim Woman Speaks.* Bangalore: Hosali Press.

Mujeeb, M.
1967 *The Indian Muslims.* London: George Allen and Unwin Ltd.

Nelson, Cynthia
1974 "Public and Private Politics: Women in the Middle Eastern World" *American Ethnologist,* vol. 1, no. 3.

Papanek, Hanna
1973 "Purdah: Separate Worlds and Symbolic Shelter." *Comparative Studies in Society and History,* vol. 5, no. 3.

Sen, Dinesachandra
1920 *The Folk Literature of Bengal.* Calcutta: The University Press.

Titus, Murray
1959 *Islam in India and Pakistan.* Calcutta: Y.M.C.A. Publishing House.
1922-232 "Mysticism and Saint Worship in India." *Muslim World,* vol.   12. pp. 129-141.

Vreeda-de-Stuers, Cora
1968 *Parda: A Study of Muslim Women's Life in Northern India.* Assen, The Netherlands: Royal Van Gorcum.

Women, Law, and Social Change in Iran

SHAHLA HAERI

The purpose of this essay is to explore possibilities under which changes in law may or may not meet the aims of social reform in creating new norms of behavior. It will be argued that in an Islamic state, the imposition of a Western code of law seems to be inadequate for creating new norms and habits. It will also be argued that whenever there are significant inconsistencies between the customary approved behavior and behavior required by law, two outcomes may follow. Either the popular demands will force a revision or modification of the new law, or under strict enforcement the law might be adopted in form but not in spirit.

As a case in point, the changes in the legal status of Muslim Iranian women will be discussed. Here my concern is with urban middle-class women. The case of Iranian women is particularly illuminating in that it demonstrates the utilization of law as a determining agent of organized action for achieving social change, and illustrates the limits of the use of such laws to induce social change. One of the noteworthy experiences of Muslim societies under the impact of the West has been in regard to their legal system. Baxbaum (1967) demonstrates that the "intrusion" of the Western laws in the developing countries has generally been superficial, with a substantial portion of the population still using traditional institutions.[1] In Iran, Western influence has been more apparent on the judiciary system of Muslim Iran than on any other system (Banani 1961).

In accordance with traditions of Iranian Shi'ism,[2] until the constitutional revolution of 1906-7 there were two systems of laws: (1) *Shari'ah*, or the Divine Law, which was concerned with human beings' social behavior and was based on the *fegh*, Islamic jurisprudence; and (2) the *Urf* — custom, known also as *Qanun* (administrative laws), which was based not only on a series of precedents or regulations but also on the orientation of the monarch in power (Arasteh 1970; Pfaff 1963: 61; Gibb 1957: 120). The function of the *Urf* courts was to have jurisdiction over matters involving the state. In practice, Banani argues, "the unstable governments of Iran had defaulted nearly all judicial authority to the *Shari'ah* courts" 1961:68.

In 1911 a bold step for the reorganization of the judiciary system was taken. Adolph Perni, a French jurist, was selected to supervise a committee for the organization and formulation of a civil code. Meanwhile, religious leaders pressured the government to guarantee and to specify that no laws that are contradictory to the *Shari'ah* (Islamic laws) should be enacted (Banani 1961: 69).

The history of "modern" Iran starts with the beginning of Reza-Shah's reign (1925-41). During this period Iranian society went through an intense phase of industrialization. The country was suddenly bursting with highly advanced technological machinery imported from the West. Western influence, which had been penetrating Iran slowly in the past two or three centuries, gained momentum and eventually dominated the country in the form of Western science and technology.

During this period the *Shari'ah*, which constituted the basis of the judiciary system in Iran, went through further significant changes. Early in 1925 a committee was formed within the Ministry of Justice that presented the *Majlis* (Parliament) with the first volume of Civil Code. The new code was a combination of a secularized *Shari'ah* and a verbatim translation of the civil code of France. In matters regarding family problems and personal status, it was a "codification, simplification and unification of the *Shari'ah*" (Banani 1961: 71). In conformity with the orthodox Islamic laws, for instance, which gave the absolute right of divorce to the husband, the Civil Code specified all *Shari'ah* causes for divorce in Articles 1057-58 and 1133-1142.

The vital legal blow to the status of *Shari'ah* came about when the *Majlis* passed laws on March 12, 1932, prohibiting the *Ulama* from registering legal documents such as transactions concerning property, marriage, or divorce. Registering documents had formerly been one of the greatest functions of the religious figures in the community and a significant source of revenue for them. These matters were subsequently placed under the authority of the civil courts, *nazmiya*. Although the power of the *Shari'ah* courts and the *Ulama* was curtailed, because of the lack of well-defined procedures for the civil courts, the *Shari'ah* courts continued to have jurisdiction over matters pertaining to marriage and divorce, *waqf* (religious endowment) guardianship, wills, and so forth. Present laws are often a perplexing mismatch of the *Shari'ah* and the Western secular codes (Banani 1961).

The influence of the West, however, has been less pronounced on the family institution, its ideology and functions than on other institutions. As Banani (1961: 80) argues, the traditional *Shari'ah* concept proved more lasting in laws pertaining to marriage, divorce, family relations, and crime against morality than in any other areas. As will be shown, the laws that have dealt specifically with family and/or women have been the least effective of all. Similarly, a series of studies of the reception of Western law in Turkey have demonstrated that Western laws are readily accepted in commercial activities, governmental bureaucracies, and business affairs. Their influence, however, is minimal in matters "involving expressive activities and basic beliefs and institutions, such as family life and marriage habits . . . despite explicit laws trying to change them" (Dror 1957: 800).

Muslim Family

Family, from the Islamic point of view, is an extended network of kin related by blood or through marriage, living and working together toward a common goal, namely the prosperity and happiness of all its members. According to Hussein Nasr (1967:16), "The Muslim family is the miniature of the whole Muslim society and its firm basis." The role of the family is emphasized in *Shari'ah*, the Divine Law, and is regarded as the stable unit of society that reflects the "patriarchal and masculine nature" of the Islamic society. Similarly, Bill and Leiden (1974) argue that the political system of patrimonialism has been prevalent in most of the Middle Eastern societies. Within the Muslim family, authority is the prerogative of the father, and the members of the household stand in an inferior relation to him. They obey him; and the patriarch, the father, commands them in the "belief that his right and their duty are part of an inviolable order that has the sanctity of immemorial tradition" (Weber in Benedix 1962: 33).

Woman, on the other hand, is the "queen" of the household, and the family domain is her undeniable world. The "Muslim man is in a sense the guest of his wife at home" (Nasr 1967: 115). She is to run the household efficiently and pleasantly. At the hands of the mother and other female relatives, young children develop the habits of discipline and learn cultural norms and values. It is her divine duty to bring up obedient and decent children. The wife's primary obligation, however, is obedience to her husband. Unlike the relationship of competition between men and women in Western societies, the relationship between the sexes in Muslim families is viewed as complementary in accordance with the unifying spirit of *Shari'ah*. (See Papanek, 1973: 104-5 on complementarity between and interdependence of men and women in Muslim Pakistan.)

The Muslim family, reflective of Muslim society, is a highly sex-segregated unit in which the division of labor is allocated along the sex lines. The concepts of honor and shame — not exclusive to Muslim societies — have influenced greatly the division of labor and role within the Muslim family. "The male of the family as father, husband, or brother, is responsible for guarding the female's sexual honor . . . His own sexual freedom is assured, but he must be always on guard against the aggression of other — equally free — males toward the women of *his* family" (Youssef 1974: 83). Clearly, from the Islamic point of view, a woman's place is at home, i.e., in the "private domain," and her duties, although not limited, are concentrated on childrearing and taking care of the household. Men, on the other hand, not only share the "private domain" — in the form of family life — with women, but they are also to participate in social, economic, and political activities outside of their homes. To men belongs the "public domain."[3]

In discussing the Muslim Iranian family, one must take note of the trichotomous structure of the Iranian society: tribal, rural, and urban. In addition, differences between socioeconomic classes, religious and ethnic identities need also to be taken into consideration. Families in different types of Iranian communities, though structurally somewhat similar, are functionally different depending on their particular mode of subsistance. In the rural and tribal setting where the family is an economic unit, women's participation in the household production is needed and complements that of men.[4] Men as well as women work actively toward "making their living"[5]. As such, the division between "private" and "public" domains is of little empirical and theoretical importance.

In urban areas, unlike the other two communities, the family is no longer a unit of economic production. With the advent of Westernization, growth of the urban centers,[6] and rapid spread of the "occupational system," the urban family has moved from a consanguine to a conjugal type of family. In the process of transition it seems to have lost its productive function and has become, economically, a consumer unit. Family members are divided into the categories of breadwinners and dependents. Men have gained higher status from employment by "earning a living" for the family, while women have had a decline in status and have been economically dependent (Women's Bureau of Social Research, n.d.).

It has been argued that "Crucial to a woman's status is the measure of her contribution to subsistence *and* her control over its products. Working hard to feed the family is not enough to secure her status, but controlling the products of subsistence is" (Beck 1974: 8). Urban women—who constitute the primary focus of this essay—participate less in the subsistence activities of the household, and have no productive roles save that of the maternal and domestic[7] (Beck 1974: 16) . It is against this background that one has to look at the recent legal changes and their subsequent impact on the status of Iranian women.

Legal Reforms And Their Impact On Iranian Women

Three major legal reforms in the status of women—the Unveiling Act of 1936, the Suffrage Act of 1963, and the Family Protection law of 1967—merit particular attention. These laws have been promulgated and used as direct agents of social change in the hope of adjusting the status of women to the rapid technological and economic changes of the country on the one hand, and to improve the international image of the society on the other. In the pages that follow I shall discuss each law in some detail.

Iranian Women Unveiled

In most of the known human societies, people have developed often elaborate norms and habits of proper dressing. The concept of covering oneself varies from culture to culture and from community to community. In Iran, covering oneself (*hejab*) is crucial for women. Muslim women, according to *Shari'ah* tradition, ought to be covered, *mahjub*, and can leave bare only their faces and the palms of their hands— still a point of dispute among Muslim theologians of different sects in Islam. Muslim Iranian girls, early in their lives, are socialized to the rules of modesty in appearance and in deed. They are taught to cover their bodies appropriately and to appear respectfully dressed in public and in the presence of men. In Iran, veiling or covering the woman's entire body, has been traditionally practiced.

In 1936 a decree from the monarch was handed down to the Iranian women that outlawed veiling, a centuries-old tradition. Veiling, a pre-Islamic practice of the aristocracy, was adopted by women of other socioeconomic classes by the time Islam was firmly established in Iran in the seventh century A.D.[8]

Veiling seems to me to be a symbolic manifestation and a further extension of the walls that surround the Iranian courtyards. The following is a brief analogy between walls and veils that may express some of the structural features and functions of veiling in Iran.

The courtyard of the Iranian house, traditional or modern, is surrounded by high walls and is "veiled" off from outsiders. The traditional houses of the middle and upper classes usually consisted of two parts: *biruni* (literally "outside"), the man's principal domain, and the *andaruni* ("inside"), inhabited predominantly, though not exclusively, by women.[9] Women in *andaruni* received guests, took care of the household, and nursed their children. For men, *andaruni* was a place where they shared comforts or discomforts of a family life with their wife or wives and could rest, dine, sleep, and seek warmth and affection. On the other hand, *biruni* was a place for business. Women were allowed to go to *biruni* only for cleaning purposes. Walls and veils are a constant reminder not only of the segregation of men and women in the family but of their related "domains" in the society.

Walls and veils are both physical symbols and reflections of the sex-segregated social structures of Muslim Iranian society. Once outside of their homes, women needed another protective device to keep the segregation of the sexes intact. The veil replaced the protective walls and became woman's shield in public. A woman without a veil (*chaddor*), like a house without walls, was indeed a conspicuous phenomenon in Iran. While walls give the house a sense of privacy and security, veils reassure, isolate, and protect women hidden behind them. A house without walls is an open invitation to trouble. Similarly a woman without a veil is vulnerable and exposed[10]. It is interesting to note that the word *manzel* (meaning house, lodging, dwelling, household) has often been used to refer to one's wife or womenfolk.

Veiling in Iran was (and is) symbolic of a way of life — not a simple fad that could be changed with fashion. It legitimized: (1) the segregation of the sexes in the family and society and prescribed for them different quarters within as well as outside the family; (2) the concept of women as the weaker sex (*zaeifeh*, literally weak) who need protection; and perhaps as a result of the other two, (3) the exclusion of women from public and professional occupations, since such jobs would inevitably place them in direct and close contact with men.

The observation of veiling concretely and visibly defined the relationship between men and women in public. Women felt secure beneath their veils, and men had little difficulty in knowing how to treat a veiled lady. Both men and women knew quite well what to do and how to do certain things (or not to do them) in the presence of a member of the opposite sex. As the veil was taken away and the old practice of veiling was broken down, confusion and uncertainty in the expected behavior sprang up. This could be attributed to the fact that unveiling was not accompanied by any meaningful political rights for women. Neither were women provided with social or economic opportunities. The few newly established schools were sex segregated (even nowadays public schools through the elementary and secondary levels are primarily segregated according to sex). In short, although the state gave women support and legitimized unveiling, the traditional and cultural patterns prevailed and neutralized the state legitimations.

In order to implement the unveiling law, Iranian women were ordered to take off their veils and to appear in public dressed in European style cloth and hats! For five successive years policemen and soldiers harrassed and molested women and tore apart anything on their heads except a European hat. Most women refused to leave their homes and some did not go out of their homes so long as the law was strictly enforced (i.e. up to 1941). The ones who dared to disobey the law and ventured outside in their veils paid an extremely high price for their insubordination. Olive Suratgar (1951:132) has made the following observations: "I was in time to see police tearing silken scarves from the women's heads and handing them back in ribbons to their owners; for anything even remotely resembling a veil was forbidden." To enforce the new norms of unveiling further, "All employees of Government bureaus, banks, municipalities and public undertakings were informed that their next month's salaries would be paid, not to themselves, but to their wives and that these ladies must come to claim them wearing hats" (ibid).

Under these conditions it requires little imagination to understand why the Unveiling Act created such an uproar of protest from people of all walks of life.

After the law was somewhat relaxed in 1941, some women resumed their traditional customs and discarded European clothing for a more familiar kind of dress. A small minority of women from higher socioeconomic classes adopted the new mode of clothing and have continued to dress in Western costumes. Women who took advantage of the new situation, however, found themselves in all kinds of predicaments. On the one hand, they had the support of the new laws and could appear unveiled in public and, even more than that, they could pursue their education and a possible profession. But on the other hand, the structure of the family, the society, and even the schooling remained sex-segregated and unchanged. These organizations sanctioned norms and patterns of behavior that were often in contradiction to the unveiling laws. Stated differently, these women did not have the support of the traditional legitimations and were left vulnerable to mistreatment and unfair judgments. Even though on the surface unveiled women appeared to "behave" unconspicuously, there was an underlying tension and extreme self-consciousness which, I believe, has persisted up to this day.

In summary, to regard the veil as the source of injustice and the cause of women's second-class citizenship in Iran is to misunderstand the fundamental obstacles—ideological as well as economic—facing women. I am not, of course, ignorant of the fettering quality that a veil can possess, nor am I by any means opposed to unveiling per se. My objections are to the method through which the law in Iran was introduced and enforced. Had the law made unveiling a voluntary matter with women first educated to the inconveniences of veiling, the aftermath of this whole process most likely would have been very different and a great deal of personal agony might have been spared.

Like the Unveiling Act, women's suffrage was a decree from the monarch, but unlike the former it marked a turning point in the legal status of Iranian women. The Suffrage Act created strong opposition from the *Ulama*, religious leaders, and the *bazaries,* merchants. Nevertheless, the Iranian Suffrage Act was proclaimed at a time when there was a relatively broader support for it.

Under the Provisions of the Iranian Constitution granted in 1906-07, the Electoral Act, Article 10, specifically stated: "Those deprived of the right to vote shall consist of all females, minors and those under guardians; fraudulent bankrupts, beggars, and those who earn their living in a disreputable way; murderers, thieves, and other criminals punished under Islamic law" (Tuba 1972:27).[11] Women were thus placed in the same category as beggars and criminals regardless of their family background and level of education.

Women's second-class citizenship was legally ended by a decree from the *Shah* on 23 January 1963. Equal electoral rights were granted to women, and subsequently six women were elected to the *Majlis* (Parliament), two of whom were appointed to the Senate. Later a woman was appointed to the Ministry of Education and joined the ranks of women in high offices.

Despite the apparent changes in women's political status, reliable statistics are lacking as to the number of Iranian women who have actually exercised their electoral rights. Duverger (in Boulding 1974: 160) demonstrates that most women around the world seem to vote as their husbands do. From his point of view, suffrage does not in itself breed autonomy in women. Perhaps an ironic result of suffrage in Iran was to give some men two votes to cast on election day! Boulding examines the impact of industrialization on the role and status of women in fifty-eight countries, including Iran, and concludes that suffrage experience does not have a strong impact on the participation of women in the developing nations. Lack of women's participation, she explains, may be attributable to the fact that giving voting rights is primarily a political decision, often undertaken with a view to a nation's international image, and is not necessarily related to existing or intended activity levels of women.

It seems quite clear that the Unveiling and the Suffrage Acts came about as by-products of the country's overall industrialization and economic expansion and not through women's own efforts and struggle.[12] Appreciative as many women are of these acts, it can hardly be claimed that the unveiling and suffrage laws improved women's rights within the family significantly. As a matter of fact, such laws sharpened the contradictions within the family and the society and widened the gap between the legally demanded and traditionally practiced behavior. This is to say that, while women could legally excel and become Ministers, Senators, lawyers, and so forth, they had no rights in matters that were directly related to their lives. They could be divorced unexpectedly, their children could be taken away, and their husbands could marry a second and a third wife. Women still had no legal and political rights within the household and were the second-class citizens within their own families.

In 1967, the socioeconomic development of the country and the slow but steady increase in the literacy rates of women had created a new sociopolitical consciousness and self-awareness among some Iranian women. Iranian women, no longer able to retreat to their protective walls of veils, but also unable to support themselves financially, requested a reform of the existing family laws. Interestingly, however, the women representatives in the Senate and *Majlis* remained quite conservative on women's issues. It was some time before they finally caught up with the rising tide of the time and addressed themselves directly to women's problems and demanded further legal reforms. In addition, and in the spirit of the previous laws, the Iranian legislators sought to update the Iranian family laws. The result was the Family Protection Law of 1967.

The Family Protection Law

The Family Protection Law (FPL) is the first set of laws formulated by the Parliament that is directly related to the needs and welfare of the family in Iran. It was passed by the *Majlis* on

June 15, 1967, and received royal assent on June 24. Contrary to the other two major laws, which were decrees from above, the FPL became law through the Parliament. In it, unlike its two predecessors, the family as a whole was considered, although the welfare of women was the central issue.

The FPL consists of twenty-three articles and one note.[13] The first five articles deal with the procedures to be followed in disputes over divorce and other family conflicts that are defined as civil disputes among husband, wife, children, paternal grandfather, executor, and guardian. Articles 6-7 deal with the duties and responsibilities of the arbitrators in matters regarding predivorce procedures. The legislators have vested jurisdiction in the courts of *Shahristan* (roughly equivalent to municipal court) and *Bakhsh* (magistrate court). The *Shari'ah* courts, however, seem to have continued "to exercise jurisdiction in disputes concerning the essential validity of a marriage or a divorce" (Hinchcliffe 1968: 517).

Orthodox Islamic law gives the absolute right of divorce to the husband. Under the provisions of the Family Law, however, though the husband still retains his right to divorce his wife, he has to apply to the court for a certificate of "incompatibility," *adam-e sazesh*. He no longer can divorce his wife without a specifically stated cause. Similarly, a woman applying for divorce must file a petition with the court for a certificate of incompatibility. Articles 8, 9, and 10 of the act specify that a couple seeking divorce must provide the court with sufficient evidence to establish grounds for issuing a certificate of incompatibility.

In addition to the conditions set forth in the Civil Code for the dissolution of marriage and divorce (arts. 1121-1142), article 11 of FPL specifies that both husband and wife can apply for a certificate of incompatibility if one or more of the following conditions be met:

(1) imprisonment of either spouse for five years or more,

(2) addiction of either spouse (for example, addiction to drugs, alcohol, gambling, and the like, which in the court's

view is harmful to the other spouse or the family),

(3) second marriage of the husband without the first wife's consent or permission,

(4) desertion of family,

(5) conviction of either spouse, by the court, for an offense that is repugnant to the honor and prestige of the family.

Article 17 of the Family Protection Law states: "the provisions of article II shall be inserted in the marriage document in the form of a condition of the contract of marriage, and an irrevocable power of attorney for the wife to execute a divorce will be explicitly provided" (Hinchcliffe 1968 : 519). The insertion of article 17 may seem meaningless at first glance. In reality, however, this article bridges the gap between *Shari'ah* and the secular law by recognizing the husband, in accordance with the orthodox *Shari'ah* and the Constitution, as the one who actually has the right of divorce. Under the FPL, the divorce is granted to a woman by her husband. She can divorce herself under her "power of attorney" on behalf of her husband. In other words, the right of the wife to divorce herself is bestowed on her by her husband, and is inserted in the marriage contract. Through this "legal strategem," the legislators have not only paid lip service to *Shari'ah*, but have also prevented a complete break with the Fundamental Law and thus the Constitution. A wife wishing to exercise her power of attorney must also obtain a certificate of incompatability (art. 9). Aside from article 11, which will be inserted in all marriage contracts, a couple can make any other conditions or provisions in accordance with article 1119 of the Civil Code (Hinchcliffe 1968: 520). It is important to note here that according to Islamic tradition, marriages in Iran had always been made in the form of a contract. Farsighted women (or their guardians) could insert conditions to further safeguard their rights.

Also, in accordance with the spirit of the *Shari'ah*, the act emphasizes the need for reconciliation of the parties. Once the certificate of incompatibility is issued, it will remain valid for only three months, during which the party must proceed to the final divorce. If the parties do not report to a "divorce notary" within this specified period, the certificate becomes invalid. According to the FPL, once the certificate of incompatability is recognized by the divorce notary, it becomes irrevocable (*Bā'en*). (A divorce is considered to be *Bā'en* when the right of the husband to revoke the divorce is curtailed.) This three-month period is equivalent to the traditional *'idda*. *'Idda* is a time, approximately three months, during which a husband who has repudiated his wife can revoke the divorce by simply going back to her. The *'idda* of a nonpregnant woman is three menstrual cycles, and of a pregnant women until the delivery of the child.

Although the woman still maintains the right to her *nafaghe* (alimony) during *'idda* under the FPL, no provisions have been made for the payment of alimony to the divorced wife beyond the three months of *'idda*. The amount of *nafaghe* during *'idda* will be decided by the court (art. 12). Islamic marriage law, however, has recognized the right of women to brideprice (*mehrieh*). *Mehrieh* is legally obligatory and women are entitled to it anytime before or after the consummation of marriage (arts. 1078-1101 of the Civil Code). Traditionally, *mehrieh* has been paid to women in the case of divorce and is meant to provide financial security for a divorced woman. Nowadays in Iran, under 40 percent of women can obtain their brideprice after their divorce (*Kayhan*, Jan. 6, 1973).[14]

According to traditional Islamic law, a mother could retain the custody of her sons until the age of two and her daughters until the age of seven. Their custody would automatically pass into the hands of their father after reaching those specified ages. Under the provisions of Family Law, the couple seeking divorce must decide and make proper arrangements for the custody of the children. However, when the court issues the certificate of incompatibility, if the parties have not decided on the custody question, the court will decide and make the necessary arrangements (art. 12). Either of the spouses or both can be responsible for the payment of the children's maintenance. Article 13 of the act allows the court, or either of the parties, or any relative of the children, or the public prosecutor to ask the court for a revision of its previous decision to change the custody of the children accordingly (Hinchcliffe 1968: 520).

Although polygyny has not been forbidden, it has been somewhat restricted (art. 14). If a man wishes to marry a second wife while still married to his first wife, he must obtain the *permission of the court*. The court, in turn, will grant permission only when assured of the man's financial ability to maintain two wives equally. Usually, the first wife is informed of her husband's plan before the court reaches a decision. If a court grants permission for a second marriage to a man while the first wife refuses to consent, the court sees this as a legitimate ground for the first wife to file a petition for divorce. (art. 11, clause C).

Notice the inconsistency between the law and cultural reality in Iran. All that the law has required, presumably to combat polygyny, is the first wife's knowledge of her husband's second marriage. Because of their culturally less favorable position and their economic dependence, in the case of a husband's second marriage, it is most likely that women will give their consent rather than apply for divorce. If a man marries a second wife without the court's permission, he may be sentenced up to two years imprisonment. The second marriage, though not validated, remains "*moa'lagh*" (afloat) until the court reaches a final decision about the disobedient husband.

Finally, under the Family Law, the husband may ask the court to intervene on his behalf to prevent his wife from engaging in a profession or occupation that is "repugnant to his family honor," or even hers (art. 15).

Immediately after the enactment of FPL, women flooded the corridors of the Ministry of Justice pleading for divorce. Apparently the number of women applicants was three times higher than that of men (*Kayhan*, June 10, 1967). Interestingly, however, most of these women did not actually pursue divorce. They were using the threat of divorce as a legal leverage to improve their bargaining position in family disputes. In actuality, more men than women obtained divorce permission (*Kayhan* July 22, 1970).

In a recent survey of 378 women applying for divorce, it was found that the divorce request in most of these cases (over 80 percent) was based on husbands' extreme cruelty. In spite of their husbands' punitive and harsh attitude, these women were willing to remain "married" if only their husbands would support them financially (Women's Bureau of Social Research, n.d.).

Professional occupations and working on paid and public jobs, outside of one's home, traditionally has been a man's prerogative. In the past two or three decades Western influence has been a major factor in encouraging the government to provide and persuade women to participate in the social and public activities outside of their household. Notwithstanding the unreliability of the statistics in Iran, the majority of women in Iran are considered to be economically "inactive" (87.5 percent according to the 1966 census, also the *Yearbook of Labor Statistics*, 1973).[15] Considering the economic dependence of women, the social stigma attached to the unmarried woman, and the strong attachment of women to their children, it is not difficult to understand why they "prefer" to remain married, no matter what.

"It has been almost ten years since the beginning of the Revolution," (White Revolution) says female Senator Manoochehrian, "but the only difference the law has made is that now men walk through corridors of the Ministry of Justice to divorce their wives" (*Zan-e-Ruz* No. 360, February 1971). There are still women divorced unexpectedly, or forced to file a divorce petition by their husband's continual harrassment. For instance, a man with two wives deceived his first wife into divorce. He promised to marry her after a divorce in order to get exemptions from the military service for their eldest son. She agreed to his deal, and was subsequently divorced. The son was not exempted and the husband did not marry her again (*Kayhan*, June 18, 1974). Lack of a social security system for women in Iran and high rates of unemployment among them deprive women of retirement benefits. A divorced woman is entitled to alimony for only three months, and that is only to ascertain whether or not she is pregnant.

Although polygyny has not been outlawed, it has been made conditional. All that the law has changed, claims Senator Manoochehrian, is "to have put the hardship of polygyny at the shoulder of judges" (*Zan-e-Ruz* No. 360, February 1971). Most men apply for a second marriage when their first wives have lost their youth and beauty and they want a "change of taste." Examples of such cases are abundant. For instance, a man who already had two wives and five children married a third young woman, for which he was imprisoned (*Kayhan*, Aug. 26, 1967). In another case, twelve men were permitted to marry second wives because the court decided they were financially able to maintain their wives equally (*Kayhan*, Dec. 11, 1967). Again, in another case, a fifty-eight-year-old man was arrested upon his wife's request. He was reported to be in another city, married to a younger woman. He had been married to his first wife for thirty-eight years (*Kayhan*, July 23, 1970).

The FPL does not make any provisions for temporary marriages. The word for temporary marriage, *mut'a*, is Arabic in origin, meaning pleasure. Temporary marriage, as practiced among the Twelver *Shi'i* Muslims, is a type of marriage in which the duration as well as the brideprice (*mehrieh*) must be specified, otherwise the marriage is void (arts. 1075-1077 and 1095 of the Civil Code). At the end of the specified period, the marriage is automatically dissolved, and the partners are freed. Whether or not temporary marriages were (or are) popular and/or much practiced among Iranians will never be fully known for two reasons. The first reason involves the rather easy process of the *mut'a*, which bypasses registration as opposed to the ritualistic process of the permanent marriage. The second reason is the cultural stigma attached to *mut'a* marriages.

Temporary marriage (*mut'a*) is unquestionably another form of polygyny. Although the FPL was silent on this very delicate matter, some of the other provisions of the law have had a noticeable impact on the structure of temporary marriage. According to the marriage laws of Iran a man, single or married, can have, through temporary marriage, as many temporary wives as he desires for as short as one hour or as long as ninety-nine years! A woman, on the other hand, can have only one temporary husband at a time, provided she is not engaged in a permanent marriage at the same time. After the dissolution of the marriage, she is to keep *'idda*, a waiting period of forty-five days or two menstruating cycles, before she can lawfully marry another temporary husband. Married women are prohibited from having temporary husbands for no matter how short a duration. Although the marriage law and *Shari'ah* have left men and unmarried women free to choose a temporary spouse with no restrictive provisions, the FPL requires that, not only every marriage must be registered with the court, but also court permission must be obtained for a second marriage. Notaries have been warned that their licenses will be canceled if the law is breached. In the case of a breach, a maximum of two years imprisonment awaits both disobedient notary and husband. Again, note the inconsistencies between the new and the old laws in Muslim Iran: on the one hand both *Shari'ah* and the civil code sanction and legitimize the institution of temporary marriage, but on the other hand the FPL, by remaining quiet on this matter, has created circumstances for which there are neither legal nor traditional solutions.

This apparent contradiction between the *Shari'ah* and the law accounts for much confusion and resentment on the part of the people. Because of the nature of temporary marriage, accurate statistics of its practice are often difficult to obtain.

However, according to the statistics of the Ministry of Justice, in the years 1965-67 temporary marriages reached their highest peak, 590 men and 613 women for the first temporary marriage.[16] In the following years, from 1968 to 1971, temporary marriages seem to have been on the decline (271 men and 249 women). This decline might be due to the regulations on marriage imposed by the FPL. People, for personal as well as ideological reasons, are unwilling to register their temporary marriages.

A temporary wife, for example, describes her case as follows: "A very kind man with sweet words and manners persuaded me to marry him on account of his wife's sickness. He told me to allow him to marry me temporarily, since the process of divorce was quite long and troublesome, and he didn't want to wait. So I married him. It has been four years since, and he still refuses to marry me permanently or to get birth certificates for our two children. Now I don't know what to do and how to send my children to school when they reach school age" (*Zan-e-Ruz* No. 484, 1974).

Children seem to have been the real victims of unregistered temporary marriages. Legally, the children of a temporary marriage have the same status as the children of a permanent marriage. Under the provisions of the new laws, however, the children of an unregistered temporary marriage have an illegitimate status.[17]

Accordingly, temporary marriage has found a black market in the cities of Iran and is on a rapid increase (*Zan-e-Ruz* June 1974). Widows often constitute the majority of temporary wives. These women, who do not have much chance of a second marriage, are often the unwilling victims or the masterminds of temporary marriages. Young girls from urban lower classes constitute the second largest number of temporary wives. Financial necessity is the major reason given for the frequent marriages of both groups.

Conclusion

Undoubtedly the Unveiling Act, the Suffrage Act and the Family Protection Law have been instrumental in providing new opportunities for some urban women in the upper strata of Iranian society. Iranian women have achieved success in all branches of public and governmental work that have been opened to them. In the light of the preceding discussions, however, it can be argued that these legal changes have not been very effective in breaking the traditional norms and habits to reach the desired goals of reform. In spite of many women's high achievements, legal equality and political rights for the majority of women have remained primarily on a theoretical level. In addition, the growing industrialization of the country and the new educational opportunities have not provided educational and economic equality for women.

The shortcomings of these laws can be attributed to at least five interrelated and interdependent factors. The most important of these factors is that the laws—unveiling, suffrage, and FPL— are inconsistent with the *Shari'ah*. The *Shari'ah* constitutes the very basis of the Islamic "legal" and ethical systems that are ingrained in Iranian culture.

The second factor is the political system of patriarchalism and the prevailing masculine attitude in the society. In the executive branch, as in the other governmental branches, male employees dominate the offices. They do not really have their hearts in the laws, and their sympathies lie with people of their own sex rather than with the law.

The third factor is the widespread economic dependence of women. From the Islamic point of view, financial responsibility rests on the man's shoulder. As such, women, i.e. primarily urban women, in most of the Muslim societies traditionally have been excluded from participating in the economic activities of the household, and consequently have been greatly dependent on their men (exceptions are to be made for women of the lower socioeconomic classes).

The fourth factor is lack of judicial control and administrative personnel to supervise and enforce the laws.

Finally, there is women's long imprisonment through illiteracy and their ignorance of the existence of the laws, and hence their inability to utilize such.

In the light of the preceding discussion, it can be strongly argued that the imposition within a society of a particular legal code, Western in this case, often bypasses the inner dynamics of that particular culture and thus fails to generate new modes of behavior. Legal reforms introduced under the conditions described fall short of achieving their aims of reform, and thus remain primarily on a theoretical level.

Addendum

This paper was written a few years before the Iranian Revolution of 1978-79. Therefore the discussion presented is to be read within the perspective of the Pahlavi regime's attempts to "modernize" the society. An analysis of the role and position of women in Iran at the present time requires a completely different approach.

Notes

1. For a similar view about the reception of the Western Law in Turkey, see *International Social Science Bulletin*, vol. 9.

2. Iranian Shi'ism has also been known as Shi'i *Ithna' ashariyah* or "Twelver" Islam.

3. Peggy Sanday makes a distinction between "private" and "public" domains. From her point of view, "the domestic domain includes activities within the localized family unit. The public domain includes political and economic activities that take place or have impact beyond the localized family unit and that relate to control of persons or control of things" (1974: 190).

4. Tribal women exercise a greater influence in the decisionmaking of the family due

to their crucial position in controlling the means of production (Frederick Barth, 1964).

5. In a recent study by Jacqueline Rudolph Tuba, it has been demonstrated that a larger portion of the rural females are "economically active" than urban females residing in the city of Arak (1973: 43). See also the *Iranian Yearbook of Statistics* (1972: 49-60).

6. Iran is among a few countries with a long history of urbanization. However, Iran's recent developments accelerated the growth of urban centers and rural migration. A comparison between the urban and rural population from 1956 to 1966 demonstrates a 7.6% increase in the total urban population from 31.4% in 1956 to 39% in 1966 (Department of Demography, Tehran University, Study No. 16 by Mahammud Mirzaei 1970: 13). By 1973, however, urban population had risen to 43% of total population. Meanwhile rural population had decreased from 62% in 1967 to 57% in 1973 (Bank Markazi Iran 1973: 93).

7. It is important here to point out that often lower-class urban women, by working as domestic servants, have contributed to the economy of the household.

8. Veiling was (and is, though not as overwhelmingly as before) primarily practiced by the urban women. Rural and tribal women did not (and do not) wear the veil; however, their local costumes are modest and covering.

9. Such architecture was more evident primarily in the structure of the house of wealthy families, but the pattern of segregation existed in all households.

10. Any unveiled woman, Iranian or foreigner, who has been in the crowded streets of downtown Tehran has at least one story to tell about being molested by young male strangers.

11. Ironically, the constitutional revolution of 1906, which promised equal rights to all citizens of Iran, ignored women's plea for liberty and equality, and legally stifled women's participation in political affairs (Tuba 1972: 27).

12. Although it is true that in Iran women's struggles and feminist movements have not been overwhelming, women have, nevertheless, helped significantly in bringing about changes not only in the laws but in the attitudes of some portions of the population as well. This essay, however, does not address itself specifically to women's movements or women's participation in social and political movements.

13. This section on Family Protection Law is primarily based on "The Iranian Family Protection Act" by D. Hinchcliffe 1968.

14. Emphasis should be placed on the unreliability of the statistical sources in Iran. *Kayhan,* a daily newspaper, like many other newspapers, may not be the best source of reference. Nevertheless, it is used here to give a general indication, however vague and unreliable.

15. Economic inactivity refers to the number of people who have, at no time, been a part of the labor force. *Iranian Yearbook of Statistics*, 1972: 47 (Salnameh Amari-e-Keshvar 1351).

16. These numbers indicate only the ones who actually cared to register their marriages. As was mentioned, many of such marriages customarily go unrecorded.

17. The International Social Science Bulletin (1957 [9] 7-81) has published a series of interesting articles in which different aspects of the reception of Western law in Turkey are explored. Of particular interest is the question of "legitimacy" or "illegitimacy" of children born of unions unregistered in a court but celebrated tradi-

tionally within the community. Because of the mounting confusion, four times since the adoption of the Swiss Civil Code in 1920s, The Grand National Assembly has passed new laws (i.e., until 1957) to legitimize children born of unregistered marriages.

Bibliography

Abbott, Nabia
    1942   "Women and State in Early Islam," *Journal of Near East Studies* 1:106-26.

Al-Ahmad, Jalal
    1961   *Garbzadegi (West-Strikenness)*, Tehran: (In Persian)

Arasteh, Reza (in collaboration with Josephine Arasten)
    1970   *Man and Society in Iran*. Leiden: E. J. Brill.

    1964   "The Struggle for Equality in Iran," *Middle East Journal*, vol. 18, no. 2 (Spring), pp. 189-205.

Banani, Amin
    1961   *Modernization of Iran, 1921-1941*, California: Stanford University Press.

Barth, F.
    1961   *Nomads of South Persia: The Baseri Tribe of the Khamseh Confederacy*, London: George Allan and Unwin.

Boulding, Elise
    1974   "Women as Role Models in Industrializing Societies: A Macro-system Model of Socialization for Civic Competence," in *Sourcebook in Marriage and the Family*, 4th ed. Edited by M. B. Sussman, Boston: Houghton Miffin Co.

Beck, Lois G.
    1974   "Theoretical Perspective on the Position of Women in Iran." Paper presented at the Eighth Annual Meeting of the Middle East Studies Association, Boston, Mass. Nov. 6-9, 1974.

Benedix, R.
    1962   *Max Weber: An Intellectual Portrait*, Garden City, N.Y.: Doubleday and Company.

Bill, J., and Leiden, C.
    1974 *The Middle East: Politics and Power*, Boston: Allyn and Bacon.

Buxbaum, David C.
   1967 *Traditional and Modern Legal Institutions in Asia and Africa.*
   Leiden: E.J. Brill.

Dror, Yehezkal
   1958 "Law and Social Change." *Tulane Law Review* 33: 158-59.

The Family Protection Law
   1973 (Quanun Hemayate Khanevadeh). Tehran: Farokhi Institution. (In Persian)

Fried, M.H.
   1967 *The Evolution of Political Societies,* New York: Random
   House.

Gibb, H. A. R.
   1962 "The Structure of Religious Thought in Islam," in *The
   Muslim World* 38, no. 3.

Hamidi, A.
   1972-73 *Iranian Civil Law (Qanun Madani),* vols. 1, 2, 3. Tehran:
   Amir Kabir Institution. (In Persian)

Hinchcliffe, Doreen
   1968 "The Iranian Family Protection Act," *International and
   Comparative Law Quarterly* 2 (April 17): 516-21.

Iran Almanac
   1971

Iranian Yearbook of Statistics
   1972-73 (Salnameh Amari Keshvar 1351).

Kayhan Iranian Daily Newapaper.

Levy, Reuben
   1957 *The Social Structure of Islam,* 2d ed. Cambridge: Cambridge
   University Press.

Nasr, Hussein
   1967 *Ideals and Realities of Islam,* New York: Frederick A. Praeger.

Papanek, Hanna
   1973 Men, Women and Work: Reflections on the Two-Person
   Career," in *Changing Women in Changing Societies.* Edited by Joan
   Huber.

Pfaff, H. R.
   1963 "Disengagement from Traditionalism in Turkey and Iran,"
   Western Political Quarterly. March, vol. 16.

Postagioglu, I. E.
   1957 "The Technical Reception of a Foreign Code of Law," *In-*

ternational Social Science Bulletin 9: 54-60.

Rahman, Fazlur
1966　*Islam.* New York: Holt, Rinehart and Winston.

Sanday, P. R.
1974　"Female Status in the Public Domain," *Women, Culture and Society,* Edited by M. Rosaldo and L. Lamphere. Stanford: Stanford University Press.

Suratgar, Olive
1951　*I Sing in the Wilderness,* London: E. Stanford.

Tipps, Dean C.
1973　"Modernization Theory and the Comparative Studies: A Critical Perspective," *Comparative Studies in Society and History* 15.

Tuba, Jacqueline R.
1973　*Macro-system Effects on the Iranian Family, its Cultural Functions and Processes in an Area Undergoing Planned Industrialization:* Arak Shahrestan, 1972, University of Tehran Project no. 15707, Plan Organization, 1973.

1972　"The Relationship Between Urbanization and the Changing Status of Women in Iran, 1956-1966," *Iranian Studies,* vol. 5, no. 1.

Women's Bureau of Social Research
n.d.　*A Case Study of the Causes of Family Disorganization in the City of Tehran.*

Yearbook of Labor Statistics
1973

Youssef, Nadia H.
1974　*Women and Work in Developing Societies,* University of California, Berkeley Publication Monograph Series 15.

Zan-e-Ruz (Today's Woman) Iranian Weekly Magazine.

The Political Mobilization of Women in the Arab World

CAROLYN FLUEHR-LOBBAN

Department of Anthropology
Rhode Island College
Providence, R.I.

Until recently the literature on Arab women has revealed more about the biases of Western writers than it has about the actual lives and activities of women in the Arab world. It has been a literature rife with prejudice, ethnocentrism, and Western chauvinism that reflect a more general and deeper anti-Arabism. The literature on Africa could hardly be said to be better.

The popular literature on Arab women is even worse. On September 9, 1973, the *New York Times* had an article in its "Travel and Resorts" section that dealt exclusively with the position of women in the Arab countries. The article was titled "Where Women Are an Annoyance that Disturbs the Symmetry of Life." Each of the four large photos that accompanied the "objective" account of the degraded position of women in Arab countries were pictures of veiled women. The clear impression conveyed was that all Arab women are veiled, and therefore downtrodden, miserable, and oppressed. The only concession to modernity was a picture of a Saudi woman veiled but wearing sunglasses. That the media project this view is not surprising — veiled women are part of the same Arab package that includes nomads crouching beside camels, obese sheikhs, and dark, shifty eyes on close-up photos of Arab men.

The scientific literature, never quite as guilty of such blatant Western chauvinism, nevertheless had room to improve its description and analysis of women in the Arab world. Increasingly the position of women is being studied by Middle Eastern and North African women, and by Western women whose contact and experience with Arab women has gone beyond the veil to touch and describe the lives of ordinary women.

Increasingly the literature is beginning to answer some of the questions that have disturbed observers of life in the Arab world who have gone beyond the tourist view of oriental rugs, camels, and veiled women. How is it that these apparently weak and pitiable women, so constrained by Arab men and Islam, often stand out as some of the strongest figures in the society? The *hareem* and the physical separation of women from men in Arab society has long been interpreted in the West as suppression of women, as entailing an inferior, degrading existence. In fact, recent ethnographic evidence suggests a different picture of traditional Arab culture, a society segregated by sex to be sure, but a society where the world of women emerges with as much integrity and scope as the world of men (Davis 1973: 12).

Women generally are excluded from formal, public politics, as are women in most of the world. But women have become involved in politics with men under the banner of nationalism, and women have acted to agitate for change in law and social tradition as they define the need for change. There are women's movements in the contemporary Arab world that have long and proud histories, but such movements are rarely discussed in the scientific literature, and are virtually absent from the popular media. The West is not accustomed to think of Arab women in the political arena, and the media are not likely to present Arab women or men in the context of their struggle for independence and national liberation. This essay is an effort to undermine the myth that Arab women are conservative or apolitical. It also seeks to make some suggestions as to the historical contexts in which Arab women are politically mobilized.

In the last several years I have written and published a number of articles dealing with the Sudanese women's movement, a movement with over a quarter century of history behind it. From this research I have become interested in the process of political mobilization of women in a broader sense and have extended my research more generally into the Middle East and Africa. A number of ideas have emerged from the Sudanese material and, in looking at other cases of political involvement of women in the Arab world and Africa, I have generated a series of hypotheses or ideas that I believe to be characteristic of women's participation in the political arena in the Arab world. Here I hope to test these ideas against the data that are available.

First, I want to set forth the hypotheses, and then return to each to support it with evidence from the literature available. The data presented will refer to countries and movements for which there is existing information, including Sudan, Egypt, Algeria, the Palestinian movement, the People's Democratic Republic of Yemen (PDRY) and some reference will also be made to Iraq.

Point 1 — That the political mobilization of women and nationalist movements are strongly associated.

Point 2 — That in countries where armed struggle has been necessary to achieve national liberation, especially in the settler colonial states, the militance demanded of women is greater.

Point 3 — That, as the struggle around nationalism intensifies, some brand of feminism also develops, and in some cases demands for the equality of women become part of the fight for national independence.

Point 4—That the struggle for equal rights for women is greatly aided by a separate women's organization within the nationalist movement: with its separate identity it keeps the woman question on the political agenda in the pre- and post-independence periods.

Point 5—That female participation in nationalist movements may originate among educated elites, but support from working class and peasant women is needed to advance nationalist and feminist political demands.

Let us examine these ideas in light of the information available on the participation of women in modern Arab politics. The first suggestion is that the emergence of women's movements is linked to the emergence of nationalist movements. There is an exceptionally strong case for this.

In Egypt, where the first Pan-Arab feminist organization emerged, women first had their political consciousness raised by a growing spirit of nationalism. In 1919 Egyptian women by the thousands joined the March of the Veiled Women as part of the first Egyptian "revolution" demanding independence from Britain. Four years later Hoda Shar'awi and others who had participated in the 1919 demonstrations organized the Egyptian Feminist Union dedicated to the struggle for the rights of women. Again in 1951, when the nationalist movement had gained tremendous momentum, 10,000 Egyptian women demonstrated at the funeral of those who had fallen in the struggles against the British (Berque 1964: 182).

It is worth noting too that the first Congress for Arab Women, which met in Cairo in 1938 and hosted representatives from many of the Arab countries, was called for the purpose of studying the worsening Palestinian situation. The resolutions passed at this first Pan-Arab women's conference dealt, not with feminist causes, but with the immediate nationalist concerns of the Palestinian people. The resolutions called for an end to the British Mandate in Palestine, an end to Jewish emigration and the transfer of Arab lands to Jews in Palestine, a rejection of any plan to divide Palestine and aid to the Palestinian cause (Rasheed, Asfahami, and Mourad 1973: 12).

In Algeria the first time in modern history that women participated in a public demonstration was in 1939, when several thousand veiled women marched under the banner "Land, Bread, and Freedom." Of course the part played by Algerian women in the final phases of national liberation is better known—this will be dealt with later. Here I want to point out that the first mass participation of Algerian women was in a nationalist demonstration, not in a civil rights protest demanding an end to the veil or the abolishing of polygyny.

In Sudan the Woman's League was formed in the same year that the Sudanese Communist party was organized, having as its primary task the ending of nearly a half- century of British colonialism. The Sudanese CP was the first political organization in the country to open its party membership to women and to establish female emancipation as part of its more general anticolonialist program.

The struggle of the Palestinian woman began as early as 1920, the year of the first Palestinian revolt against the British Mandate in Palestine in which women joined in protests and demonstrations. In 1929 a general conference of Palestinian women held in Jerusalem was attended by 300 women. Resolutions were passed demanding the withdrawal of the Balfour Declaration and the prohibition of Zionist emigration into Palestine. As a result of this conference the Palestine Women's Federation was formed. The birth of the first Palestinian women's organization was simultaneous with the beginning of the resistance to Zionist penetration of Palestine.

As an early manifestation of Arab solidarity among women, in Iraq the first organized political action by women was in 1948 at the Queen Aliya College, where a demonstration was staged in an effort to have the Iraqi government send troops to assist in the defense of Palestine (*Baghdad Observer* Mar. 15, 1975).

Other examples could be cited of the emergence of women in the context of rising nationalist consciousness. These examples are prominent ones for which information exists. More stories of the courage and determination of Arab women fighting for independence will surely come to light when a new breed of Middle Eastern scholars considers in more depth the rule of women in nationalist struggles.

Let us consider the second point, that the militance demanded of women is greater in the countries where armed struggle has been necessary to achieve national liberation, and especially in the settler colonial states. The settler colonial states are of course Algeria and Palestine.

Settler colonialism is more tenacious because the economic stakes are higher, and frequently armed struggle is necessary to eliminate it. This was the case in Algeria and is a current reality in Palestine.

In Algeria the decision within the F.L.N. (National Liberation Front) to involve women as an integral part of the revolution was a major step because it was understood that this tactic, if not handled properly, could alienate large sectors of the traditional Muslim population. First, married men were contacted, later widows and divorcees, but the flood of unmarried women who wanted to join the FLN was so great that these restrictions had to be dropped (Fanon 1965: 51). The veil and customs related to female dress and public behavior were turned into weapons of struggle, perhaps most heroically in cases where Algerian women donned European dress and carried bombs into the French Quarter. The urban guerrilla phases of the involvement of women in the Algerian national liberation movement is best known, but the support women gave to the armed struggle in the countryside was also critical. Women assumed the responsibilities for village affairs that had been emptied of men either taken by the French as forced labor or fighting against the French. Women themselves were arrested and tortured for collaboration with the nationalists, and in the end the French terrorists even took to shooting indiscriminately at women as well as men on the streets of Algiers (Gordon 1968: 53). Within the FLN, women cadres served as nurses, spies, commandos, and even in some cases combatants. However, it was not until after independence that a separate women's organization, the UNFA (National Union of Algerian Women) was formed.

As the fate of Palestine was sealed and the Palestinian nation was transformed into a settler colonial state under Zionist leadership in Israel, the resistance of the Palestinian people, including Palestinian women, grew. During the 1936 armed revolt against the British, women participated actively, not only by demonstrating against the British, but also by carrying arms and provisions to the fighters. During one battle at Azzoun (July 26, 1936), Fatima Khalil Ghazal was slain by British colonialist bullets.

During the 1948 war, Palestinian women formed a division and volunteered to join the fighting forces. In addition to the scores of women and men and children massacred at Deir Yassin, others, including women, lost their lives fighting the Zionists.

During twenty-seven years of Zionist occupation, a number of Palestinian liberation movements emerged, and with them the role of women took on even more significant proportions, particularly after the 1967 war. Inside occupied Palestine, women formed the nucleus of the resistance against the occupation forces. By the beginning of 1968 many women had joined the ranks of the freedom fighters and carried arms. These activities of women were suppressed the same as those of men—for example, five women were arrested in Nablus in January 1968 and accused of participation in the armed struggle and of hiding Fateh (Palestine National Liberation Movement) fighters as well as acting as liaison personnel for Fateh in the occupied territories.

After 1967 the development of women as cadres, i.e., militants attached to a political party, greatly increased. As members of nationalist political organizations, women are involved in national liberation in the fields of political education, health, and hygiene, as agents in covert operations and even as combatants. Fateh organized the General Union of Palestinian Women, which is open to all Palestinian women; its second conference in Beirut in 1974 was held under the banner "Organizing the efforts of the Palestinian women is essential to the Battle of Liberation" (PLO Information Bulletin 1974).

Historically the Yemeni women took part in the national liberation struggle against British colonialism which gained independence for southern Yemen in 1967. During the anti-colonialist guerrilla war, women participated by acting as intelligence agents, by hiding soldiers and arms and by distributing NFL (National Liberation Front) literature. During the final days preceding independence, women joined in the mass demonstrations demanding independence.

To return to the central point, that the militance demanded of women is greater in the area where armed struggle has been the necessary tactic to gain independence, requires that *militance* be defined. Even though many women in the Palestinian movement, in colonialist-occupied Algeria and Yemen have aided in the wars of independence, I do not necessarily equate female militance with the use of force or armed violence. The development of female militance is a type of political involvement where women *cadres* are linked to political parties, even taking on leadership roles within that party. It is a type of political involvement that cannot be matched by participation in street demonstrations or even in national strikes, both of which are tactics which are temporary, no matter how dramatic. Women as cadres have a commitment to struggle and a dedication to the success of the nationalist program with the knowledge and understanding of women's reward in that freedom.

This leads logically to the third point, that some brand of

feminism develops as the nationalist struggle intensifies.

The Egyptian Feminist Union grew out of the participation of women in the 1919 nationalist demonstrations; the Sudanese Women's Union came into being simultaneously with the nationalist movement; the UNFA in Algeria emerged from the years of protracted struggle against French colonialism; the Palestinian Women's Federation emerged at the beginning of the anti-Zionist protests in Palestine in the 1920's; and the Yemeni Women's Union was formed in 1968 by women militants from the National Liberation Front once independence was achieved. In each of these cases political associations of women had not existed prior to the political events which set them into motion, namely the deepest sentiments of nationalism. In each of these cases a separate women's organization emerged from the nationalist movement and dedicated itself to the twin goals of national sovereignty *and* emancipation for women. The link between nationalism and feminism is a clear and strong one; however, the development of feminist demands and the political consciousness within these organizations depends very much on the leadership and on the political direction that the larger movement takes.

In the Palestinian example, despite many courageous acts by individual Palestinian women, the demand for the full emancipation of women has only been part of the leftist political programs of the PFLP (Popular Front for the Liberation of Palestine) and the DPFLP (Democratic Front).

In Egypt, the Feminist Union developed a life of its own separate from the nationalist movement out of which it sprang, and it raised many demands concerning the rights of women in education, suffrage and in traditional family life.

In the Sudan, the Women's Union agitated for changes in the laws affecting working women, e.g. equal pay for equal work, maternity leave and government pensions for women, while they also campaigned for reforms in the family laws, especially the Islamic divorce laws and the polygyny rule. The

Women's Union also began a program of education to attempt to dissuade women from continuing the practice of customs considered harmful to women, for example, female circumcision and facial scarification for the purpose of ethnic identification. Linked to the Sudanese Communist Party, the Women's Union proposed these changes within an independent and socialist Sudan.

The Women's Union in the People's Democratic Republic of Yemen, which emerged from the national liberation movement, has integrated itself thoroughly with the Yemeni revolution while raising the special demands of women within it. In July 1974 at the first Congress of the Women's Union, a great emphasis was placed on the full incorporation of women in the political, economic and social life of southern Yemen. A special emphasis was placed on increasing participation of women in the People's Militia and on the total eradication of illiteracy among women.

But the greatest victory for the Yemeni woman has come with the new Family Law which was a product of the work of the Women's Union and was promulgated in 1974. Under the new Family Law: 1) forced marriage, especially that of a young girl, has been abolished - only the consent of a woman 16 years of age or more and a man 20 years of age or more is required; 2) polygyny has been outlawed; 3) divorce must be applied for equally by the man and the woman, and child support and alimony depend on which spouse is capable of making such payments; 4) everything in the traditional law dealing with the forced obedience of the wife has been eliminated; 5) bridewealth payments may not exceed the equivalent of $300 and there is some discussion of eliminating all such payments in marriage. Such reforms have been made possible by an alliance between feminist demands and a national liberation movement that has come to state power.

Although the UNFA (National Union of Algerian Women) was not formed until after Algerian independence, it nevertheless drew its support from the high degree of nationalist and feminist consciousness that developed among women during the many years of struggle against French colonialism. In 1965, the year the UNFA was established, it organized a demonstration on March 8, International Woman's Day, in which 10,000 Algerian women of all ages and social backgrounds marched through the streets of Algiers in a show of support for women's rights and in solidarity with the international women's struggles (Ottaway and Ottaway 1970). Feminism in these cases is only roughly analogous to the rise of feminism in modern times in the West. Feminist movements in the Western European countries and in the United States have not been linked to nationalist movements and otherwise progressive political parties. In fact, in some of the movements in the West in which nationalism has been a key feature, the reactionary content of chauvinism, both male chauvinism and national chauvinism, has been dominant. While women both in the Arab countries and in the West are not first-class citizens of nations, they are nevertheless exploited by different social and political systems. In modern politics the main struggle in the Arab world has been anticolonialist and even antifeudalist, and women's political mobilization takes place within the context of larger political struggles around these issues. Women in the West are exploited by capitalism and its ideology of male supremacy, but too often the main struggle has been around the ideology alone rather than the economic system that produces it.

The fourth point is that a separate women's organization greatly aids in the actual achievement of equal rights for women. With its separate identity, an independent women's organization is able to keep the "women question" on the political agenda in the nationalist struggle and in the post-independence phase.

After several decades of existence the Feminist Union established itself as a political force in Egyptian national politics. When Nasser came to power he instituted a number of reforms regarding the status of women that the Union had stressed over the years. Universal suffrage was made law, equal pay for equal work was instituted, and educational and professional opportunities were equalized in law for women. The Feminist Union and its social program, together with the massive participation of women in the final years and months leading up to independence, secured a high priority for women's rights in Nasser's program of reform.

Similarly in Sudan, twenty-five years of agitation for reform, plus the massive involvement of women in the 1964 revolution, brought reforms for women. After 1964 women won the vote and, some years later with the "May Revolution" government of Numieri, reforms in the work laws and in selected areas of the Shari'a were also instituted. While the Women's Union had strong ties to the Sudanese Communist party, it retained a large measure of autonomy and controlled the arena of women and politics in Sudan for well over a quarter century. The existence of the organization and the instituting of reforms by various governments are linked: over the years the Women's Union developed a broad membership with progressive leadership that kept the women's question on the political agenda of Sudanese national politics.

In Algeria during the war of national liberation, women related primarily to the FLN; only after independence was the UNFA launched. Perhaps one measure of the lack of enforcement of progressive gains after the revolution was the lack of a strong, independent women's group during the national liberation struggle. Once UNFA was formed, it adopted a rather passive position within the Ben Bella regime. After the Boumediene counterrevolutionary coup in June 1965, the UNFA opposed the coup but failed to mount an organized opposition. For a time the union ceased functioning altogether because the leadership was paralyzed by indecision as to how to react to the Boumediene traditional and Islamic "revolution." Individual strong members of the union, however, did respond to the new family code proposed in 1966, a code so conservative that it had to be dropped due to vigorous protests from Algerian feminists (Ottaway and Ottaway 1970: 37). In March 1966 the police had to be called in to prevent a massive walkout of UN-FA women from a speech by Boumediene in which he said women should not be treated equally with men in employment opportunities (Humbaraci 1966: 87). Finally UNFA elected a moderate leadership that declared its allegiance to the party of Boumediene, and a split resulted in which the most militant feminists withdrew from the UNFA. Apparently after this UNFA lost its political base among urban progressive women and began proselytizing for the government in the rural areas by recruiting these women into its ranks.

The final point is that female participation in nationalist movements may originate among educated elites, but support from working class and peasant women is needed to advance nationalist and feminist political demands. Educated women, traditionally from the wealthier sectors of the society, have the leisure time and exposure to public affairs that lead to involvement in the nationalist movement by a progressive sector of the local elites.

In Egypt the Feminist Union was formed by women who were basically from bourgeois or petit-bourgeois backgrounds, and the movement retained this character throughout its more than a half century of existence up to the present. Hoda Shar'awi herself was the daughter of a prominent general who had been governor of Upper Egypt; she was well educated and spoke French and Turkish by the time she was thirteen. Her husband was a wealthy merchant, but also an activist in the nationalist movement. Many of the early supporters of the Feminist Union were Cairo University students. And in 1952 it was a contingent of women from the middle class who blockaded the door of the main Barclay's Bank in Cairo to enforce a boycott of the colonialist bank. Essentially the activities of the Feminist Union have been confined to social and cultural affairs, and its fifty-year history has been one where it has acted mainly as a political pressure group agitating for equal rights for women.

Djamila Bouhired and Djamila Boupacha, two women

whose names are among the most famous associated with the Algerian revolution, were both from middle-class backgrounds and were French educated. Others who joined cells in the early days of the struggle were law students, teachers, medical students — individuals whose position would have been privileged had they not opted for involvement in the nationalist movement.

And in the Sudan the first organized group of women formed in 1946 after a nationalist demonstration at Omdurman Secondary School for Girls was broken up by colonialist police. Women were not admitted to the university at this time, so the women in the vanguard were high school students. The Sudanese Women's League was originally based among urban, literate women, but in 1951 it was reorganized as the Sudanese Women's Union, and its membership was extended to working and peasant women. The Women's Union began to penetrate the trade union movement and was heavily responsible for the organizing of the Nurses' Trade Union and the Government Elementary School Teachers' Union. So while the movement did not begin in the working classes, it saw the necessity early on to establish ties there.

The First Congress of the Women's Union of the People's Democratic Republic of Yemen which announced the new Yemeni Family Law was held in the relatively remote region of the Fifth Governorate in the east. Here a special campaign was underway to mobilize the peasant women of the religion. The Women's Union which grew most readily in the capital city of Aden had already mobilized working women into its ranks. The Congress also commemorated the uprisings a year before which overturned the feudal sultans in the region and returned the land to the peasants. After the promulgation of the new Family Law, a major task of the Women's Union has been the education of all Yemeni women to the gains which they have made in the legal arena.

As a final observation, nationalist and feminist politics often emerge among the elite or local bourgeoisie, but if the movement remains in this class the result is limited goals with limited gains for women.

Final Remarks

We have discussed these several points with reference to the mobilization of women in modern Middle Eastern politics, specifically national independence movements. To conclude this discussion, a few more observations could be made.

It is clear that Arab women have had a role, in some cases a major role, to play in the nationalist movements. This should do away with the myth that Arab women are conservative or apolitical.

Further we have seen that Arab women cannot possibly conduct a struggle for emancipation in isolation from the larger struggle for national independence. To be sure, under colonialism the position of women did not improve — education was provided last to women, if at all, and males among the colonized population were favored with the low-level colonial administrative jobs. Although colonialism exacerbated previously existing inequalities in Arab society, it did not create them. And the political programs of several of the nationalist movements have recognized this and have made considerable efforts to do away with exploitation and oppression in all of its forms.

It is interesting to note that in some respects the greatest advances have been made in some of the most "backward" areas, that is, in the countries where the local colonial power or the feudal regime has neglected local and economic development. I refer to southern Yemen and to Algeria before independence. Here a couple of factors are involved. In the first place, in armed struggle the mobilization of a greater percentage of the population is required, so the involvement of women is needed to handle increased personnel demands for the "normal" operation of society and the waging of war. In this situation, women are called upon to do things they have never done before — conducting village affairs, acting as the sole economic support of families, and even joining the liberation armies. In this situation of general social upheaval, which is a concomitant of armed nationalist struggle, opportunities for major change on a grander scale seem possible.

It is essential that women and men in the West not judge the liberation of women in the Arab world by Western standards. Many Europeans who have visited Algeria since independence have been shocked to see that the use of the veil is still in existence. From Westerners, who are accustomed to equate the veil with female suppression, this reaction is predictable. While I think that there are a number of reasons why gains for women in Algeria have not advanced in the post-independence phase, I do not think the continued use of the veil is critical among them. Political failures of organization and the overthrow of the Ben Bella regime are more important actions.

Others in the West take a superficial view and identify a liberated woman as one who wears miniskirts, works as a stewardess or secretary, smokes and drinks and perhaps refuses to marry, i.e., an Arab woman who approximates the behavior and manner of a "liberated" woman in the West. The emancipation of women has also been linked to the accumulation of degrees, particularly university degrees, which are regarded as certificates of emancipation. The women's movement of FRELIMO, the Mozambican liberation movement from which the Arab liberation groups could learn a great deal, has criticized this attitude. They say that genuine emancipation comes as women participate in the transformation of a social order as part of a party seeking national independence and liberation for women. To seek individual liberation through higher degrees is a false and misleading path.

And finally, spontaneous outbursts or uprisings of women are not enough to achieve liberation. Organization must replace spontaneity, and a constant vigilance must be maintained to see that women are effectively represented in social, political, and economic institutions, and in this way real equality between man and woman will be achieved.

Bibliography

Baghdad Observer
   1975   "Reminiscences from Pre-revolutionary Struggle of Iraqi Women," March 15.
Berque, Jacques
   1964   *The Arabs*, New York: Praeger.
Davis, S.S.
   1973   "A Separate Reality; Moroccan Village Women," Paper read at the Middle East Studies Association, Milwaukee, Wisconsin.
Fanon, Frantz
   1967   *A Dying Colonialism*. New York: Grove Press.
Fluehr-Lobban
   1977   "Agitation for Change; the Sudanese Women's Movement," in *Sexual Stratification*, A. Schlegel, Ed., Columbia University Press.
   1978   "People's Yemen Since Independence," paper read at Arab-American University Graduates' meeting, Minneapolis, Minn.
Gordon, David
   1967   *Algeria: An Essay on Change.* Harvard Middle East Monographs.
Humbaraci, Arslan
   1966   *Algeria: The Revolution that Failed.* New York, Praeger.
Palestine Resistance Bulletin
   1971   "DPFLP Women," October.
Ottaway, David and Ottaway, Marina
   1970   *The Politics of a Socialist Revolution.* Berkeley: University of California Press.
PLO Information Bulletin
   1974   *Palestine Images,* October.
Rasheed, Baheega; Asfahami, T.; and Mourad, Samia
   1973   "The Egyptian Feminist Union," Anglo-Egyptian Bookshop.
Some Aspects of the Yemeni Women's Struggle, published by the Ministry of Information, People's Democratic Republic of Yemen on the occasion of the International Women's Year, 1975.
People's Democratic Republic of Yemen, Ministry of Information, "A

Summary of the Experience of the Revolution in Democratic Yemen,"
1974.

In addition to the above sources, additional information was gathered
through personal interviews with leaders of the Yemeni Women's
Union in Aden in 1975.

Bibliography

Abaden, Nermin. "Turkey." *Women in the Modern World*. Edited by Raphael Patai. New York: The Free Press, 1967, pp. 82-105.

Abdul-Rauf, Muhammad. *The Islamic View of Women and the Family*. New York: Robert Speller and Sons, 1977.

— — —.*Marriage in Islam*. Jerico, N.Y.: Exposition Press, 1972.

Abu-Lughud, Janet, and Amin, Lucy. "Egyptian Marriage Advertisements: Microcosm of a Changing Society." *Marriage and Family Living* 23, no. 2 (1961): 127-36.

Abu-Zahra, Nadia M. "On the Modesty of Women in Arab Muslim Villages: A Reply." *American Anthropologist* 72, no. 5 (1970): 1079-88.

Afetinan, A. *The Emancipation of the Turkish Woman*. Paris: UNESCO, 1962.

Afza, N. "Woman In Islam." *Islamic Literature* 13, no. 10 (1967): 5-24.

Ahmed, Feroz. "Age at Marriage in Pakistan." *Journal of Marriage and the Family* 31, no. 4 (1969): 799-807.

Ahmed, Kazi Nasir-ud-Din. *The Muslim Law of Divorce*. Islamabad: Islamic Research Institute, 1972.

Ahmed, Shereen Azia. "Pakistan." *Women in the Modern World*. Edited by Raphael Patai. New York: The Free Press, 1967, pp. 42-58.

Ali, Zahida Amjad. "The Status of Women in Pakistan." *Pakistan Quarterly* 6, no. 4 (1956): 46-55.

Amar, Hamed. *Growing up in an Egyptian Village*. London: Routledge, Kegan Paul, 1954.

Antoun, Richard T. "On the Modesty of Women in Arab Muslim Villages: A Study in the Accommodation of Traditions." *American Anthropologist* 70, no. 4 (1968): 671-97.

— — —. "Antoun's Reply to Abu-Zahra." *American Anthropologist* 72, no. 4 (1970): 1088-92.

Arasteh, Reza. "The Struggle for Equality in Iran." *The Middle East Journal* 18, no. 2 (1964): 189-205.

Baer, Gabriel. *Population and Society in the Arab East*. New York: Frederick Praeger, 1964, pp. 34-69.

Bean, Lee L. "Utilization of Human Resources: The Case of Women in Pakistan." *International Labour Review* 97, no. 4 (1968): 391-410.

Beck, D.F. "The Changing Moslem Family of the Middle East." *Marriage and Family Living* 19 (1957): 340.

Beck, Lois G., and Keddi, Nikki, eds. *Women in the Muslim World.* Cambridge Mass.: Harvard University Press, 1978.

Berger, Morroe. *The Arab World Today.* Garden City, N.Y.: Doubleday and Co., 1962, pp. 117-53.

Bevan-Jones, V. *Women in Islam: A Manual with Special Reference to Conditions in India.* Lucknow: Lucknow Publishing House, 1941.

Bhattacharya, D.K. "A Note on Authority and Leadership in a Matrilineal Society." *The Eastern Anthropologist XXVI* (1973):95-99.

Boserup, Esther. *Woman's Role in Economic Development.* London: George Allen and Unwin, Ltd., 1970.

Camilleri, Carmel. "Modernity and the Family in Tunisia." *Journal of Marriage and Family* 29 (1967): 590-95.

Carlaw, Raymond W. et al. "Underlying Sources of Agreement and Communication between Husbands and Wives in Dacca, East Pakistan." *Journal of Marriage and the Family* 33, no. 3 (1971): 571-83.

Chamberlayne, J.H. "The Family in Islam." *Numen* 15, no. 2 (1968): 119-41.

Charnay, Jean-Paul. *Islamic Culture and Socio-Economic Change.* London: E.J. Brill, 1971.

Churchill, Charles W. "The Arab World." In Raphael Patai, ed., *Women in the Modern World.* New York: The Free Press, 1967.

Dearden, Ann, ed. *Arab Women.* Report No. 27. London: Minority Rights Group, December 1975.

Desanti, Dominique. "No More Veils." Translated by V. Reeves. *Atlas* 9 (1965): 91-93.

Dicaprio, J.M. "The Family in Islam." *Islamic Culture* 12, no. 10 (1966): 37-48.

Djebar, Assia. *Women in Islam.* London: Andre Deutsch, 1961.

Dodd, Peter C. "The Effect of Religious Affiliation on Women's Role in Middle Eastern Arab Society." *Journal of Comparative Family Studies* 5, no. 2 (1974): 117-29.

— — —."Family Honor and the Forces of Change in Arab Society." *International Journal of Middle East Studies* 4, no. 1 (1973): 40-54.

— — —."Youth and Women's Emancipation in the United Arab Republic." *The Middle East Journal* 22, no. 2 (1968): 159-72.

Esposito, John. "Muslim Family Law Reform: Towards an Islamic

Methodology." *Islamic Studies* 15 (1976): 19-51.

— — ."Women's Rights in Islam." *Islamic Studies* 14 (1975): 99-114.

Farrag, A. "Social Control amongst the Mzabite Women of Beni-Isguen." *Middle East Studies* 7, no. 3 (1971): 317-28.

al-Faruqi, Lamia L. "Women's Rights and the Muslim Women." *Islam and the Modern Age* 3, no. 2 (1972): 76-99.

Fawzi, S. "The Role of Women in a Developing Sudan." Proceedings of the Institute of Differing Civilizations, Brussels, 1958.

Fernea, Elizabeth W. *Guests of the Sheik*. Garden City, N.Y.: Doubleday Anchor Book, 1969.

Fernea, Elizabeth W. and Basima Bezirgan. *Middle Eastern Muslim Women Speak*. Austin: University of Texas Press, 1977.

Fernea, Elizabeth W. and Robert A. "Variation in Religious Observance Among Islamic Women." In *Scholars, Saints and Sufis,* edited by Nikki Keddi. Berkeley, Calif.: University of California Press, 1972.

Forget, Nelly. "Attitudes toward Work by Women in Morocco." *UNESCO: International Social Science Journal* 14, no. 1 (1962): 92-123.

Fox, Greer Litton. "Some Determinants of Modernism among Women in Ankara, Turkey." *Journal of Marriage and the Family* 35, no. 3 (1973): 520-29.

"Freedom of Choice in Algerian Marriages." *Muslim World* 55 (1965): 279-81.

Fuller, Anne H. *Buarij: Portrait of a Lebanese Muslim Village*. Cambridge, Mass. Harvard University Press, 1961.

Galadanci, S.A. "Education of Woman in Islam with Reference to Nigeria." *Nigerian Journal of Islam* 1, no. 2 (1971): 5-10.

Goode, William J. *World Revolution and Family Patterns*. New York: Collier-Macmillan Free Press, 1963.

Goody, Jack, and Tambiah, S.J. *Bridewealth and Dowry.* Cambridge: At the University Press, 1973.

Gordon, David C. *Women of Algeria: An Essay on Change*. Cambridge, Mass.: Harvard University Press, 1968.

Granqvist, Hilma. *Marriage Conditions in a Palestinian Village*. 2 vols. Helsinki: Holsingsfors Akademische Buchhandlung, 1931-35.

Graziani, Joseph. "The Momentum of the Feminist Movement in the Arab World." *Middle East Review,* Winter 1974-75, pp. 26-33.

Haddad, Yvonne. "Palestinian Woman: Patterns of Legitimation and Domination." *Palestinian Sociology,* edd. Elia Zureik and Khalil Nakhleh. London: Croom, Helm Ltd., 1979.

Hansen, Henry Harold. *Daughters of Allah: Among Moslem Women in Kurdistan*. London: Allen and Unwin, 1960.

— — — .*The Kurdish Woman's Life: Field Research in Muslim Society, Iraq.*

Copenhagen: National Museet, 1961.

Heggoy, Alf Andrew. "Cultural Disrespect: European and Algerian Views on Women in Colonial and Independent Algeria." *Muslim World* 62, no. 4 (October 1972):323-34.

— — —."Algerian Women and the Right to Vote: Some Colonial Anomalies." *Muslim World* 64, no. 3 (July 1974): 228-35.

Hilal, J. "The Management of Male Dominance in 'Traditional' Arab Culture: A Tentative Model." *Civilisations* 21, no. 2 (1971): 85-95.

Huber, Joan. *Changing Women in Changing Societies.* Chicago: University of Chicago Press, 1973.

Hudson, B.B. et al. "Cross-cultural Studies in the Arab Middle East and the United States: Studies of Young Adults." *Journal of Social Issues* 15, no. 3 (1959).

Hussain, Igbalunnisa. *Changing India: A Muslim Woman Speaks.* Bangalore: Hosali Press, 1940.

— — —.*Purdah and Polygamy: Life in an Indian Muslim Household.* Bangalore: Hosali Press, 1944.

Hussein, Aziza. "The Role of Women in Social Reform in Egypt." *Middle East Journal* 7 (1953): 440-50.

Ingrams, Doreen. *A Time in Arabia.* London: John Murray, 1970.

— — —."The Position of Women in Middle Eastern Arab Society." In Michael Adams, ed., *The Middle East: A Handbook.* New York: Praeger, 1971.

Jacobs, Sue-Ellen. *Women in Perspective: A Guide for Cross-cultural Studies.* Urbana, Ill.: University of Illinois Press, 1974.

Jones, V.R. et al. *Women in Islam.* Lucknow: Lucknow Publishing House, 1961.

Keyser, James, "The Middle Eastern Case: Is There a Marriage Rule?" *Ethnology* 42, no. 3 (1974): 293.

Khalaf, S. *Prostitution in a Changing Society: A Sociological Survey of Legal Prostitution in Beirut.* Beirut: Khayats, 1965.

Lichtenstadter, I. *Islam and the Modern Age.* New York: Bookmen Associates Twayne Publishers, 1958.

— — —."The Muslim Woman in Transition, Based on Observations in Egypt and Pakistan." *Sociologus* 7, no. 1 (1957): 23-28.

Magnarella, Paul J. "Conjugal Role Relationships in a Modernizing Turkish Town." *International Journal of Sociology of the Family* 2, no. 2 (1972): 179-92.

Maher, Vanessa. *Women and Property in Morocco.* Cambridge: At the University Press, 1974.

Malik, F.H. "Woman in Islam." *The Muslim Digest* 21, no. 10 (1971): 20-23.

Many Sisters. Edited by Carolyn J. Matthiasson. New York: Free Press, 1974.

Melikian, L. "The Dethronement of the Father." *Middle East Forum* 36, no. 1 (1960): 23-26.

Mernissi, Fatima. *Beyond the Veil*. Cambridge, MA: Schenkman Publishing Company, 1975.

— — —. "The Moslem World: Women Excluded from Development." In Irene Tinker and M. B. Brauman, Eds., *Women and World Development*. Washington, D.C.: AAAS, 1976.

— — —."Women, Saints, and Sanctuaries." *Signs* 3, no. 1 (1977): 101-12.

Milburn, Josephine F. *Cross National Comparisons of Women's Legal Status*. American Political Science Association, 1973.

Mohd, Ahamad Bin I. "The Administration of Family Law in Indonesia." *Islamic Culture* 43, no. 2 (1969): 109-24.

Muhyi, I.A. "Women in the Arab Middle East." *Journal of Social Issues*, no. 3, 1959, pp. 45-57.

Nagavi, Sayyid Ali. "Modern Reforms in Muslim Family Laws: A General Study." *Islamic Studies* 13 (1974): 235-52.

Nelson, Cynthia. "Changing Roles of Men and Women: Illustrations from Egypt." *Anthropology Quarterly* 41, no. 2 (1968): 57-77.

Papanek. Hanna. "Purdah in Pakistan: Seclusion and Modern Occupations for Women." *Journal of Marriage and the Family*, August 1971, 517-30.

— — —."The Woman Field Worker in a *Purdah* Society." *Human Organization* 23, 2 (1964), 160-63.

Pastner, Carroll. *Sexual Dichotomization in Society and Culture; the Women of Panjgur, Baluchistan*. Ann Arbor, Michigan: Published on demand by University Microfilms, 1974.

Patai, Raphael. *Golden River to Golden Road: Society, Culture and Change in the Middle East*. Philadelphia: University of Pennsylvania Press, 1962.

Perlmann, M. "Women and Feminism in Egypt." *Palestine Affairs* 4, no. 3 (1949): 36-39.

"Preliminary Paper on Integration of Women in Development." Social Development Division of the United Nations, February 1972.

Prothro, Edwin Terry, and Najib Diab, Lutfy. *Changing Family Patterns in the Arab East*. Beirut: American University of Beirut, 1974.

Rejwan, N. "The Intellectuals in Egyptian Islam." *New Outlook* 7, no. 8 (1964):33-44.

Rivlin, Benjamin et al. *The Contemporary Middle East*. New York: Random House, n.d.

Rosenfeld, H. "Change, Barriers to Change, and Contradictions in the Arab Village Family." *American Anthropologist* 70, no. 4 (1968): 732-52.

— — —."On Determinants of Status of Arab Village Women." *Man*, (London), May 1960, pp. 66-70.

Sabri, M.A. *Pioneering Profiles: Beirut College for Women*. Beirut: Khayats, 1967.

Saleh, Saneya. "Women in Islam: Their Status in Religious and Traditional Culture." *International Journal of Sociology of the Family*, March 1972, pp. 35-42.

Sayegh, R. "The Changing Life of Arab Women." *Middle East Journal* 8, no. 6, (1968): 19-23.

Schneider, Jane. "Of Vigilence and Virgins: Honor, Shame and Access to Resources in Mediterranean Societies." *Ethnology* 10 (1971): 1-24.

Shafik, Doria. "Egyptian Feminism." *Middle Eastern Affairs*, August-September 1952, pp. 233-38.

Smock, Audrey C., and Haggag, Nadia Y. "Egypt: From Seclusion to Limited Participation." In Janet Z. Giele and Audrey C. Smock, eds., *Women: Roles and Status in Eight Countries*. New York: John Wiley, 1977.

Smock, Audrey, and Giele, J. eds. *Women and Society in International and Comparative Perspective*. New York: John Wiley, 1977.

Sultana, Farrukh. "Status of Women in Iqbal's Thought." *Islamic Literature* 17, no. 1 (1971): 49-54.

Sweet, L.E. "The Women of 'Ain ad-Dayr." *Anthropology Quarterly* 40, no. 3 (1967): 167-83.

al-Talib, N. "Status of Women in Islam." *Islamic Literature* 15, no. 6 (1969) : 57-64.

Tomeh, A. "Cross-cultural Differences in the Structure of Moral Values: A Factorial Analysis." *International Journal of Comparative Sociology* 11, no. 1 (1970): 18-33.

— — —."Patterns of Moral Behaviour in Two Social Structures." *Sociology and Research* 55, no. 2 (1971): 149-60.

Ungor, B. "Women in the Middle East and North Africa, and Universal Suffrage." *Annals of the American Academy of Political and Social Science*, no. 375, 1968, pp. 72-81.

van Ess, D. *Fatima and Her Sisters*. New York: John Day, 1961.

Vreeda-de-Stuers, Cora. *Purda: A Study of Muslim Women's Life in Northern India*. Assen, The Netherlands: Royal Van Gorcum, 1968.

Women, Culture and Society. Edited by M. Z. Rosaldo and L. Lamphere. Stanford, Calif.: Stanford University Press, 1974.

Woodsmall, Ruth Frances. *Moslem Women Enter a New World*. New York: Round Table Press, Inc., 1936.

— — — .*Study of the Role of Women in Lebanon, Egypt, 'Irāq, Jordan and Syria, 1954-1955.* Woodstock, Elm Tree Press, 1956.

— — — .*Women and the New East.* Washington D.C.: The Middle East Institute, 1960.

Youssef, Nadia H. *Women and Work in Developing Societies.* Berkeley, Calif.: University of California, Berkeley, Publication Monograph Series 15, 1974.